# THE
# KEY
# TO YOUR OWN
# NATIVITY

# The Rational Basis of Astrology.

*As each copy of this book is likely to come into the hands of a great number of people who here find their first introduction to the subject of* ASTROLOGY, *or at least their first incentive to a serious consideration thereof, it is thought well to devote this fly-leaf to a brief setting forth of the foundational principles upon which the science rests, and also of the claims of Astrology as a basis for character study. There will be many to whom the mere sublimity of the subject will at once appeal; but there are others whose attitude of mind is philosophical rather than devotional, and it is to these that we address ourselves here.*

The *first principle* upon which the science of astrology rests is, that the whole Universe is actually what the term implies—a unity; and that a law which is found in manifestation in one portion of the Universe must also be equally operative throughout the whole. The consequent to this major premise is, that our own solar system being in itself a complete whole, those laws which are operative among the major constituents of that system, *viz.*, the planetary bodies, are also in force among the lesser components of the same system—to wit, ourselves, and the other objects on this earth, whether solid, fluid, or gaseous, whether human, animal, vegetable or mineral.

The *second principle* is, that by a study of the motions and relative positions of the planets the operations of these laws may be observed, measured, and determined.

From these two first principles, aided by present-day observation and a mind capable of a metaphysical grasp of the metaphysical significance of phenomena, the whole science of Astrology as now expounded can be deduced. It is a mistake far too prevalent even among thoughtful and unprejudiced people to suppose that the present interest in Astrology is merely the decadent revival of an ancient superstition, based entirely on accepted tradition.

Nevertheless, since Truth is the same in all times, the learning of the ancients, transmitted to us by tradition—largely in the form of myth —is of the greatest value to the modern student. Indeed, the astrologer who had to depend entirely on the two first principles given above would certainly have a herculean task before him of observation, tabulation and induction before he would be even so well equipped as the reader who procures an elementary text-book such as this and intelligently applies its principles. For while the attributes of the various planets, Mars, Venus, Jupiter and Saturn for instance, are daily shown to be in entire accordance with the *dicta* of the ancients,—this is a fact that is quite lost sight of by the ordinary critic,—yet the arrival at such conclusions by sheer experimental methods alone would be nearly as long deferred as some of the modern theories about matter and force, which are seen when understood to be after all mere corollaries of the elementary principles of mechanics, already centuries old.

Having thus considered the philosophical, or perhaps one should rather say the scientific grounds for this study, as a means of comprehending nature's laws, we will briefly enumerate the claims of astrology as regards its practical application to ordinary life. It will be noted that we have carefully avoided all reference to the grandeur of the subject and have treated the matter from the dispassionate standpoint of pure reason. And, if the principles here alluded to be not considered proven, it is at least impossible for the most ingenious casuist to demonstrate their impossibility, or reasonably to argue their *a priori* unlikelihood.

The Claims of Astrology then are, that it offers first and foremost a means of general character-study entirely surpassing the combined advantages of ordinary anthropological methods, being at once more comprehensive and more subtle. Secondly, and this is pre-eminently its greatest, its divine use, a means for the unbiassed examination of one's own character, and the most effective means of strengthening it. Thirdly, a knowledge of times and seasons appropriate for certain works, and a means of *testing* one's development of character. Lastly and leastly, though unfortunately by many made firstly and solely, a means to some extent—indeed, with those specially fitted, to a very remarkable extent—of forecasting future events.

The utility of the study of this ancient, this *synthesised* wisdom is by no means exhausted in the above condensed statement, but these are the chief features which entitle the subject to claim the attention of every earnest and thoughtful person.

Finally we may add that, while in reality the profoundest of studies, it is so based upon simplicity that anyone can in a short while become sufficiently proficient, not only to "cast a horoscope" (in itself a mere question of reckoning), but also to some extent to "judge a nativity."

# Titles in the Alan Leo Astrologer's Library

# The Key to Your Own Nativity

by

## ALAN LEO

DESTINY BOOKS
Rochester, Vermont

Destiny Books
One Park Street
Rochester, Vermont 05767

First U.S. Edition 1983
This edition reprinted in 1989 by Destiny Books


Library of Congress Cataloging-in-Publication Data

Leo, Alan.
    The key to your own nativity : analytical readings of every
position in a nativity, based on scientific principles / by Alan
Leo.
        p.   cm. — (Alan Leo astrologer's library)
    ISBN 0-89281-179-X :
    1. Natal astrology.   I. Title.   II. Series: Leo, Alan. Alan Leo
astrologer's library.
BF1719.L465   1989
133.5—dc20                                                89-16935
                                                             CIP


Printed and bound in the United States

10  9  8  7  6  5  4  3  2  1

Destiny Books is a division of Inner Traditions International, Ltd.

Distributed to the book trade in the United States by Harper and Row
Publishers, Inc.

Distributed to the book trade in Canada by Book Center, Inc., Montreal, Quebec

# FOREWORD.

It must not be supposed because this is termed the Sixth Volume of the " Astrology for All " Series, that the study of the five former books need necessarily precede the use of this. On the contrary, the steadily widening demand for astrological literature necessitated the addition of a simpler volume to this now well-known series ; and the favourable reception that was accorded to the first edition of this book, especially by practical students and professors of astrology, shows that it filled a real want and supplied information that was needed in actual practice. As stated in the Explanatory Introduction on page xiii, this book is intended for the use of those who have no knowledge of Astrology at all, as well as for those who are already students of some experience. However, a few inquiries that have reached the author, chiefly from beginners who have not quite understood the purpose of the work, make it desirable to explain *what it is not* as well as *what it is.*

## WHAT THIS BOOK IS NOT.

This volume is not intended to give instructions how to cast a horoscope, or elementary information concerning the twelve houses, or the nature of the signs of the Zodiac, or the things signified by the planets. It is assumed that the reader desiring further acquaintance with these matters, all of which have been fully explained in the previous volumes of this Series and (in a more condensed form) in the smaller Astrological Manuals, will refer to those books.

## WHAT THIS BOOK IS.

Apart from the more or less mechanical use that may be made of the book by those who—however ignorant of astrology—have procured one of the Special Charts referred to on page 305, and are thereby enabled to obtain at once the reading of the horoscope (be it their own or any one else's), this book has a value for the student, whether elementary or advanced. In fact, the more experienced the student, the more fully is he likely to appreciate the advantages to be derived from its use.

To the beginner, however, it is a *sine qua non.* For, having calculated a horoscope, or having been supplied with one by someone else, and knowing something of the meaning of signs, houses, aspects and planets, the task of writing out a delineation of it in full is sure to fall to the lot of every student who wishes to become practically efficient. In order that this may be done, it is necessary to have the fullest information as to the meaning of any and every position and combination that can be found in the map ; the horoscope must be analysed, split up into all its constituent parts, and the signification of each understood in detail. The results that follow from their combinations under such headings as personal, characteristics, health, occupation, money matters, parentage, marriage, children, friends, and so on, have then to be considered and the information furnished by the combinations of the various factors taken into account.

This book is intended to supply precisely that kind of information and it is written not from the point of view of the scientist, or the philosopher, or the occultist, but from that of the practical astrologer, *i.e.*, one who is actually engaged in delineating character and fortune. It approaches astrology from a standpoint somewhat similar to that of a physiognomist or a phrenologist, except that it studies the horoscope instead of the personal appearance.

### How this Book came to be Written.

Its compilation was the result of the popularity that attended the advent of the short " Test Horoscopes " issued in thousands at the beginning of the present century. These in their simplest form originally consisted of descriptions of character and temperament as associated with the rising sign, the rising planet, and the ruler of the ascendant ; and they met with such success that a great demand arose for their extension and for much further information of a similar kind concerning other parts of the horoscope. It would have been a hopeless task for one person to cope with the ever increasing work thus entailed, had not a method been devised by which a series of analytical judgments could be used to supply the kind of information demanded.

The original stock of separate judgments consisted of OVER A THOUSAND different mimeographed sheets, each being subjected to continuous careful revision during ten years' constant use. The method has thus been subjected to a practical test that could not have been applied in any other way ; and, making allowance for occasional discrepancies (such as one dealt with in Chapter XXXIV), it has been found more satisfactory in every respect than the old-fashioned unsystematic way of giving a more or less haphazard judgment, which was liable to vary according to the personal equation of the astrologer and his frame of mind at the moment of writing.

Out of the original stock of judgments, the best and most applicable have been selected and are now given to the world, so as to be accessible to both inquirers and students for general use. Given a map of the heavens at birth, anyone of ordinary intelligence may refer to the numbered paragraphs in this book and give an unbiased reading of any horoscope equal in value to that of a professional astrologer—a reading moreover that shows in what way the judgment has been arrived at, thus adding greatly to its value.

ALAN LEO.

*London, Autumn,* 1917.

ERRATA.—On p. XVII, line 14, from foot *F* and 452, should be *C* and 451. On p. 282, line 5, from foot, *How to Judge a Nativity, Part II.*, should be *The Art of Synthesis.*

*The* FIRST EDITION *of this book being issued in the year* 1910 *explains the reference to the year of King George's ascension on page* 284. *The present edition is in all respects the same as the former.*

# TABLE OF CONTENTS.

# EXPLANATORY INTRODUCTION.

A VERY little attention will make clear the purpose of this book, which is so arranged as to be practically self-explanatory. It is intended for two classes of readers :—

(1) Those who have no knowledge whatever of how to judge a nativity.

(2) Students who though knowing the rules and capable of some independent judgment, require a handy method of quickly obtaining a delineation as a basis for further exposition.*

## READERS IN CLASS (1).

As for the first class, those entirely ignorant of Astrology, no explanation is required. They will be readers who have taken advantage of the Offer advertised on p. 305, and they will have before them FULL INSTRUCTIONS, with a list of numbers indicating the paragraphs to be studied, and the order in which they should be read. Their course therefore is quite plain, and they may " skip " the remainder of this Introduction, as it hardly concerns them at their present stage. But they will do well to read the preliminary remarks at the head of each chapter before studying the particular paragraph of that chapter set down for their perusal. The IMPORTANT NOTE on p. xxi should be read with attention.

## READERS IN CLASS (2).

Readers in the second of these two classes, however, will naturally look for some explanation of the plan of the book, and a few hints as to how to make the best use of it. It has been described as self-explanatory

---

* The necessary rules for Casting the Horoscope will be found in *Astrology for All Part II.*, or in the small Shilling Manual, *What is a Horoscope and How is it Cast ?*

and there is no doubt that without any introduction an intelligent student could manage quite well, for a study of the EXAMPLE CHART of King George's Horoscope, facing title page, gives a very fair idea of how the book is used, and a similar chart needs only to be prepared for any horoscope of which a Delineation is desired. The number of the paragraph required can at once be seen from the REFERENCE CHART on pp. xxii, xxiii.

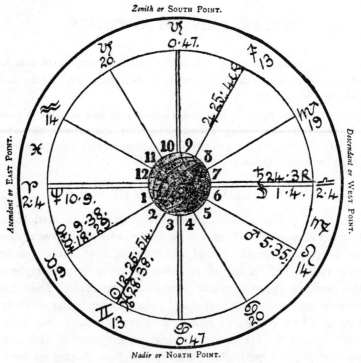

KING GEORGE V. *Horoscope of Birth. June 3rd, 1865, 1.18 a.m.,*
*51°30′N., 37 secs. W.*

But perhaps a few additional words of explanation may be useful. In the ten or twelve years of every-day astrological practice, of which this book is the outcome, a scheme of judgment was gradually evolved in which the delineation was treated under seven main heads or sections, these being:—(1) the RISING SIGN and RULING PLANET, Ruler's House- and Sign-Position, and Aspects to the Ruler; (2) the INDIVIDUAL CHARACTERISTICS, as represented by the Sign-Position and Aspects of the Sun ; (3) the PERSONAL CHARACTERISTICS, as indicated by the Sign-Position and Aspects of the Moon ; (4) the MENTAL QUALIFICA-TIONS, as shown by the Sign-Position and Aspects of the planet Mercury. These four sections comprised what may be termed the ground-work of the delineation ; and (5) a brief treatment was then accorded to each of THE HOUSES OF THE HOROSCOPE under the heading of Finance, Travel, Environment, etc., judged from either a planet in, or the condition of the ruler of, the house concerred ; followed by (6) a SUMMARY of the general trend of the horoscope, indicating the main tendencies to encourage or repress. Finally a few pages were generally added upon (7) the FUTURE PROSPECTS for the ensuing four or five years.

The EXAMPLE CHART of King George's nativity illustrates this method of delineation in a very effective manner, and it need only be pointed out that a certain amount of judgment is called for in selecting the aspects, house-rulers, etc., so as to secure the best " all round " reading of the horoscope. The first four items, for instance, are quite plain sailing but when we come to the Ruler's Aspects we find □ ♀, △ ♀, ✳ ☽, ✳ ☉, and we naturally pause to enquire if all of these should be given here, and if not, which. A little consideration will show that ♂ ✳ ☉ and ♂ ✳ ☽ will come usefully under heads (2) and (3) as Individual and Personal Characteristics, while as for the ♂ △ ♀, that is of a nature so contradictory to ♂ □ ♀ that it will be better to omit that for the delineation at this point, and in fact leave it out altogether in that form, this Neptune influence being best treated under head (2) as ☉ ✳ ♀.

The aspects in Chapter XVIII. are arranged thus :— ♂, *b*, *a*, which stand for *conjunction, benefic, adverse*, the adverse aspects being

☍ □ ∠ ⚼ and perhaps ☌

while the benefic are

△ ✳ and perhaps ⚺

though ☌ and ⚺ are perhaps better omitted altogether from consideration in most cases. Aspects to the Sun are first given, in this order,

☽ ☿ ♀ ♂ ♃ ♄ ♅ ♆ ;

then aspects of the Moon to those planets following, ☿ ♀ ♂, etc. ; then Mercury to ♀ ♂ ♃, etc. And so on. Hence an aspect of any planet to the Sun appears as an aspect of the Sun to that planet. All this will be made quite clear by a little study of the Reference Chart on pp. xxii and xxiii.

It is better to err on the side of *sparseness* as regards aspects, that is, it is better to give too few than too many ; pick out the ʻboldest,ʼ and give those only.

The question next arises as to whether ☽ ☍ ♅ should be included under head (3), Personal Characteristics. The answer is, No. The aspect is not exceedingly close, and it is somewhat modified and cast into the shade by ☽ ⚹ ♂ and by ♅ *rising*, which latter will be found under the "supplementary paragraphs" ; we therefore content ourselves with ☽ ⚹ ♂ only. Again, if ☽ ⚺ ☿ came under consideration we should include it under Mental Qualifications, rather than under Personal Characteristics, as the aspects between the Moon and Mercury have much to do with the facility with which the brain is able to express the thoughts. In the present case, the delineation of this aspect can usefully be omitted, as Mercury is rising and almost within the Ascendant, and hence more active than would otherwise be the case, while the Moon too is in close touch with the Ascendant by aspect.

These few remarks will probably suffice to make clear all that is likely to need explanation. The student is urged to study the Example closely, reading the whole through several times and noting how the *balance* of the whole judgment is maintained. For it is in the first makıng out of the chart that the real art of delineation consists ; the rest follows almost automatically.

With regard to the " Polarities " given in Chapter XXXIII, they should be included under head (3), after the Lunar Aspects. It is not always necessary to include the Polarity, and the student should use his own judgment as to whether it is of advantage to do so.

The first four heads of the delineation being disposed of, the Houses come under special consideration as follows :—ii., *Finance;* iii., *Travel;* iv., *Environment;* v., *Enterprise;* vi., *Sickness;* vii., *Marriage;* viii., *Legacies;* ix., *Philosophy;* x., *Profession;* xi., *Friends;* xii., *Occultism.* The other meanings of each house, not included under these general terms, come in for a certain amount of incidental treatment in the delineations.

The general plan is to take the planet ruling the sign occupying the house or on its cusp, as ruler ; but if there should be a planet occupying the house, then take that as ruler in preference to the lord of the sign on the cusp ; and if more than one planet be in the house, then take the chief of them, according to its general strength, as ruler. This plan however is not invariably followed, as a study of the REFERENCE CHART will show, and it will be a useful exercise for the student's intuition if he will ask himself why. Thus, in considering the Second House, if there be no planet in the second, do not take ruler of the cusp, but see if either Venus or Jupiter be angular, and if so take it, but if not, then take the sign on the cusp, cardinal, fixed or mutable as the case may be. Similarly with the Third House, and the Tenth House.

In the case of the Seventh House, if there be no planet in that house, take the sign-position of Venus and judge by that. And for the Eleventh House, if there be no planet there, see if the sign occupying it, or on the cusp, be of the Fiery, Earthy, Airy or Watery triplicity, and judge by that. In the case of the Twelfth House, there is a special delineation, *N.P.*, which may be given when there are no planets in the twelfth.

The Summaries will sufficiently explain themselves: *C.*, *F.*, *M.*, respectively mean the *majority of planets* in cardinal, fixed, or mutable signs; but two letters coupled together, such as *C. and F.*, has a quite different signification, implying that the Sun is in a cardinal and the Moon in a fixed sign; *F. and C.* would mean Sun fixed and Moon cardinal, of course. These are very useful where the planets are evenly distributed, or nearly so, among the three qualities. Similar remarks apply to the triplicities. Where there is a clear majority of planets in a certain type of sign (*e.g.*, 5 in cardinal and 4 in watery), the appropriate paragraphs should be given; but if there is any doubt as to which type of sign is most strongly represented, then go by Sun and Moon,—as for instance in King George's nativity, *M. and F.*, and *A.* (pars. 452, 441) Paragraphs 440 to 445 may (with suitable modification of wording) be used where both Sun and Moon are in same type of sign.

In this, as in all other matters, the student's own judgment should be brought into play, but as a general rule the Summary should include (*a*) planets' mundane positions (*rising, setting, above* or *below*) and (*b*) majority or Sun-and-Moon sign positions (*C.F.M.*, *F.E.A.W.*, etc.), though if found mutually contradictory (*e.g.*, *planets rising, majority mutable*), then the question must be well judged and one or other selected in accordance with the decision arrived at.—Planets termed

*rising* are those in x., xi., xii., i., ii., iii.
*below* ,, ,, ,,       i., ii., iii., iv. v., vi.
*setting* ,, ,, ,,       iv. v., vi., vii., viii., ix.
*above* ,, ,, ,,       vii., viii., ix., x., xi., xii.

As regards the FUTURE PROSPECTS, sufficient hints are given in the Chapter that deals with them. Here, as elsewhere, what to omit needs to be known, as well as what to include, and it is perhaps even more important.

In writing out a delineation for a friend, it is advisable to give each paragraph a brief explanatory title, in some such fashion as followed on the Example Delineation in the Appendix.

This, then, concludes the Introduction, and the student may now be left to explore the remainder of the book at his pleasure, assured that although in a sense he may be said to have before him " ready-made judgments," yet he never need feel that the opportunity for the exercise of his own independence of thought and power of combination is wanting, or that he is not in a very real manner developing, in proportion to his earnestness and application, the power to " Judge a Nativity " for himself.

———

Perhaps a word or two may not be out of place as to the literary form which these Delineations take.

Let us consider how they came to be written. A man full of his subject is dictating to a stenographer, who follows as rapidly as pen will permit and at the end of each page summarily interrupts the speaker who has perforce to turn to a new theme. Each sentence is thrown out white-hot from the brain, and caught, as it were, by the paper. The idea is everything to the speaker, the form nothing. His mind is working rapidly, and the quicker his thoughts can be transferred to paper the better ; a clerkly finish can be given to them at any time, if necessary. And why then, the critic will naturally ask, has not this been done ?

The answer is simple, but conclusive. It *has* been done. During the time the system of Delineations embodied in this book was in progress, a graduate of London University was employed in its revision, and so much modification did he at first consider necessary that many paragraphs were entirely rewritten. The result, however, was altogether disappointing. The attempt to express wide and elastic ideas—such as a description of the influence of Aries as a Rising Sign for example—in precise phraseology was doomed to failure. The rewritten paragraphs were clear and definite enough ; too definite, in fact, for when comparison was made and they were tested alongside the originals, it was found that they produced upon the reader the effect of a dry statement of fact instead of a new and palpitating idea. This was so patent even to the scholar in question, that in going through the remainder of the series he confined himself to altering a word or sentence here and there, realising that with all their literary shortcomings the paragraphs in their original form were better suited to convey the IDEAS intended, than any more elegant form into which literary skill could turn them. Even a certain amount of periphrasis was found to be not without its value in giving what may be termed the *feel* of the idea which the speaker had desired to convey. And the same remark applies to such usages as "liable" where "likely" would be more 'correct' and yet fail to suggest the intended idea so well. He might make the experiment with paragraph 271, and see if he can improve "ancient and antiquated, old and antique" which he will at first condemn as tautological.

Having this experience in mind, therefore, it will be understood that in preparing this book for the press no attempt has been made to divest the Delineations of their original spontaneous and impromptu character ; for the author has realised that to be too precise is as mischievous as being too vague. But it is not pretended that no improvement is possible and the student can hardly have a better exercise, literary or astrological, than the endeavour to express in his own wording the ideas he gathers as he reads.

It has been said that the delineations were, in the first instance, dictated. The necessity for brevity has caused one or two sentences to take a form which may at first convey little or no meaning to the reader unless he is naturally intuitive, but a little pondering will usually show what is meant. As an instance may be cited "make the thing action when its usefulness has passed by," from paragraph 452, where what is meant is that decision may be postponed until the action decided on comes too late to be of any service, but has to be undertaken neverthe-less. Thought has in the end to become action, that is the law of thought, and dilatoriness in arriving at a decision does not alter that law although it may render the action nugatory.

It is found in practice that a delineation in the SECOND PERSON makes as a rule a far more direct and vivid appeal to the average man or woman than if it were put in a more or less impersonal manner. For that reason these Delineations have not been re-worded in this respect (counsels to the contrary notwithstanding), the original " you " and " your " having been retained throughout.

### "SUNRISE HOROSCOPES."

Should it be desired to give the horoscope of some person whose time of birth is not known, the best plan is to calculate the horoscope for the moment of *sunrise.*\* The reason for this being that the moment of sunrise at any place is full of a special energy, which to some extent pervades the whole day, and hence a horoscope calculated for that moment will contain much of truth for every person born on that day, at that place, and would certainly be more correct than any other unless the correct horoscope were obtained by " rectification," which is a long and difficult process requiring much skill.

Where a written delineation of such a horoscope is being given it will be well to preface it with paragraph 630B.

*\** *A General Reference Chart showing the scheme of the whole work will be found on pp. xxii, xxiii, a copy of the Special Chart on p. 283, and an Example Delineation in Full on p. 284. *\**

---

\* This is easily done by turning to the Table of Houses for the birthplace, noting the Sidereal Time at which the degree of the zodiac occupied by the Sun is on the cusp of the First House, and finding the time of day by subtracting this S.T. from the S.T. at Noon as given in the Ephemeris. The horoscope is then calculated for this time in the usual way.

Suppose for example King George (see page xiv) : S.T. when Ⅱ 13° is on cusp of First House in the Latitude of London, is 20.41.41, and S.T. at Noon, June 3rd, 1865, is 4.47.49 ; difference 8.6.8. That is, sunrise was about 8.6.8. *before noon*, or 3.54, a.m.. for which time calculate the " Sunrise Horoscope."

# IMPORTANT NOTE.

## APPARENT CONTRADICTIONS.

IT will often be found that one part of a Delineation will be apparently in direct contradiction to a statement made in another part of the same Delineation. Those who have made any considerable study of Astrology will be fully prepared for this, will understand how it happens, and will find little difficulty in modifying one or other of the conflicting paragraphs—as regards its *wording*, that is to say—so as to remove the apparent discrepancy. But readers to whom the whole subject is new, and who feel, perhaps, something of the same vague astonishment and distrust when first confronting a "horoscope" that the author himself felt on a like occasion, may at first be inclined to think such a discrepancy tantamount to actual disproof of Astrology, and to fancy all that has gone before either "coincidences" or "generalities."

The fact is, some such contradictions as these exist in every nature, and are to be found (if we search deep enough) in even the best balanced and broadest minded characters. In some, these paradoxical contradictions are more marked, and where that is so Astrology shows the nature of the two opposing tendencies, and points out which is likely to win. Some men are parsimonious in the household and extravagant in business, others large-handed at home and niggling at the office.—Why? Astrology, and Astrology alone, supplies a clue to such anomalies of character.

It is hardly the place here to go into such matters of detail. Enough to remind the reader that where he meets with conflicting statements in his Delineation he should remember that such conflicting tendencies exist in the character of the person whose Nativity is being studied, and that in order to find out which of two opposing influences is likely to be the stronger, it will be well to appeal to the judgment of a more experienced student.

Where a delineation is being written out for a friend, if he is at all of a critical temperament, it will be wise to call his attention to any discrepancies of this kind, rather than leave him to discover them for himself. See paragraphs 630 *Fa* and 630 *Fb*.

# Reference Chart

## Section 1

**Rising Sign**

| | |
|---|---|
| ♈ | 1 |
| ♉ | 2 |
| ♊ | 3 |
| ♋ | 4 |
| ♌ | 5 |
| ♍ | 6 |
| ♎ | 7 |
| ♏ | 8 |
| ♐ | 9 |
| ♑ | 10 |
| ♒ | 11 |
| ♓ | 12 |

*Ruling Planet*

| | |
|---|---|
| ☉ | 13 |
| ☽ | 14 |
| ☿ | 15 |
| ♀ | 16 |
| ♂ | 17 |
| ♃ | 18 |
| ♄ | 19 |
| ♅ | 20 |
| ♆ | 21 |

*House Position of Ruler*

| | |
|---|---|
| I. | 22 |
| II. | 23 |
| III. | 24 |
| IV. | 25 |
| V. | 26 |
| VI. | 27 |
| VII. | 28 |
| VIII. | 29 |
| IX. | 30 |
| X. | 31 |
| XI. | 32 |
| XII. | 33 |

*Sun as Ruler in Signs*

| | | |
|---|---|---|
| ☉ | ♈ | 34 |
| ☉ | ♉ | 35 |
| ☉ | ♊ | 36 |
| ☉ | ♋ | 37 |
| ☉ | ♌ | 38 |
| ☉ | ♍ | 39 |
| ☉ | ♎ | 40 |
| ☉ | ♏ | 41 |
| ☉ | ♐ | 42 |
| ☉ | ♑ | 43 |
| ☉ | ♒ | 44 |
| ☉ | ♓ | 45 |

*Moon as Ruler in Signs*

| | | |
|---|---|---|
| ☽ | ♈ | 46 |
| ☽ | ♉ | 47 |
| ☽ | ♊ | 48 |
| ☽ | ♋ | 49 |
| ☽ | ♌ | 50 |
| ☽ | ♍ | 51 |
| ☽ | ♎ | 52 |
| ☽ | ♏ | 53 |
| ☽ | ♐ | 54 |
| ☽ | ♑ | 55 |
| ☽ | ♒ | 56 |
| ☽ | ♓ | 57 |

*Mercury as Ruler in Signs*

| | | |
|---|---|---|
| ☿ | ♈ | 58 |
| ☿ | ♉ | 59 |
| ☿ | ♊ | 60 |
| ☿ | ♋ | 61 |
| ☿ | ♌ | 62 |
| ☿ | ♍ | 63 |
| ☿ | ♎ | 64 |
| ☿ | ♏ | 65 |
| ☿ | ♐ | 66 |
| ☿ | ♑ | 67 |
| ☿ | ♒ | 68 |
| ☿ | ♓ | 69 |

*Venus as Ruler in Signs*

| | | |
|---|---|---|
| ♀ | ♈ | 70 |
| ♀ | ♉ | 71 |
| ♀ | ♊ | 72 |
| ♀ | ♋ | 73 |
| ♀ | ♌ | 74 |
| ♀ | ♍ | 75 |
| ♀ | ♎ | 76 |
| ♀ | ♏ | 77 |
| ♀ | ♐ | 78 |
| ♀ | ♑ | 79 |
| ♀ | ♒ | 80 |
| ♀ | ♓ | 81 |

*Mars as Ruler in Signs*

| | | |
|---|---|---|
| ♂ | ♈ | 82 |
| ♂ | ♉ | 83 |
| ♂ | ♊ | 84 |
| ♂ | ♋ | 85 |
| ♂ | ♌ | 86 |
| ♂ | ♍ | 87 |
| ♂ | ♎ | 88 |
| ♂ | ♏ | 89 |
| ♂ | ♐ | 90 |
| ♂ | ♑ | 91 |
| ♂ | ♒ | 92 |
| ♂ | ♓ | 93 |

*Jupiter as Ruler in Signs*

| | | |
|---|---|---|
| ♃ | ♈ | 94 |
| ♃ | ♉ | 95 |
| ♃ | ♊ | 96 |
| ♃ | ♋ | 97 |
| ♃ | ♌ | 98 |
| ♃ | ♍ | 99 |
| ♃ | ♎ | 100 |
| ♃ | ♏ | 101 |
| ♃ | ♐ | 102 |
| ♃ | ♑ | 103 |
| ♃ | ♒ | 104 |
| ♃ | ♓ | 105 |

*Saturn as Ruler in Signs*

| | | |
|---|---|---|
| ♄ | ♈ | 106 |
| ♄ | ♉ | 107 |
| ♄ | ♊ | 108 |
| ♄ | ♋ | 109 |
| ♄ | ♌ | 110 |
| ♄ | ♍ | 111 |
| ♄ | ♎ | 112 |
| ♄ | ♏ | 113 |
| ♄ | ♐ | 114 |
| ♄ | ♑ | 115 |
| ♄ | ♒ | 116 |
| ♄ | ♓ | 117 |

*Uranus' House Position*

| | | |
|---|---|---|
| ♅ | I. | 118 |
| ♅ | II. | 119 |
| ♅ | III. | 120 |
| ♅ | IV. | 121 |
| ♅ | V. | 122 |
| ♅ | VI. | 123 |
| ♅ | VII. | 124 |
| ♅ | VIII. | 125 |
| ♅ | IX. | 126 |
| ♅ | X. | 127 |
| ♅ | XI. | 128 |
| ♅ | XII. | 129 |

*Neptune's House Position*

| | | |
|---|---|---|
| ♆ | I. | 130 |
| ♆ | II. | 131 |
| ♆ | III. | 132 |
| ♆ | IV. | 133 |
| ♆ | V. | 134 |
| ♆ | VI. | 135 |
| ♆ | VII. | 136 |
| ♆ | VIII. | 137 |
| ♆ | IX. | 138 |
| ♆ | X. | 139 |
| ♆ | XI. | 140 |
| ♆ | XII. | 141 |

## Section 2

**Individuality**

| | | |
|---|---|---|
| ☉ | ♈ | 142 |
| ☉ | ♉ | 143 |
| ☉ | ♊ | 144 |
| ☉ | ♋ | 145 |
| ☉ | ♌ | 146 |
| ☉ | ♍ | 147 |
| ☉ | ♎ | 148 |
| ☉ | ♏ | 149 |
| ☉ | ♐ | 150 |
| ☉ | ♑ | 151 |
| ☉ | ♒ | 152 |
| ☉ | ♓ | 153 |

## Section 3

**Personality**

| | | |
|---|---|---|
| ☽ | ♈ | 154 |
| ☽ | ♉ | 155 |
| ☽ | ♊ | 156 |
| ☽ | ♋ | 157 |
| ☽ | ♌ | 158 |
| ☽ | ♍ | 159 |
| ☽ | ♎ | 160 |
| ☽ | ♏ | 161 |
| ☽ | ♐ | 162 |
| ☽ | ♑ | 163 |
| ☽ | ♒ | 164 |
| ☽ | ♓ | 165 |

*Moon in Houses*

| | | |
|---|---|---|
| ☽ | I. | 166 |
| ☽ | II. | 167 |
| ☽ | III. | 168 |
| ☽ | IV. | 169 |
| ☽ | V. | 170 |
| ☽ | VI. | 171 |
| ☽ | VII. | 172 |
| ☽ | VIII. | 173 |
| ☽ | IX. | 174 |
| ☽ | X. | 175 |
| ☽ | XI. | 176 |
| ☽ | XII. | 177 |

## Section 4

**Mental Qualifications**

| | | |
|---|---|---|
| ☿ | ♈ | 178 |
| ☿ | ♉ | 179 |
| ☿ | ♊ | 180 |
| ☿ | ♋ | 181 |
| ☿ | ♌ | 182 |
| ☿ | ♍ | 183 |
| ☿ | ♎ | 184 |
| ☿ | ♏ | 185 |
| ☿ | ♐ | 186 |
| ☿ | ♑ | 187 |
| ☿ | ♒ | 188 |
| ☿ | ♓ | 189 |

*Mercury in Houses*

| | | |
|---|---|---|
| ☿ | I. | 190 |
| ☿ | II. | 191 |
| ☿ | III. | 192 |
| ☿ | IV. | 193 |
| ☿ | V. | 194 |
| ☿ | VI. | 195 |
| ☿ | VII. | 196 |
| ☿ | VIII. | 197 |
| ☿ | IX. | 198 |
| ☿ | X. | 199 |
| ☿ | XI. | 200 |
| ☿ | XII. | 201 |

### ASPECTS

**Solar Aspects**

| | | |
|---|---|---|
| ☉ ☽ | ☌ | 202 |
| | b | 203 |
| | a | 204 |
| ☉ ☿ | ☌ | 205 |
| | b | 206 |
| | a | 207 |
| ☉ ♀ | ☌ | 208 |
| | b | 209 |
| | a | 210 |
| ☉ ♂ | ☌ | 211 |
| | b | 212 |
| | a | 213 |
| ☉ ♃ | ☌ | 214 |
| | b | 215 |
| | a | 216 |
| ☉ ♄ | ☌ | 217 |
| | b | 218 |
| | a | 219 |
| ☉ ♅ | ☌ | 220 |
| | b | 221 |
| | a | 222 |
| ☉ ♆ | ☌ | 223 |
| | b | 224 |
| | a | 225 |

**Lunar Aspects**

| | | |
|---|---|---|
| ☽ ☿ | ☌ | 226 |
| | b | 227 |
| | a | 228 |
| ☽ ♀ | ☌ | 229 |
| | b | 230 |
| | a | 231 |
| ☽ ♂ | ☌ | 232 |
| | b | 233 |
| | a | 234 |
| ☽ ♃ | ☌ | 235 |
| | b | 236 |
| | a | 237 |
| ☽ ♄ | ☌ | 238 |
| | b | 239 |
| | a | 240 |
| ☽ ♅ | ☌ | 241 |
| | b | 242 |
| | a | 243 |
| ☽ ♆ | ☌ | 244 |
| | b | 245 |
| | a | 246 |

*Mercury*

| | | |
|---|---|---|
| ☿ ♀ | ☌ | 247 |
| | b | 248 |
| | a | 249 |
| ☿ ♂ | ☌ | 250 |
| | b | 251 |
| | a | 252 |
| ☿ ♃ | ☌ | 253 |
| | b | 254 |
| | a | 255 |
| ☿ ♄ | ☌ | 256 |
| | b | 257 |
| | a | 258 |
| ☿ ♅ | ☌ | 259 |
| | b | 260 |
| | a | 261 |
| ☿ ♆ | ☌ | 262 |
| | b | 263 |
| | a | 264 |

*Venus*

| | | |
|---|---|---|
| ♀ ♂ | ☌ | 265 |
| | b | 266 |
| | a | 267 |
| ♀ ♃ | ☌ | 268 |
| | b | 269 |
| | a | 270 |
| ♀ ♄ | ☌ | 271 |
| | b | 272 |
| | a | 273 |
| ♀ ♅ | ☌ | 274 |
| | b | 275 |
| | a | 276 |
| ♀ ♆ | ☌ | 277 |
| | b | 278 |
| | a | 279 |

*Mars*

| | | |
|---|---|---|
| ♂ ♃ | ☌ | 280 |
| | b | 281 |
| | a | 282 |
| ♂ ♄ | ☌ | 283 |
| | b | 284 |
| | a | 285 |
| ♂ ♅ | ☌ | 286 |
| | b | 287 |
| | a | 288 |
| ♂ ♆ | ☌ | 289 |
| | b | 290 |
| | a | 291 |

*Jupiter*

| | | |
|---|---|---|
| ♃ ♄ | ☌ | 292 |
| | b | 293 |
| | a | 294 |
| ♃ ♅ | ☌ | 295 |
| | b | 296 |
| | a | 297 |
| ♃ ♆ | ☌ | 298 |
| | b | 299 |
| | a | 300 |

*Saturn*

| | | |
|---|---|---|
| ♄ ♅ | ☌ | 301 |
| | b | 302 |
| | a | 303 |
| ♄ ♆ | ☌ | 304 |
| | b | 305 |
| | a | 306 |

*Uranus*

| | | |
|---|---|---|
| ♅ ♆ | ☌ | 307 |
| | b | 308 |
| | a | 308A |

## Section 5

**Finance**

| | | |
|---|---|---|
| ☉ | II. | 309 |
| ☽ | II. | 310 |
| ☿ | II. | 311 |
| ♀ | II. | 312 |
| ♂ | II. | 313 |
| ♃ | II. | 314 |
| ♄ | II. | 315 |
| ♅ | II. | 316 |
| ♆ | II. | 317 |
| | Card. | 318 |
| | Fixed | 319 |
| | Mut. | 320 |
| ♀ | Ang. | 321 |
| ♃ | ,, | 322 |

**Travel**

| | | |
|---|---|---|
| ☉ | III. | 323 |
| ☽ | III. | 324 |
| ☿ | III. | 325 |
| ♀ | III. | 326 |
| ♂ | III. | 327 |
| ♃ | III. | 328 |
| ♄ | III. | 329 |
| ♅ | III. | 330 |
| ♆ | III. | 331 |
| | Card. | 332 |
| | Fixed | 333 |
| | Mut. | 334 |

**Environment**

| | | |
|---|---|---|
| ☉ | IV. | 335 |
| ☽ | IV. | 336 |
| ☿ | IV. | 337 |
| ♀ | IV. | 338 |
| ♂ | IV. | 339 |
| ♃ | IV. | 340 |
| ♄ | IV. | 341 |
| ♅ | IV. | 342 |
| ♆ | IV. | 313 |

**Enterprise**

| | | |
|---|---|---|
| ☉ | V. | 344 |
| ☽ | V. | 345 |
| ☿ | V. | 346 |
| ♀ | V. | 347 |
| ♂ | V. | 348 |
| ♃ | V. | 349 |
| ♄ | V. | 350 |
| ♅ | V. | 351 |
| ♆ | V. | 352 |

**Sickness**

| | | |
|---|---|---|
| ☉ | VI. | 353 |
| ☽ | VI. | 354 |
| ☿ | VI. | 355 |
| ♀ | VI. | 356 |
| ♂ | VI. | 357 |
| ♃ | VI. | 358 |
| ♄ | VI. | 359 |
| ♅ | VI. | 360 |
| ♆ | VI. | 361 |

# Reference Chart—*continued.*

**MARRIAGE**

☉ VII. *362*
☽ VII. *363*
☿ VII. *364*
♀ VII. *365*
♂ VII. *366*
♃ VII. *367*
♄ VII. *368*
♅ VII. *369*
♆ VII. *370*
♀ ♈ *371*
♀ ♉ *372*
♀ ♊ *373*
♀ ♋ *374*
♀ ♌ *375*
♀ ♍ *376*
♀ ♎ *377*
♀ ♏ *378*
♀ ♐ *379*
♀ ♑ *380*
♀ ♒ *381*
♀ ♓ *382*

**LEGACIES**

☉ VIII. *383*
☽ VIII. *384*
☿ VIII. *385*
♀ VIII. *386*
♂ VIII. *387*
♃ VIII. *388*
♄ VIII. *389*
♅ VIII. *390*
♆ VIII. *391*

**PHILOSOPHY**

☉ IX. *392*
☽ IX. *393*
☿ IX. *394*
♀ IX. *395*
♂ IX. *396*
♃ IX. *397*
♄ IX. *398*
♅ IX. *399*
♆ IX. *400*

**PROFESSION**

☉ X. *401*
☽ X. *402*
☿ X. *403*
♀ X. *404*
♂ X. *405*
♃ X. *406*
♄ X. *407*
♅ X. *408*
♆ X. *409*
CARD. *410*
FIXED *411*
MUT. *412*

**FRIENDS**

☉ XI. *413*
☽ XI. *414*
☿ XI. *415*
♀ XI. *416*
♂ XI. *417*
♃ XI. *418*
♄ XI. *419*
♅ XI. *420*
♆ XI. *421*
Fiery sign *422*
Earthy ,, *423*
Airy ,, *424*
Watery ,, *425*

**OCCULTISM**

☉ XII. *426*
☽ XII. *427*
☿ XII. *428*
♀ XII. *429*
♂ XII. *430*
♃ XII. *431*
♄ XII. *432*
♅ XII. *433*
♆ XII. *434*
N.P. *435*

## Section 6

**SUMMARIES**

Rising *436*
Setting *437*
Above *438*
Below *439*

Fire *440*
Air *441*
Water *442*
Earth *443*

Card. *444*
Fixed *445*
Mut. *446*

C. & F. *447*
C. & M. *448*
F. & C. *449*
F. & M. *450*
M. & C. *451*
M. & F. *452*

F. & A. *453*
F. & W. *454*
F. & E. *455*
A. & F. *456*
A. & W. *457*
A & E. *458*
W. & F. *459*
W. & A. *460*
W. & E. *461*
E. & F. *462*
E. & A. *463*
E. & W. *464*

**SUPPLEMENTARY PARAGRAPHS**

*Rising Planets*

☉ *465*
☽ *466*
☿ *467*
♀ *468*
♂ *469*
♃ *470*
♄ *471*
♅ *472*
♆ *473*

*Personal Colouring*

☽ ♈ *474*
☽ ♉ *475*
☽ ♊ *476*
☽ ♋ *477*
☽ ♌ *478*
☽ ♍ *479*
☽ ♎ *480*
☽ ♏ *481*
☽ ♐ *482*
☽ ♑ *483*
☽ ♒ *484*
☽ ♓ *485*

**POLARITIES**

☉♈-☽♈ *486*
☉♈-☽♉ *487*
☉♈-☽♊ *488*
☉♈-☽♋ *489*
☉♈-☽♌ *490*
☉♈-☽♍ *491*
☉♈-☽♎ *492*
☉♈-☽♏ *493*
☉♈-☽♐ *494*
☉♈-☽♑ *495*
☉♈-☽♒ *496*
☉♈-☽♓ *497*
☉♉-☽♈ *498*
☉♉-☽♉ *499*
☉♉-☽♊ *500*
☉♉-☽♋ *501*
☉♉-☽♌ *502*
☉♉-☽♍ *503*
☉♉-☽♎ *504*
☉♉-☽♏ *505*
☉♉-☽♐ *506*
☉♉-☽♑ *507*
☉♉-☽♒ *508*
☉♉-☽♓ *509*
☉♊-☽♈ *510*
☉♊-☽♉ *511*
☉♊-☽♊ *512*
☉♊-☽♋ *513*
☉♊-☽♌ *514*
☉♊-☽♍ *515*
☉♊-☽♎ *516*
☉♊-☽♏ *517*
☉♊-☽♐ *518*
☉♊-☽♑ *519*
☉♊-☽♒ *520*
☉♊-☽♓ *521*
☉♋-☽♈ *522*
☉♋-☽♉ *523*
☉♋-☽♊ *524*
☉♋-☽♋ *525*
☉♋-☽♌ *526*
☉♋-☽♍ *527*
☉♋-☽♎ *528*
☉♋-☽♏ *529*
☉♋-☽♐ *530*
☉♋-☽♑ *531*
☉♋-☽♒ *532*
☉♋ ☽♓ *533*
☉♌-☽♈ *534*
☉♌-☽♉ *535*
☉♌-☽♊ *536*
☉♌-☽♋ *537*
☉♌-☽♌ *538*
☉♌-☽♍ *539*
☉♌-☽♎ *540*
☉♌-☽♏ *541*
☉♌-☽♐ *542*
☉♌-☽♑ *543*
☉♌-☽♒ *544*
☉♌-☽♓ *545*
☉♍-☽♈ *546*
☉♍-☽♉ *547*
☉♍-☽♊ *548*
☉♍-☽♋ *549*
☉♍-☽♌ *550*
☉♍-☽♍ *551*
☉♍-☽♎ *552*

**POLARITIES**—*continued*

☉♍-☽♏ *553*
☉♍-☽♐ *554*
☉♍-☽♑ *555*
☉♍-☽♒ *556*
☉♍-☽♓ *557*
☉♎-☽♈ *558*
☉♎-☽♉ *559*
☉♎-☽♊ *560*
☉♎-☽♋ *561*
☉♎-☽♌ *562*
☉♎-☽♍ *563*
☉♎-☽♎ *564*
☉♎-☽♏ *565*
☉♎-☽♐ *566*
☉♎-☽♑ *567*
☉♎-☽♒ *568*
☉♎-☽♓ *569*
☉♏-☽♈ *570*
☉♏-☽♉ *571*
☉♏-☽♊ *572*
☉♏-☽♋ *573*
☉♏-☽♌ *574*
☉♏-☽♍ *575*
☉♏-☽♎ *576*
☉♏-☽♏ *577*
☉♏-☽♐ *578*
☉♏-☽♑ *579*
☉♏-☽♒ *580*
☉♏-☽♓ *581*
☉♐-☽♈ *582*
☉♐-☽♉ *583*
☉♐-☽♊ *584*
☉♐-☽♋ *585*
☉♐-☽♌ *586*
☉♐-☽♍ *587*
☉♐-☽♎ *588*
☉♐-☽♏ *589*
☉♐-☽♐ *590*
☉♐-☽♑ *591*
☉♐-☽♒ *592*
☉♐-☽♓ *593*
☉♑-☽♈ *594*
☉♑-☽♉ *595*
☉♑-☽♊ *596*
☉♑-☽♋ *597*
☉♑-☽♌ *598*
☉♑-☽♍ *599*
☉♑-☽♎ *600*
☉♑-☽♏ *601*
☉♑-☽♐ *602*
☉♑-☽♑ *603*
☉♑-☽♒ *604*
☉♑-☽♓ *605*
☉♒-☽♈ *606*
☉♒-☽♉ *607*
☉♒-☽♊ *608*
☉♒-☽♋ *609*
☉♒-☽♌ *610*
☉♒-☽♍ *611*
☉♒-☽♎ *612*
☉♒-☽♏ *613*
☉♒-☽♐ *614*
☉♒-☽♑ *615*
☉♒-☽♒ *616*
☉♒-☽♓ *617*
☉♓-☽♈ *618*
☉♓-☽♉ *619*
☉♓-☽♊ *620*
☉♓-☽♋ *621*
☉♓-☽♌ *622*
☉♓-☽♍ *623*
☉♓-☽♎ *624*
☉♓-☽♏ *625*
☉♓-☽♐ *626*
☉♓-☽♑ *627*
☉♓-☽♒ *628*
☉♓-☽♓ *629*

## Section 7

**FUTURE PROSPECTS**—*Solar Aspects*

☉ ☽ ☌ i.
b ii.
a iii.
☉ ☿ ☌ iv.
b v.
a vi.
☉ ♀ ☌ vii.
b viii.
a ix.
☉ ♂ ☌ x.
b xi.
a xii.
☉ ♃ ☌ xiii.
b xiv.
a xv.
☉ ♄ ☌ xvi.
b xvii.
a xviii.
☉ ♅ ☌ xix.
b xx.
a xxi.
☉ ♆ ☌ xxii.
b xxiii.
a xxiv.

**FUTURE PROSPECTS**—*Interplanetary or Mutual Aspects*

☿ ♀ ☌ xxv.
b xxvi.
a xxvii.
☿ ♂ ☌ xxviii.
b xxix.
a xxx.
☿ ♃ ☌ xxxi.
b xxxii.
a xxxiii.
☿ ♄ ☌ xxxiv.
b xxxv.
a xxxvi.
☿ ♅ ☌ xxxvii.
b xxxviii.
a xxxix.
☿ ♆ ☌ xl.
b xli.
a xlii.
♀ ♂ ☌ xliii.
b xliv.
a xlv.
♀ ♃ ☌ xlvi.
b xlvii.
a xlviii.
♀ ♄ ☌ xlix.
b l.
a li.
♀ ♅ ☌ lii.
b liii.
a liv.
♀ ♆ ☌ lv.
b lvi.
a lvii.
♂ ♃ ☌ lviii.
b lix.
a lx.
♂ ♄ ☌ lxi.
b lxii.
a lxiii.
♂ ♅ ☌ lxiv.
b lxv.
a lxvi.
♂ ♆ ☌ lxvii.
b lxviii.
a lxix.
♃ & ♄ b lxx.
a lxxi.
♃ ♅ ☌ lxxii.
b lxxiii.
a lxxiv.
♄ ♅ ☌ lxxv.
b lxxvi.
a lxxvii.

*Moon's progress through Signs*

☽ ♈ lxxviii.
☽ ♉ lxxix.
☽ ♊ lxxx.
☽ ♋ lxxxi.
☽ ♌ lxxxii.
☽ ♍ lxxxiii.
☽ ♎ lxxxiv.
☽ ♏ lxxxv.
☽ ♐ lxxxvi.
☽ ♑ lxxxvii.
☽ ♒ lxxxviii.
☽ ♓ lxxxix.

**FUTURE PROSPECTS**—*Moon's Progress*

☽ 1st xc.
☽ 2nd xci.
☽ 3rd xcii.
☽ 4th xciii.
☽ 5th xciv.
☽ 6th xcv.
☽ 7th xcvi.
☽ 8th xcvii.
☽ 9th xcviii.
☽ 10th xcix.
☽ 11th c.
☽ 12th ci.

**FUTURE PROSPECTS**

☽ ☉ ☌ cii.
b ciii.
a civ.
☽ ☿ ☌ cv.
b cvi.
a cvii.
☽ ♀ ☌ cviii.
b cix.
a cx.

**FUTURE PROSPECTS**—*Moon's Progress (continued)*

☽ ♂ ☌ cxi.
b cxii.
a cxiii.
☽ ♃ ☌ cxiv.
b cxv.
a cxvi.
☽ ♄ ☌ cxvii.
b cxviii.
a cxix.
☽ ♅ ☌ cxx
b cxxi.
a cxxii.
☽ ♆ ☌ cxxiii.
b cxxiv.
a cxxv.

AN HONEST TALE SPEEDS BEST BEING PLAINLY TOLD.

*Shakespeare: King Richard II.*

# The Key to your own Nativity.

§ 1.—*The Ruling Planet, etc.*

## CHAPTER I.

### THE ASCENDANT AND THE RISING SIGN.

THE term ASCENDANT is a name for the first of the twelve houses of the horoscope. It is due east of the place of birth; and the beginning or cusp of the house is the eastern horizon. The Rising Sign is that sign of the zodiac which is on the cusp of the Ascendant at birth. This is usually the most important sign in the horoscope, and it gives a description in general terms of the personal appearance and the character, although this is subject to modification according to the positions of the planets—especially the Ruling Planet, and any planet or planets that may be rising in or near the Ascendant.

**1.** ARIES was rising at your birth. This is a cardinal, movable, and fiery sign. This gives much energy and activity both of body and mind, much impulse and enthusiasm, with many changes in the course of life. You are courageous, enterprising, frank and outspoken. You can face difficulties promptly and bravely; you know your own mind, and are seldom at a loss what to do or say when called upon to decide. You are ambitious, self-reliant, and adventurous; and you will win your way in the world largely through these qualities and through your confidence in your own ability to succeed. You are a great lover of freedom and independence, and you get along badly when you are in any way hampered, restricted, or interfered with. You are generous and quickly responsive to appeals to the emotions. You are a zealous and energetic supporter of any person or cause that enlists your sympathies. Most of your misfortunes will arise through too much hastiness and impulse, whether in action, in judgment, or in the feelings. You are somewhat lacking in coolness, in calm deliberation, and self-restraint; and you do not find it

See descriptions on page 8.

easy to give way to others even when justice or prudence demands it. Mars is the ruling planet of the sign Aries.

**2.** TAURUS was rising at your birth; a fixed earthy sign. In disposition you are loving and affectionate, fond of pleasure, and an admirer of beauty in all things. The sign Taurus often gives a love of music or art, with good taste in colour, in melody, in dress, in ornaments, and elegance generally. You are cool, self-contained, firm, and strong-willed; a lover of peace, quiet, and harmony. You are also practical and desirous of putting everything to the test of practice and experience, and you value persons, things, and ideas largely for the use to which they can be put. You have much perseverance and quiet firmness, are somewhat reserved and self-centred, and you can show great obstinacy upon occasion. You do not change very easily, and are a little lacking in adaptability. Your course of life tends to move from day to day and even from year to year in its accustomed channels with comparatively little alteration. You are not easily influenced by other people, but are a persistent and patient worker in your own way and according to your own ideas. You are slow to anger but are apt to harbour resentment. You have fixed opinions, keen feelings and desires, and are capable of strong passions; but are also good natured and fond of comfort and repose. Venus is the ruling planet of the sign Taurus.

**3.** GEMINI was rising at your birth; a sign belonging to the element air and to the common or mutable quality. You have good mental abilities and an active and flexible mind. This is one of the intellectual signs, and those who are born under it usually have abilities for writing, studying, speaking or thinking. You are fond of books and reading, you can learn easily from books or lectures, you can apply your mind to a variety of subjects and are ingenious and inventive. You are suitable for receiving a good education and are adapted for almost any literary pursuit or clerical work. You have good reasoning powers, a thoughtful mind, and are fluent either of speech or pen. You have ability for languages and science and are also fond of travel. You have comprehensiveness of mind and a quick adaptability to various pursuits and studies, but you are somewhat lacking in concentration and perseverance. You are rather irresolute, uncertain, and changeable at times, do not feel sure of yourself and may even hold or express contradictory

See descriptions on page 8.

opinions.   You are liable to worry and irritation and are easily upset by little annoyances.   You are kind, humane and sympathetic, but you know what it is to have fits of shyness, nervousness, and reserve, when you withdraw into yourself.   Reason and understanding are your strong faculties, but you are liable to lack continuity and strength of will. Mercury is the ruling planet of the sign Gemini.

**4.**    CANCER was rising at your birth ; a sign belonging to the element water and to the cardinal or movable quality.   This gives you much sensitiveness and receptivity, active feelings and emotions, and love of sensation and novelty.   You have a strong domestic and social nature, warm affections, and are fond of home life.   You are easily influenced by those whom you love or admire, but are apt to be cold, reserved, and distrustful to those you do not know well or whom you dislike.   You have an active imagination and fancy, and often live the past over again in your mind and anticipate the future.   You have much prudence and forethought, are careful and cautious, and have a good deal of tenacity and firmness.   You have some natural ability for trade and business management and might gain success in this direction, as you have a sense of value and economy.   You have a practical mind and you put everything ultimately to the test of practical use, and with care you may make a reputation as a useful and practical person in your own line of life.   You live a good deal in the senses, and at times are changeful and capricious, but you also have patience and perseverance.   The Moon is the ruler of the sign Cancer.

**5.**    LEO was rising at your birth ; a sign belonging to the element fire and of the fixed quality.   This gives you an open, candid and honourable disposition, magnanimous and generous.   You have dignity and self-confidence that will sustain you in trouble and difficulty, and that will bring you to the front in life if you use your opportunities wisely. You do not under-rate your own value, but are ambitious and masterful with large and far-reaching aims and schemes.   You have some degree of pride and fondness for display and ostentation at times, and the sense of the dramatic is strong in you.   You have a warm heart and ardent affections and make a very faithful friend, one not liable to change or vacillate.   You are compassionate, tender and sympathetic, and anxious to give help to those who need it and to protect those who need protection.

See descriptions on page 8.

Your pride is rather easily touched, and anger is sometimes quick to rise, but you are a forgiving enemy and prefer peace to war. You have a firm strong will and do not readily change your course when you have once decided on it, but are capable of persistent effort extended over a long period. You are cheerful, hopeful, sociable and companionable. Your feelings and emotions are quickly roused, you are rather fond of luxury and pleasure, and may need to put some curb upon this side of your nature. The Sun is the ruler of the sign Leo.

**6.** VIRGO was rising at your birth; a sign belonging to the earthy element and to the common or mutable quality. This gives a disposition quiet, retiring, modest and reserved. You are careful and prudent, and are capable of exercising much forethought before you act. You are sympathetic and kind, but you do not wear your heart on your sleeve; and although you are very adaptable and almost capable of being all things to all men, you seldom show your real nature openly, and are at times difficult to understand. You have good mental abilities, can learn readily and are of a studious nature. You have a logical mind, good reasoning faculties, and have much adaptability for scientific or literary pursuits; but you are able to develope a fair amount of practical ability also, and can attend to small details skilfully and methodically. You are apt at times to worry unnecessarily, and to vacillate and change your mind. You are diffident and lacking in self-confidence and are too ready to give way before difficulties. You are not sufficiently hopeful. You will work best and be most fortunate if you follow a leader and rely upon him. Virgo is the sign of the servant, not the master. Mercury is the ruling planet of the sign Virgo.

**7.** LIBRA was rising at your birth; a sign belonging to the element air and to the cardinal or movable quality. This gives you a courteous, gentle, affable and kind disposition. Your feelings and affections are strongly developed and are likely to play an important part in your life. You are able to make many friends; you associate easily with other people; the social side of your nature is active and your growth will best be served by cultivating it wisely. You will be less fortunate if you live alone or dissociate yourself from others. You have a refined mind, are fond of beauty and orderliness, with a taste for music or painting. Your surroundings influence you very much and you are not happy unless they

See descriptions on page 8.

are neat, elegant and harmonious. Your mind is susceptible of considerable cultivation especially in connection with the more imaginative and idealistic subjects; but you have more intuition than reason, and emotion and affection are more to you than cold intellect. You are rather fickle and changeable, your likes and dislikes vary a good deal, and your ideas change with your moods. You are not quite constant either to persons or to ideas, and you are likely to experience many changes in your life. Companionship, friendship, partnership, association, and marriage are the keynotes of your nature, and you will not attain to your fullest possibilities without them. Venus is the planet ruling the sign Libra.

**8.** SCORPIO was rising at your birth; a sign belonging to the element water and to the fixed quality. This gives you a strong and forceful character, positive and decided. You generally know your own mind and are clear and emphatic in your ideas and opinions. Irresolution is not usually one of the weaknesses of this sign. You are brave and courageous and do not shrink from controversy or dispute if it is thrust upon you. You are self-reliant and do not shirk responsibility. You have strong likes and dislikes towards both persons and ideas, and you do not easily change either your opinions or your habits of life. You have much strength of will; and although feelings, emotions, and passions sometimes sway you intensely, you have much endurance and persistence and you can work hard and long to achieve your ends. You have a good deal of pride and dignity, and are capable of much anger if either of these is wounded. You should have considerable executive ability and are capable of becoming a good practical worker if you turn your attention in this direction. You are a good fighter, and the critical, sarcastic, and analytical sides of your nature are active. You are ingenious and resourceful; at times too brusque and emphatic in manner and not sufficiently conciliatory towards those who differ from you; and you are ambitious and masterful. You have some taste for things mystical, occult, curious and secret. Mars is the planet that rules the sign Scorpio.

**9.** SAGITTARIUS was rising at your birth; a sign belonging to the element fire and to the mutable or common quality. This gives you an honourable and open-minded disposition, frank and candid. You are generous, kind and sympathetic, truthful and just. You have much

See descriptions on page 8.

sense of dignity and like neatness, orderliness, precision and correctness both in person and surroundings. You have also a love of beauty in form and outline and have much taste in clothes, ornaments, and decorations. You are a lover of freedom and independence; are generally active and restless, as well as hopeful and cheery. You are fond of out-door sports and exercises and may gain a good deal of skill in this direction. You are somewhat impulsive and fiery, sometimes a little too brusque and abrupt, but usually only when offended; for as a rule you are very ceremonious in your behaviour and dislike anything like a breach of etiquette. You are generous, humane, and benevolent. You are versatile in mind, and have a natural ability to cultivate the mind in the direction of the higher or more difficult branches of learning, such as philosophy, theology or law. You have the sense of reverence and devotion and have much natural religion whether you cultivate it or not. Jupiter is the planet ruling the sign Sagittarius.

**10.** CAPRICORN was rising at your birth; a sign belonging to the element earth and of the cardinal or movable quality. This gives you a quiet, steady, and persevering disposition, patient, enduring and tactful. You are at times inclined to melancholy and to too serious a frame of mind; are a little lacking in cheerfulness, hopefulness, and buoyancy; and sometimes look too much on the dark side of things. You have much practical executive ability, are a steady useful worker and will carry out faithfully any work you undertake. You have much self-control and strength of will, and can pursue your ends persistently in the face of many obstacles. You believe in justice, economy, caution and prudence, and you usually think before you act. You are ambitious of power and are capable of exercising it; are self-possessed and can order, direct and manage subordinates very efficiently, although you are apt to be more respected than loved by them. You possess reserve and restraint; you do not make friends very easily, but you are very faithful to those you possess and are a stern and rather pitiless enemy. You have a quiet persistence and steadfast determination that will enable you to do almost anything you set your mind on. Saturn is the planet ruling the sign Capricorn.

**11.** AQUARIUS was rising at your birth; a sign belonging to the element air and of the fixed quality. This gives you good mental and

See descriptions on page 8.

intellectual abilities, and you should possess tastes that may be cultivated for either science, literature or art. You have a strong will, strong and decided opinions, and do not change very easily. You are patient and persevering, firm and quietly determined. Your disposition is open, candid, frank and truthful; and if at times you can be very silent and self-contained you are not usually given to melancholy but are genial, cheerful, and ingenuous. You are likely to make many friends and are constant and faithful in your attachments and you will benefit a good deal through friends and acquaintances and take much pleasure in their society and companionship. You have a good memory and are capable of receiving a good education, and you have abilities capable of cultivation in a variety of directions. You have some inclination for the occult and mysterious and might easily make headway in such directions. Saturn is the planet ruling the sign Aquarius.

**12.** PISCES was rising at your birth; a sign belonging to the element water and to the common or mutable quality. This makes you kind, sympathetic, benevolent and generous. You have a humane and charitable disposition, your feelings are easily roused, and you are disposed to help those who need your help. You are sociable and friendly and are able to make acquaintances easily and to get on with people. You have a strong imagination and a fertile fancy, are impressionable and emotional, and you would be suited for any course in life that would develope this side of your nature; for the theatre, singing, music, painting or for imaginative literature, as you have some taste in these directions. You like to take life easily and enjoy yourself, are good-natured and easy going and like to be well-disposed to all people, and you usually are so. You have some sense of dignity and pride, and are observant of forms, ceremonies and etiquette, and are considerate of the feelings of others. You are a lover of beauty and refinement; you cannot bear ugly or inharmonious surroundings; and you have much artistic taste. You are sensitive, intuitional, and receptive. Jupiter is the planet ruling the sign Pisces.

See descriptions on page 8.

### Approximate Description of Personal Appearance
### Produced by the Sign Rising.

*N.B.—These descriptions are considerably modified by (1) the sign which the Moon occupies at birth, and (2) the sign in which the lord of the Ascendant or Ruling Planet is placed. They are here given as general hints merely. To correctly judge appearance from the horoscope requires much skill.*

ARIES RISING produces a dry and rather lean body ; middle stature ; strong limbs, large bones, a face somewhat like a *ram*, often dark and usually thick eyebrows, quick sight, fairly long neck, dark or ' fiery ' complexion, rough and wiry hair, often curly and usually brown, sometimes reddish ; fairly broad shoulders. The first half of the sign gives a taller and fuller build, the last half a smaller type and usually much darker.

TAURUS RISING produces a short, full, well-set body ; full face and eyes, short thick neck, full lips, wide nostrils and mouth, shining face often somewhat swarthy ; large strong shoulders, short thick broad hands, dark sometimes black hair, usually inclined to be curly especially in the front, with often a little tuft on the forehead.

GEMINI RISING gives a tall, upright, straight body ; long arms ; hands and feet generally thin and nervous, usually dark complexion, dark or blackish hair ; eyes hazel with a sharp quick active look, and usually very bright.

CANCER RISING gives a moderate stature, full and usually round face, pale and with a delicate appearance ; features small, and generally a nose of the type termed cogitative ; sad brown hair, and small grey eyes. The Moon's sign-position greatly affects the appearance and indeed the whole character in this case, but those born under Cancer are usually timid and retiring.

LEO RISING. Fair stature inclining to fulness of body ; usually well formed, with upright carriage ; broad shoulders well set ; eyes bright and glowing, with quick sight ; and usually of a brown hazel or hazel brown colour ; plenty of hair of fairish colour, ranging from flaxen to brown of varying shades ; oval to round face, ruddy or sanguine complexion, firm step, and usually dignified and autocratic bearing.

VIRGO RISING. Middle stature, well formed, rather slender; neat and compact, sometimes very prim. Dark, ruddy complexion and pleasing face, nose long and projecting from the base. The mercurial nose is unmistakable.

LIBRA RISING. Fair statue, sometimes tall, in the first half of the sign; in the latter half, stouter and shorter. A graceful body, well formed; hair smooth and glossy, sometimes jet black, though if Venus is in a fair sign the hair is quite light; face round and lovely, fine clear red-and-white complexion, eyes ranging from blue to green, but always large and clear. Persons born under this sign are usually very good looking, women especially. A pleasing and graceful bearing, and very polite in address.

SCORPIO RISING. Medium size, thick, well-set body, strong and robust; face square or broad, complexion dark or dusky, hair dark brown, usually rough, curling, bushy and plentiful. Eyes dark, sometimes grey and rather small, with a shrewd look. Walk is rather snake-like or sinuous, especially in women.

SAGITTARIUS RISING. Well-formed body, rather tall; long, oval face, high forehead and long nose; fine clear eyes, often a dull glazed brown, very round and open looking and of an unmistakable type; good complexion, open countenance; hair chestnut or light brown. Fond of walking and of a good carriage.

CAPRICORN RISING. Short slender body, not as a rule well formed; long thin face, generally plain. Chin long and often protuding, small thin wry neck, hair very dark brown or black, sometimes a blue black, and lanky; narrow breast and usually weak knees.

AQUARIUS RISING. Middle stature, sometimes stout, and well set, robust and strong; long face; good, clear, sanguine and sometimes very delicate complexion; hazel eyes; fair hair from flaxen to light brown. This sign gives to males as much personal beauty as Libra gives to females.

PISCES RISING. Short stature, thickish build, round shoulders and stooping gait; large, pale face, clear and lucid skin, hair dark or darkish; sleepy or fishy or protruding eyes, very mobile features and soft speech.

# CHAPTER II.

## THE RULING PLANET.

WITH each sign of the zodiac one of the planets is associated as lord or ruler of the sign. An account of the Rising Signs has been given in Chapter I., and particulars of the influence of the planets that rule these signs follow here.

**13.** THE SUN is ruler of the sign Leo. Its influence is to give vitality and fire to the whole nature, physically and mentally. It contributes towards dignity, self-reliance, and strength of will; giving ambition and a desire to achieve worthy results in action. You will wish to be at the head of affairs in your own particular sphere, and you will not find it congenial to occupy subordinate positions. You are able to organise and manage affairs and people, and you do not shrink from responsibility. You are kind-hearted and generous, admiring what is noble and scorning what is mean or base. The social and affectional side of your nature is well developed, and you can easily attract to yourself friends and companions. You like comfort, pleasure, and luxury; and you must not let weaknesses either of the heart, or it may be of the desire nature, run away with you. Internal harmony realised in outer life is the key to this influence, which belongs chiefly to the individuality.

**14.** THE MOON is ruler of the sign Cancer. Its influence is to form, nourish and sustain, and it pertains to the personality. The domestic and home-loving side of your nature is strong, and you are drawn towards family and parents. Your imagination is well developed, and plays a large part in your life. Feeling and sensation are active with you, and you are rather liable to change and fluctuate in your moods from day to day, and to lack energy and persistence. You have the ability to become practical and to deal with affairs as you find them in a capable manner. You could adapt yourself to a variety of subjects according to your training; for domestic life, business, practical science and applied art all supply spheres for the activity of those who are born under the Moon. You are careful and prudent, and inclined to economy and foresight in all things, and are practical and capable when you do not let your imagination or your feelings run away with you.

**15.** The planet MERCURY is the ruler of the signs Gemini and Virgo. Its influence is over the brain and nerves, and it has more to do with the mind than with the senses. It gives you good mental ability, ingenuity and adaptability, fertility of resource and wit, and probably a good memory. You should be apt at speech and argument, plausible and fluent in conversation ; but along with this there sometimes goes a degree of subtlety, and secrecy, as well as reserve or retirement. Your whole nature will seldom be shown to the world, and there will be one side which you will never show even to your most intimate friends. Your mind is active but a little lacking in concentration and perseverance ; and you are liable to occupy yourself with too many subjects, to change a little too rapidly, and to have too many irons in the fire. You can adapt yourself readily to the moods and opinions of people, and can see truth under quite opposite disguises. Mercury takes upon itself to some extent the nature of other planets ; therefore you need to pay attention to the sign occupied by Mercury at your birth and the aspects it receives ; for these may modify what has been here stated.

**16.** The planet VENUS is the ruler of the signs Taurus and Libra. It is the planet of love and beauty. It strengthens the affections and it will make the social side of your nature active and strong. You are warm-hearted and companionable, fond of the society of friends and relatives, of a loving and peaceable disposition, and favouring all that is harmonious and refined. You are fond of ease and comfort, of pleasure and luxury, and you may need to exercise some restraint over this side of your nature. Venus generally gives those who are born under it good taste and a love of beauty, of fine surroundings, clothes, ornaments, decorations, and an appreciation of neatness and orderliness. You probably have the ability to develope the æsthetic side of your nature in the direction of singing, music, art, poetry, etc. ; if you care to do so. The influence of the planet can also be adapted to a business life, as it gives some financial ability and good luck. The disposition is usually cheerful, hopeful, and good natured, and brings popularity and many friends.

Venus is the chief significator of love and marriage. It also has some influence over money matters and general prosperity as well as giving a sense of beauty.

**17.** The planet MARS is the ruler of the signs Aries and Scorpio. It is the planet of fire, energy, and expansion. It gives you a disposition that is ardent, active, positive, impulsive, and impetuous. You are a lover of freedom and independence, and cannot endure restraint, confinement or delay. You are generous and frank, an admirer of openness, bravery and courage, both physical and moral. You have much self-confidence, and are usually able to hold your own easily, being prompt in word and action. You need to beware of being too rash and headstrong, for you are rather inclined to be aggressive and self-willed ; and you are likely to bring many troubles upon yourself through this. You have a good deal of pride, which is easily wounded, and you do not find it easy to remain cool and self-restrained under provocation. You are an active and energetic worker and can accomplish much in a short time, and you have it in you to become very practical and capable in the world if you exercise a little self-discipline.

Mars is the planet of fire, energy, impulse, and action. Its position by sign indicates the channel through which these qualities will flow. It also has some significance in connection with the kind of death.

**18.** The planet JUPITER is the ruler of the signs Sagittarius and Pisces. It tends to give a hopeful, buoyant and cheerful disposition which should go far towards making you popular and gaining you many friends. You can gain social esteem and success and will be popular and generally liked. You are benevolent, generous and humane, and are always ready to help those who deserve it and to assist worthy causes. You have a regard for law, order, and propriety and for the rules and conventions of customs ; you dislike incivility, awkwardness, or bad taste in opinions or conduct as much as you do ugliness or inharmony in your surroundings. You have a reverence for beauty both in outward form and in ideas ; you like beautiful surroundings and comfort and elegance in all things. You have energy, enthusiasm, ardour and faithfulness. You have a natural respect for law and religion, and you take kindly to ritual, ceremonial, and etiquette, and are a little too liable to be bound by formalities. You have power to cultivate the higher faculties of the mind in the direction of law, religion, or philosophy, if you care to do so.

Jupiter is a very favourable planet when well placed. It governs social and general prosperity, religion, law, benevolence and good will ;

and gives some appreciation of beauty, harmony, imagination, and ideality.

**19.** The planet SATURN is the ruler of the signs Capricorn and Aquarius. It tends to give you a disposition that is sober, serious, and thoughtful. It is the planet that naturally rules old age, and its best influence is not usually seen until youth is passed. It gives you self-control, reserve and restraint, as well as some natural inclination to frugality, prudence and cautiousness. You should also gain from it strength of will and a patient, persevering disposition, with calmness, fortitude and serenity. You may at times be a little lacking in buoyancy and cheerfulness, and you do not unbend socially so easily as some persons can, or produce so much mirth, fun and jollity, although you can appreciate these when they come your way. You have a good deal of practical ability and can manage things and persons ably and economically. You are ambitious, and can form far-reaching plans and schemes and spend a long time in carrying them out. The best lesson that Saturn teaches is self-control, prudence, patience, chastity, thrift, and the meditative mind, as well as to distinguish between real worth and superficial pretentiousness.

Saturn is considered an unfortunate planet owing to its power to limit and restrict, it therefore has a binding and restraining influence. It is the bridge between the emotions and the mind and governs them until self-control is secured.

\*         \*         \*         \*

The above are the seven rulers of the signs of the zodiac according to the rules handed down from antiquity. In addition to these there are two other planets discovered in modern times—Uranus and Neptune. These are not yet proved to rule any of the signs in quite the same sense as the other planets do. Uranus is considered by some to have a good deal of sympathy with Aquarius, and may perhaps sometimes rule that sign but only in the more highly developed of humanity; it is also well placed when in Aries and Gemini. Neptune seems to have some sympathy with Pisces and is perhaps well placed in Cancer also.

**20.** The planet URANUS gives a strong, self-reliant and positive disposition in which all sides of the nature are capable of being fully developed. It gives a strong and original intellect; one that thinks out things for itself and does not copy other people. It gives ability for higher mental studies, whether scientific, metaphysical, or literary. To the emotional side of the character it gives force and energy, enthusiasm and determination, and great zeal on behalf of any person or cause that may attract. It renders the will strong and indomitable and gives the ability to work hard and actively. Those who are born under this planet are very independent, they dislike rules, restraints, and conventions, and frequently break or ignore these. They generally come to the front and are more or less notable persons in their sphere of life, as they can direct, control, and rule, and take responsibility. The planet also gives some leaning toward the occult and mysterious, and sometimes brings strange and unusual experiences. Sudden changes occur in the life; and the good and evil that Uranus bestows are both likely to come about very unexpectedly.

Uranus is the synthetic planet. It governs the will to a large extent and is responsible for magnetic changes in the body and nervous system ; it brings changes in consciousness and corresponding changes in life.

**21.** The planet NEPTUNE is difficult to understand, and seems very elusive. It has largely to do with the psychic and the emotional sides of the nature. It generally gives some psychic or mediumistic experiences, such as remarkable dreams, visions, intuitions, impressions, second sight, thought transference, etc., and some inclination towards these or similar subjects. It sometimes gives taste for music or art. It renders active the feelings, emotions, and the senses ; and in some cases there is danger of too much indulgence in this side of the nature, which may require restraint and purification. The will is often not very strong, and the nature is plastic and receptive ; and although it gives good nature and amiability there is liable to be irresolution and a disinclination to face difficulties and to remain firm and steadfast. Very little is actually known concerning the planet Neptune as its influence appears to affect the subconscious mind more than actual physical events, and it only affects to any considerable extent those who are very receptive, and somewhat mediumistic or psychic.

# CHAPTER III.

## The Position of the Ruling Planet in the Houses.

The influence of the Ruling Planet, as described in Chapter II., is subject to modification by its position in the houses and the signs and also by the aspects it receives from other planets. Any Aspects to the Ruling Planet (pars. 202 to 308) should therefore be considered, jointly with its sign- and house-position, under this head as explained in the Introduction.

The meaning of the position of the ruler in the twelve houses is given in the present Chapter.

**22.** The ruling planet rising in the Ascendant. This is a strong position and it is fortunate both for character and events. It means that the nature of the ruler, which has been previously described, may be expected to be very prominent in your character, and to operate with the least possible amount of hindrance and obstacle. This adds strength and uniqueness to the character also, marking you off clearly from other types. The influence of the ruler will also be seen clearly in the events of your life, both those which you cause yourself, and others which are brought upon you by the actions of people with whom you come in contact. If you learn thoroughly the nature of your ruler, you will be prepared for the effects it will produce when in this position. Its whole character is not likely to be shown at once ; for the more superficial traits belong to youth and the deeper and fuller influences to maturity.

**23.** The ruling planet is in the Second House. This brings financial matters and all questions relating to money and possessions prominently forward. You will have anxieties concerning money matters ; and either you will take considerable interest of your own accord in questions of finance or else circumstances will necessitate your doing so. Generally speaking the position is a fairly fortunate one and indicates ability to gain money through occupations or persons that are signified by the planet and by the sign in which it is placed. This good fortune will be increased by every good aspect the planet receives but either essene or interfered with by every bad one. This position of the ruler also increases somewhat the strength of will and the emotional or desire nature.

**24.** The ruling planet is in the THIRD HOUSE. This position makes thought and intellect more active in the life and makes it probable that the occupation or amusements or hobbies may be more of the mind than they would otherwise be. Books, writings, letters, documents, may be very important; perhaps much reading, writing or studying. This position also gives a good deal of travelling, chiefly short journeys; frequently much correspondence, and many changes of opinion or of mental outlook. You will be bound by family ties, and your brothers and sisters will either help or hinder you according to the agreement or disagreement of your horoscope with theirs.

**25.** The ruling planet is in the FOURTH HOUSE. This gives domestic and home ties that bind you, especially in the early part of your life ; some close link with one of the parents—probably the mother—that exerts a strong influence over you and affects your life a good deal. If this is not so, some circumstances in your environment will hamper you somewhat and may not be removed until middle age is passed. This position favours the acquisition of land, property, houses, and the products of the land, and is good for those who follow occupations connected with these things. The fourth house governs the latter years of life and old age in general ; and often the matters indicated by this position may not be experienced to their full extent until then. This point of the horoscope is somewhat psychic and occult, having a close relation with the astral plane, and you may be drawn toward psychic matters at the latter part of life or have some very unusual experiences.

**26.** The ruling planet is in the FIFTH HOUSE. This brings out the social and pleasure-loving side of the nature, giving warmth to the affections and ardour to the feelings. Amusements and occupations are taken up because they give you pleasure rather than for any use you intend to put them to, and you extract a good deal of enjoyment from life. In some cases the person who has this position at birth follows some pursuit or takes up some hobby that gives pleasure to others, such as music, art, the theatre, etc., and there is often decided taste in one of these directions. You must beware of going too far in matters of pleasure and the senses. You may be able to gain through judicious speculation when under favourable directions. You will be interested in children and fond of them. Your love nature will be strong and easily moved. You are generous, sincere, and honourable. Vitality and bodily health are strengthened by this position.

**27.** The ruling planet is in the SIXTH HOUSE. This is a good position for you if you are a worker, whether in a high or low position of life. You may have others working under you, and you will be able to manage and organise them successfully ; but this position oftener indicates one who is at his best when serving rather than when commanding, and who is most fortunate when he associates himself with someone else as manager, partner, or occupies some position under another rather than working alone. This applies both to business and professions. Sometimes a government servant may have this position, or one who is in a large firm or undertaking, or who is in some way not wholly his own master. Your health is liable to be affected adversely by such an influence as this and to delay your prospects in some way or bring you misfortune.

**28.** The ruling planet is in the SEVENTH HOUSE. This is likely to bring you before the public to some extent, as it contributes to the acquisition of friends and acquaintances, attracts attention to you, and will be good if you follow any career that brings you before the public. This especially attracts you towards the opposite sex and you are likely to be popular with them. It inclines strongly towards marriage and renders it unlikely that you will remain single. In business' or other undertakings you are likely to work best in partnership or in company with others rather than quite alone, and you can easily attract other people to you and get on with them. At such times as you are under bad directions you may have enemies as the result of this position, and suffer from opposition, rivalry, jealousy, or contention.

**29.** The ruling planet is in the EIGHTH HOUSE. This is a position that is rather liable to imperil the health or even the life during infancy and youth, especially when under bad directions. If this period is successfully passed, it increases your energy and strength of body as well as the activity and forcefulness of your nature. You are likely to gain money by association with other people, through partnership or otherwise ; and also to gain by marriage, if you marry. Money by legacy is very probable. You may have to do with wills or the goods of the dead ; the death of some friend or relative may have an important influence upon you ; and you may be brought in touch with death in many ways. A taste for psychism or occultism sometimes accompanies this position, and you may meet with unusual experiences in connection with spiritualism or the dead.  It is a good position for such people as surgeons, chemists, undertakers, coroners, or those who have to do with the dead either directly or indirectly.

**30.**  The ruling planet is in the NINTH HOUSE.  This will attract you towards religion at some time in your life and bring you in touch with people connected with religion or churches.  You may also interest yourself in philosophy or other profound subjects, as this position has much to do with the higher nature and the more abstract side of the mind and its cultivation.  You may have to do with authorship or publication either on your own account or by association with others.  You will probably travel a good deal or have to do with the sea or shipping, and may take a long voyage, and changes involving journeys will come into your life.  This position enriches and develops the mind and promotes the cultivation of knowledge and wisdom.

**31.**  The ruling planet is in the TENTH HOUSE.  This indicates that you are ambitious, aspiring, enterprising, and desirous of holding power and gaining recognition, and that you will probably succeed in doing so.  You are likely to rise in life, and to achieve honour, reputation, fame or position according to the nature of the efforts you put forth.  You will gain the favour of those who are older or more highly placed than yourself ; of business, professional, and social superiors ; and will benefit and derive pleasure from association with them.  Opportunities for achievement and success will occur to you and, if you live up to the possibilities that are in you, you may accomplish much.  Sometimes this indicates a close link with the father, or a resemblance to the father in appearance, disposition or occupation.

**32.**  The ruling planet is in the ELEVENTH HOUSE.  You will have many friends and acquaintances and will be rather a popular person in your own sphere of life.  You make friends easily among people who are of the type signified by your ruling planet ; they will be congenial, and you will derive both pleasure and benefit from them, as they will be willing to help you if you need assistance at any time.  At the same time you should exercise some discrimination in choosing friends, because when you are under bad directions you may suffer through them.  Friends are likely to influence you a good deal in one way or another.  You have some degree of ambition and of desire for success, as well as of worth and dignity, and you are likely to rise in life and meet the fulfilment of your ambitions.

**33.** The ruling planet is in the TWELFTH HOUSE. This is not wholly a fortunate position, because when you are under bad directions you will be liable to suffer from fraud, imposture, enmity, treachery, and malice. The evils that follow from this house are usually difficult or impossible to foresee and therefore are unexpected and often disastrous. Sometimes they will result from some lack of prudence or foresight on your own part and you may yourself be the cause of them; for which reason this house has been called that of "self-undoing." You may be hampered and restricted in your life through this influence, and have a feeling of thwarted hopes, or some degree of retirement or seclusion may be forced upon you at some time, with or without your desire. You may be in danger of false accusations, false friends, or even false imprisonment. While under good directions you may receive help and assistance if you need it and you will be willing to afford it to others, as you are sympathetic and charitable. Some inclination for occultism or psychic matters often accompanies this position, the joining of secret societies, and matters that involve secrecy, mystery, or the unexpected may enter into your life.

# CHAPTER IV.

## The Position in the Signs of the SUN as Ruler.

**34.** The Sun is in ARIES. This increases the energetic, active, and impulsive side of your nature, in so far as the rising sign can exhibit these qualities. You will be to some extent ambitious and aspiring, as well as quick to take advantage of your opportunities. You possess some independence and self-confidence; you are capable of filling positions of responsibility and prominence; and can direct and manage other people. When you meet with opposition you are inclined to be rather wilful, rash, and pugnacious. Your natural position is in the forefront and you do not readily take a back seat, or subordinate yourself to others easily. You are capable of working hard for any person or cause that attracts you and of sacrificing much. This is a fairly fortunate position for vitality as well as for rising in life.

**35.** The Sun is in TAURUS. This increases your self-reliance and ambition, but accompanying these there will be much perseverance and determination, and you will be more likely to act cautiously than impulsively. You are apt to be rather fixed and unyielding at times, not sufficiently adaptable and responsive to new ways and ideas. Your natural tendency is to follow one course of life for a long time with comparatively little change; but this enables you to pursue your purpose with steadfastness, patience, and quiet persistence; and you may achieve much in this way. These characteristics may be directed either towards public affairs or money matters, and will tend to bring you prominence or success in the long run. You are affectionate and warm-hearted, but can also be quiet and self-contained at times.

**36.** The Sun is in GEMINI. This will increase the mental side of your nature, making your mind positive and strong but also versatile, restless, and fond of change. This may give you some inclination for reading, writing, educational, clerical or literary work of some kind; and you might meet with success in an occupation having to do with one of these. You are sympathetic and intuitive, but are a little lacking in continuity and a little irresolute at times. You can adapt yourself to people readily, and understand people ; you can also persuade and argue with them but are not quite so successful at managing or commanding them. You may travel a good deal because of this position, mainly short journeys by land. The intellectual and scientific side of your nature is strong, and you will probably make friends among such people as writers, students, intellectual or literary folk.

**37.** The Sun is in CANCER. This increases feeling and sensitiveness in you and gives you an inclination for home life and domesticity. You are naturally reserved and cautious, and you do not show your whole nature on the surface. You can make headway in life by the exercise of prudence, care and economy ; and this position gives some degree of business instinct and forethought, also adaptability for practical matters, whether in the household, in more public affairs, or in applied science. You have tact and management and might achieve success through these qualities. This is favourable for gain through the parents, and it inclines to the acquisition of house or land property and to dealing in these. In the case of elderly people this position is rather good for comfort and prosperity in old age. Your success in life will depend more than with most people upon a favourable environment ; because if circumstances oppose you, you are apt to feel keenly a sense of being hampered, thwarted and restricted.

**38.** The Sun is in LEO. This gives you ambition, aspiration, ardour, and determination. You possess good organising ability ; can manage and direct other people ; are fitted for being at the head of affairs ; and able to assume authority and command. If you exercise self-control you may achieve much success through strength of will and personal magnetism, and you will find you have much advantage over other people in these respects. You have much sense of personal dignity, but you are warm-hearted, good-natured, sociable, generous and magnanimous. This position is likely to lead you into some more or less responsible or prominent position where you will have to direct or employ others, and you are likely to have success therein. Your feelings and desires are ardent, you have a strong sense of the dramatic, and a love of beauty and luxury. It is difficult for you to subordinate yourself to others or to occupy any position of inferiority, as you are a natural leader.

**39.** The Sun is in VIRGO. This tends to give method, tact and ingenuity to your character ; you can adapt yourself to people, understand them and sympathise with them.  You have many sides to your nature and are not tied down to one line of thought or activity only, but have a good deal of adaptability and plasticity.  This position, if considered alone, does not give very great strength of will and sometimes goes with some degree of vacillation or tendency to change and fluctuate both in moods and actions.  It signifies one who is probably better as a servant than as a master and who is most successful when he works under a superior or with a partner than when left quite alone.  You should have good mental abilities and could cultivate intellectual pursuits with success.  You have shrewdness, discrimination, and critical ability; but have a tendency to reserve and seriousness, and you sometimes lack buoyancy and fire.

**40.**  The Sun is in LIBRA.  This increases the social side of your nature, and gives you the inclination to associate with other people. You will probably be more successful in this way than by working alone. Friendship, society, partnership, co-operation and association with others are indicated here.  Some other person is likely to come into your life in one of these ways or by marriage and influence your life greatly.  You are affectionate and friendly, and you have a love of beauty, ornaments, colour, music or art, and you might meet with success in cultivating these.  You should have good powers of perception and observation, and you are intuitive and critical but just.  You are fond of travel and change.  This position also helps to give cheerfulness, hopefulness, good-humour and buoyancy, with some degree of independence and activity.

**41.**  The Sun is in SCORPIO.  This position increases your strength of will and positiveness of character, making you strong, determined, and firm.  You naturally tend to resist outside influences, and are not easily swayed by other people, but rather go on your own way and make up your own mind.  This also gives you energy, impulse, and some amount of combativeness both physical and mental, as well as a tendency to wit or sarcasm and criticism of others.  You are a generous, faithful, and devoted friend but a dangerous and rather unforgiving enemy.  You have dignity, self-confidence, and some reserve; you can stand on your own dignity and keep your own counsel when necessary.  This position makes the planet Mars of importance in your character and life, and may fit you for one of the occupations ruled by this planet.  You may meet with success towards the close of life.

**42.** The Sun is in SAGITTARIUS. This adds to the sincerity, candour, frankness and honesty of your nature, and tends to make you just, humane, benevolent and sociable. It will help you to gain friends and acquaintances and to win the confidence of others, by whom you will be much influenced, and you will influence them in your turn. You are companionable, and your natural instinct is not to live alone but to associate a good deal with others, and you have respect for the forms, customs, and conventions of society. There is some amount of impulse in your nature, and at times you speak and act a little too hastily, and you need to cultivate forethought and prudence. You have much hopefulness and buoyancy, with activity and restlessness of mind and body. You are original and inventive, and although fond of change can work hard and complete lengthy tasks. There is some likelihood of travelling or voyaging. You have taste for beauty in nature and are fond of pleasure. You are a respecter of religion and have some philosophical ability.

**43.** The Sun is in CAPRICORN. This position increases the gravity and seriousness of the mind, and tends to thoughtfulness, reserve, and self-control. You may succeed by cultivating forethought, prudence, and tactfulness. You have practical capacity, ability to attend to detail, and sufficient strength of will to pursue your ends perseveringly and steadily for years in order to achieve what you desire. You are desirous of power and are fitted for acting as a head or ruler over others, although you would also make a faithful servant and worker or manager. You will gain more by plodding and quietly working with a given end in view than by excitement or hurry. This position may also tend to isolate you somewhat at times either through the force of circumstances or because you adopt an attitude of reserve. You need to cultivate cheerfulness and resist any tendency to depression.

**44.** The Sun is in AQUARIUS. This planet will help to lift you up in the world, to bring you before people, so that you will know many people and be known to many, and are likely to have many friends and acquaintances. You possess ability and power, and will do well to cultivate your faculties and ambitions, and not be too retiring or reserved. You have a strong and independent nature and are capable of standing alone and working out your own destiny. This position broadens both the mind and the feelings, making you free, humane and spirited, as well as endowing you with good intellectual abilities if you will only cultivate them. You are suited for a public life and would succeed better in some large sphere of action than in a smaller or more retired one. You should have a good memory and be a good judge of character and human nature.

**45.** The Sun is in PISCES. This position increases that side of the nature that belongs to feeling, emotion, and sensation, and makes these active and important in your character. You are able to sympathise with others, and are naturally humane, charitable, and helpful to those who are in trouble or ill-health. You are easy-going, adaptable, and receptive of impressions ; and your success or the reverse will be largely dependent upon the persons with whom you come in contact and your environment generally ; for you are more likely to mould yourself to circumstances than to compel things to your will. At times you are a little apt to worry as well as to show vacillation and a wavering indecision. You are a respecter of law and order, and have regard for social customs. You like comfort and luxury and are an admirer of beauty and elegance.

# CHAPTER V.

## THE POSITION IN THE SIGNS OF THE MOON AS RULER.

**46.** THE Moon is in ARIES. This increases the restlessness and love of change of your nature; and it tends to make you live in fits of enthusiasm, impulse, emotion, and fire rather than by cold, calculating, or plodding methods. You have ambition and great desire to excel, and to some extent this desire is likely to be realised; for this position holds out a possibility of your rising in life or at least of your becoming a person of some note in your sphere of life. To succeed you must cultivate stability and patience, and learn to control emotion and impulse. You are imaginative and somewhat highly strung, and you live largely in an ideal world, in the mind and the emotions. You are somewhat disobedient and independent, dislike restraint, and do not easily take up a subordinate position. This gives some slight tendency to feverish complaints, mental overwork, or affections of the head.

**47.** The Moon is in TAURUS. This is a fortunate position, as the Moon is exalted in this sign. It brings you friends and acquaintances through whom you will have much pleasure and who may be of credit or assistance to you in life. Your acquaintances will have more effect upon your career than is the case with most people; and you have it in your power to make and maintain very lasting friendships. This position is fairly fortunate for money matters, especially for money gained through houses or property in land or through a parent. It tends to give a sociable disposition, in which tenacity, patience, and a quiet firmness play a part; but you are liable to exhibit jealousy, pride, and undue obstinacy at times, and may stand in your own light in this way. Your habits are rather fixed and unchanging and lacking in adaptability.

**48.** The Moon is in GEMINI. This increases the strength of the intellectual side of your nature and makes you more impressionable through thought than through feeling. You have a capacity for attending to a multiplicity of details, and you can occupy yourself with more than one subject, whether in study or in practical occupation, because you can

25

easily change from one thing to another. You have a good deal of versatility and changefulness which may at times become lack of persistence and thoroughness. This position inclines you to books, writing, study, science, or literature, and gives the likelihood of some success in one of these directions. You may travel frequently, but chiefly short journeys, and you are fond of movement, walking, or going about. You are active in mind and body and may be skilful with your hands. You will gain in tact and diplomacy as life advances and will live more in the mind than in the feelings.

**49.** The Moon is in CANCER. With this position you will be very greatly influenced by your surroundings and by the people with whom you come in touch; you will be very sensitive to inharmonious conditions, and be more liable to be upset by them than most people. You are attached to home and are very domesticated, and although circumstances may lead you to travel you are always happiest in your own home. You will have many changes in your life and may go a voyage; you like variety and your moods and humours vary a good deal from day to day. You have some tendency to thrift, economy, and carefulness; you value money, and property, and do not like to see them wasted; and you have some ability for management, whether in domestic affairs, business, or otherwise, and would make a good and useful servant and manager. This position often gives a close link with the mother and her side of the family, and you may take after your mother a good deal.

**50.** The Moon is in LEO. This gives you ambition, independence, self-reliance, and a strong and positive will. You are very desirous of succeeding in life, and you are adapted to occupy some position of authority or responsibility where you will be at the head and have others under you. You have dignity, assertiveness, and ambition to do great things, and if you can add method and prudence to your enthusiasm and energy you may make a name for yourself. You have imagination, ideality, generosity and candour. You are a sincere friend and lover and have the ability to make yourself popular. This position is moderately fortunate in money matters, but you need to guard against extravagance. You are fond of pleasure, of luxuries, of society, ornaments and beauty, and you have a good deal of taste.

**51.** The Moon is in VIRGO. This increases your mental ability and especially the practical side of your mind, and fits you for any occupation in which adaptability, ingenuity and a grasp of method and detail are required. So far as this position is concerned you would probably be more fortunate as a servant than as a master, although you may achieve considerable success, especially if you associate yourself with others or work under a head. You may gain friends and popularity, but you should not be too ambitious or eager to rise, as you will do best by living quietly and not coming too much to the front; you should adapt yourself to circumstances and not seek to force them to your will. You will probably travel a good deal. You are inclined to worry and be over anxious at times and you need to cultivate hopefulness and equanimity.

**52.** The Moon is in LIBRA. This position should bring you many friends and acquaintances, and increase your popularity generally. It is opposed to isolation or separation, and brings you into touch with the many, tending to bring you before the public, so that you would be more fitted for a wide sphere of activity than for a restricted one. It is to some extent fortunate for marriage, partnership, and companionship, and you may gain through these channels. It gives you some liking for music or painting, with taste for ornaments, the blending of colours, the decoration of rooms, and artistic pursuits generally. It tends to give an agreeable and sociable disposition, and makes the emotional side of the nature active, but you must beware of becoming too easy-going and indifferent. It forms a link between yourself and a parent, probably your mother, and shows a likelihood of gain through parents.

**53.** The Moon is in SCORPIO. This increases the firmness and positiveness of the nature, gives you very strong likes and dislikes, and brings you much under the sway of the feelings and impulses. You tend to live a good deal in sensation, and you have powerful motives for all your actions; and as you are rather strong-willed you are prepared to go to considerable lengths in carrying out whatever you have decided upon. This should also give you some practical ability and capacity for energetic working, although you also appreciate a comfortable life and an easy time. You can be rather abrupt and plain spoken at times, and are capable of some amount of angry feeling. You are rather averse to change and are fixed in your habits, and not easily influenced by others. While under good directions you may possibly make money by speculation, or by partnership or association with others.

**54.** The Moon is in SAGITTARIUS. This tends towards activity and restlessness of manner, makes you quick and impulsive, and you move rapidly in whatever you do whether at work or play. You are high spirited and aspiring, and there is sometimes with this position some danger of injuring the health through over-work or hastiness and impulsiveness.　You are liable to be rather too enthusiastic or anxious in what you do, whether your activities are social, business, or intellectual; you throw too much of yourself into what you do; and you are just as eager for the interests of others as for your own.　There is some likelihood of your travelling, a voyage is possible, and you may change your residence a good many times.　A change of occupation is possible. You have the ability to develope some psychic gift such as clairvoyance, dreaming, etc.　You may have ability for music or painting or a natural attraction to religion.

**55.**　The Moon is in CAPRICORN.　This gives you a good deal of self-control and reserve; you have a tendency at times to wrap yourself up in yourself a good deal and not to wear your heart on your sleeve; and although other moods may vary with you, this characteristic of being self-contained and cold will return at times.　You have patience and perseverance in following what you have set your mind on, and although you may meet with many anxieties and trials you will show much persistence.　You have prudence and caution, also some practical administrative ability and business instinct, and are careful and economical. This position may bring you before the public in some way, as it has more to do with the many than the few, and it will attract you towards other people by way of association, partnership, friendship or marriage. You need to cultivate hopefulness and enthusiasm.

**56.**　The Moon is in AQUARIUS.　This makes you original and independent in your ideas, and may give taste or ability for some occult pursuit.　You are inclined to investigate things that are out of the common, and if you do so while under good directions you may gain considerable success in this direction or may develope some psychic faculty. You have some determination and perseverance and do not easily change your habits.　This position increases the imagination and intuition and gives an insight into human nature.　It brings you before the many, the multitude, and may give many friends and acquaintances and a good deal of social success through which you may rise in the world.　You have some abilities for political, educational, and scientific work.　The loss or death of a friend may affect you greatly.

**57.**　The Moon is in PISCES.　This position increases the emotional side of the nature, making the feelings active and receptive.　You are impressionable and sensitive and a good deal influenced by your surroundings, especially in domestic or social matters. You accommodate yourself to people and your comfort is largely dependent upon the kind of people who surround you and the circumstances of daily life. You are quiet and easy going, but changeable and fond of variety, and, so far as this position goes, a little lacking in energy, resolution and persistence. You are probably somewhat mediumistic and might develope some psychic faculty. When under bad directions you may incur opposition or enmity or suffer from loss, treachery, or underhand conduct. There is likelihood of travelling, possibly a voyage, and many changes of residence.

# CHAPTER VI.

## The Position in the Signs of MERCURY as Ruler.

**58.** MERCURY IN ARIES. This gives you a fiery, restless and ambitious type of mind, quick, witty and enthusiastic, with more impulse and energy than prudence or forethought. It will make you clever and self-assertive, apt and ingenious in argument, prompt in decision, fertile in ideas and original. You may gain success through these qualities in various directions and may make your mark in life. Your mind could be trained in various directions, and you could probably become either a speaker or a writer. You are likely to make friends among literary people or those associated with books in some way. You are a little lacking in mental concentration and steadfastness, and are fond of change and variety in things of the mind. You have some tendency to exaggeration and to sarcasm and may meet with trouble through these qualities. A good deal of travelling is likely, chiefly short journeys.

**59.** MERCURY IN TAURUS. This indicates an intellect of the patient and persevering type, not prone to change easily. You are not so adaptable or versatile in thought as are some people; it takes a good deal to induce you to change your opinions and habits of thought, and you are not very prompt in decision; but when you have once grasped what you believe to be right or true you do not easily give it up, but are very tenacious and unyielding. You have a good deal of intuition and some taste for music or art, and can take much pleasure in beautiful things. You are not always so ambitious or energetic as you might be, and your feelings are rather liable to bias your judgment; but you can accomplish a good deal in intellectual matters through your persistence and determination not to give way. There is some ability to earn money through writings, studies, or skilled occupations. Some travelling is indicated but mainly for some definite purpose such as business, money matters, health, etc., rather than mere love of travel.

**60.** MERCURY IN GEMINI. This strengthens the intellectual side of your nature, giving you a quick wit, a versatile and ingenious mind, and an appreciation of all things intellectual. You could take a good education and your mind could adapt itself to almost any subject involving thought or skill. Reading, writing, studies, books, science or literature will appeal to you and you may have ability for any or all of these subjects. You are somewhat liable to divide and scatter your energies by too much change or by trying to attend to two or more subjects at once instead of by concentrating your mind on one. You will be fond of variety in matters of the mind, and may exhibit some lack of decision, too much versatility and desultoriness. You are fond of travel, especially short journeys, and are likely to travel frequently. You have real ability and can accomplish much if you concentrate your energies, and you might achieve some public success or fame. You are original and ingenious and would succeed at the study of astrology.

**61.** MERCURY IN CANCER. This adapts the mind to practical and utilitarian ends whether in business or worldly affairs or in science; use and purpose are always to the front and some advantage is expected to accrue from whatever study the mind may engage in. You have the ability to make money through travelling, writings, or study or through some occupation in which the mind is largely engaged. You will make friends among literary or business people and those who are signified by the planet Mercury. You have some amount of intuition and you are mentally flexible, changeable and restless; you should have a good memory, and your mind if sometimes a little slow is sure and tenacious. You are likely to travel a little, possibly by water, and you may have several changes of residence. When under bad directions you may suffer or even lose money through house or land and through brothers or sisters.

**62.** MERCURY IN LEO. This gives positiveness, vitality, and firmness to the intellect. You will form great schemes and large plans, and will take comprehensive and widely reaching views of things, but will not be so apt or ingenious in small matters or little details; for these you will be liable to overlook or forget. You have imagination and ideality, some sense of the dramatic and imposing, and might rise considerably in any occupation in which these qualities were needed. You have strength of mind, and when you have once formed your plans you are not liable to change but can spend a long time and exert much energy in carrying them out, as you have intellectual concentration and power. You have ability for work in connection with public bodies or enterprises, with theatres, concerts, schools, and are capable of managing or directing others in such affairs.    You may travel a good deal, for pleasure or through your occupation.

**63.**  MERCURY IN VIRGO.    This gives a subtle and ingenious mind that can adapt itself to many subjects and pursuits.    You should be fitted to receive a good education or you could develope your own powers yourself with a little help from others.    You should have a good memory, you can learn readily either from books or from teaching, and you have abilities that could be turned either to literature, science, or practical affairs.    You might adapt yourself to almost any occupation requiring intellectual ability and ingenuity, professional or otherwise. Reading, writing, study, books, secretarial work, clerical work, are all suitable activities for you ; and you would be likely to succeed if you could co-operate with some one else or work under a superior or employer ; for you would make a good servant in mental matters.    You have much tact and adaptability of thought, but you may need to cultivate candour and openness.    You have method and orderliness of mind and can attend to many subjects and manage small details without confusion.

**64.**  MERCURY IN LIBRA.    This position increases the activity of the mind and also helps to refine it.    The social faculties should be strengthened in you, agreeableness, friendship, and mirth should be active, and those tendencies that draw people together should easily be cultivated. You will be most fortunate when you co-operate or associate with one or more others, for you will learn more and gain and achieve more in this way than by isolated action.    You have artistic or musical tastes which are susceptible of cultivation, and your mind could adapt itself either to literary or scientific activities.    You have intuition, imagination, and taste ; the perceptive faculties and comparison are strong in you ; and many forms of mental refinement are congenial to you.    You are fond of travelling.    Your pleasures are largely those of the mind.    You have the ability to earn money through some intellectual pursuit, especially if undertaken in partnership or association with someone else.

**65.**  MERCURY IN SCORPIO.    This makes your mind active, positive, and persistent.    You may exhibit considerable determination and strength of will, but this position of Mercury also gives some circumspection and will lead you to adapt means to ends and to exercise tact and diplomacy and not to rely upon determination only.    You should have considerable power of mental concentration and can control and disguise your feelings if necessary.    You have powers of wit and sarcasm and might develope rapid and fluent speech either by tongue or pen. You have ability for drawing, sculpture, or for mechanics, engineering, or almost any occupation in which manual skill and mental activity are combined. You would make a successful mesmerist as your mind is of the positive type, and you might develope practical occult power of some kind.

**66.** MERCURY IN SAGITTARIUS. This adapts your mind naturally to religion or philosophy, and you have abilities for dealing with abstruse or complicated subjects such as law, abstract science, or history. You could easily acquire critical ability as applied to art, music, or literature, and might develope a good style and sense of form in writing. You are somewhat impulsive in speech at times and may make enemies through your tongue or pen. You are somewhat changeable in mind and are more likely to dabble in a number of subjects than to confine yourself to one, and may occupy yourself with two lines of study at the same time. You have ability for writing or studying but you would be more successful by working with someone else or by association with others in some way than by working alone. This gives you love of change and you are likely to travel a good deal.

**67.** MERCURY IN CAPRICORN. This makes your mind strong, resolute, and firm, and gives you mental concentration, endurance, and continuity. You should have a good memory, and you can store your mind with a great variety of either practical experience or extensive learning upon which you can draw as occasion requires. Your mind is clear, practical, and tenacious, and when you have made a subject your own you do not easily give it up or forget it. You are cautious and profound and have abilities that could be exercised upon abstruse subjects or that could make you very practical and tactful in life. While under good directions you may rise considerably through the exercise of your mental abilities and might gain some fame through tongue or pen or powers practically applied. You have some faculty for speaking or writing and it could be developed by a little training. Your mind is of the solid and serious rather than the brilliant or superficial kind.

**68.** MERCURY IN AQUARIUS. This indicates an intellect that is strong, positive, independent and original. You incline rather to form your own conclusions and think things out for yourself than copy your opinions from other people. You should have a good memory and have no difficulty in learning by heart; you have good mental abilities that might be directed either to science, art or literature ; and you might gain some recognition, reward, or fame through your mind. You might succeed in the study of mystical or occult subjects, also at the study of languages. You are likely to travel a little and may go a voyage. You could succeed at teaching or training others ; also as an agent, manager, or worker on behalf of another. You have intuition and might develope considerable will power and mesmeric ability.

**69.** MERCURY IN PISCES. You have good intellectual ability but have a tendency to scatter your energies among many subjects rather than confine yourself to one, to be a little lacking in concentration or in power of application, and you try to follow two lines of study or pursuit at the same time. You should have a good imagination, an appreciation of the beautiful, artistic tastes, and a sense of order, method, neatness and fitness, both in ideas, in words, and in things. This will be of use to you in writing or speaking, and will give you good powers of expression. You will be apt to meet with some delay or difficulty in matters of education, studies, and literary affairs, and when you are under bad directions you will be liable to disappointments and may incur opposition or enmity, untrue reports, difficulties in employment or with those in your employ. Under good directions you may gain success or even fame through literature, imaginative or artistic work. You are likely to travel a little but may have trouble connected with it.

# CHAPTER VII.

## THE POSITION IN THE SIGNS OF VENUS AS RULER.

**70.** VENUS IN ARIES. This position will enable you to make friends easily, and will increase the number of your friends and acquaintances. It bestows to some extent the gifts of popularity, geniality ability to please and to win approval. The affections are active and ardent, love is easily called forth, and the feelings and emotions are deep and intense, so that in some cases it is not easy to restrain or rein them in, and imprudence may result from this. There is some amount of good fortune in money matters promised and the position is good for success in general, but it does not necessarily indicate that you have financial ability; and there is generally some degree of extravagance, free expenditure, generosity or wastefulness; which may either spring from your own character, and will then need checking, or may be forced upon you by circumstances. You should have some taste for music, or painting, and are fond of ornaments, and beautiful things.

**71.** VENUS IN TAURUS. This is considered a fortunate position for the planet Venus. It gives constancy to the affections, faithfulness in love, and, although the feelings are strong, the nature is fixed and not liable to change easily. Both likes and dislikes are maintained tenaciously, and while you can be an enduring friend you are also rather loth to give up feelings of prejudice or hostility. The social side of your nature is well developed and you can gain friends and be popular in your own circle. If you apply yourself to business or financial matters this position would be fortunate because it would help to win you the good opinion of people with whom you dealt and so would smooth your path. It is slightly favourable for money matters generally, especially through legacy, partnership, or marriage. You have some ability for dealing with money, but you can also be generous and kind.

**72.** VENUS IN GEMINI. This position gives some amount of social popularity and increases the number of friends. You may gain friends among literary people, the well-educated, or travelled people. It

35

sometimes gives some inconstancy in love matters or else two love affairs or two marriages. It forms a link between yourself and brothers, sisters, and cousins; and your relations with these should be pleasant and harmonious. It favours travelling whether for pleasure or arising out of your occupation, and it is fortunate for money derived from writing, books, literature, speaking, education, profession rather than business. It clears and refines the mind, and inclines you somewhat to religion. It gives you some sense of order and method, not only in every day matters but in the arrangement and expression of ideas and attention to detail.

**73.** VENUS IN CANCER. This position increases the affectional side of the nature and renders you home loving, companionable, and domesticated, at least so far as the feelings are concerned, although you may possibly have other and different characteristics in other departments of your nature. You appreciate the comforts and protection of home life, and you have the parental instinct to afford help and protection towards children or those who are much younger or weaker than yourself. This influence sometimes brings about marriage for the sake of a home or social comforts. It is fortunate for the acquisition of money or property through marriage or partnership, as well as from some family source either on your own side or on that of the marriage partner. You should have some amount of business instinct and are not inclined to waste what you possess extravagantly. You could manage money matters and should be fortunate in house or land property.

**74.** VENUS IN LEO. This gives warm and sincere affections, a very deep love nature, and a great amount of faithfulness and constancy with it. It may bring about an early marriage, if other circumstances do not interfere, and it tends in the direction of "love at first sight." It is a fortunate influence socially and may bring you many pleasant friends and acquaintances through whom you may obtain enjoyment or profit. It is apt to make you a little extravagant, both in the matter of the feelings, which tend to be too active, and of money matters as well. You have much generosity, kindness, and magnanimity. You have a cheerful, hopeful nature, fond of pleasure, company and luxury. You would benefit through any occupation having to do with entertainments, public affairs, company, society, or the drama; and you could gain through speculative investments if you add prudence to your enterprise. This brings some degree of popularity and the good-will of superiors.

**75.** VENUS IN VIRGO. This is a fortunate influence for commercial and business matters, especially if you associate yourself with others as servant, manager, or partner ; for it will bring you more success through co-operation with others in some way than it will if you seek to work alone. You will gain through servants, partners, and those in your employ ; and this position would prosper you as a servant or manager for someone else. You may also gain through prudent investments or speculations if conducted while you are under good influences. It sometimes brings about delay or hindrance in matters of love and marriage, or some kind of incompatibility after marriage, but this may be overcome under good influences. The love nature is equable, quiet, well disposed, sensible, and not blind to the faults of the loved one. You would make a kind parent.

**76.** VENUS IN LIBRA. This is favourable for marriage and all kinds of association with others; it increases the number of your friends and acquaintances, gives sociability and some amount of social popularity or ability to acquire it. It contributes to some extent to the refinement of the mind and gives some taste for pursuits of the nature of Venus such as music, poetry, singing ; as well as helping to develope the mind in the direction of imagination, ideality, a sense of beauty and good taste, so that ugliness or coarseness offends you. Love and affection are here blended with thought rather than with desire, and the æsthetic faculties make their appearance. You could earn money by an occupation of the nature of Venus, especially if in partnership with someone else or as a manager or agent for someone. This may give money through marriage.

**77.** VENUS IN SCORPIO. This is not altogether a fortunate position for the planet. It tends to make feeling, desire, and sensation rather too active and impulsive so that they are likely to need some restraining and regulating. You are a little too fond of pleasure, luxury, and indulgence at times. It gives a strong love nature and a decided attraction to the opposite sex. There is some danger of trouble in love or marriage, hasty or imprudent attachments, liability to the breath of scandal, inharmony or jealousy in love or marriage, separation from or death of the loved one. If you can exercise self-control, the worst of these troubles will not happen, and you will then show a generous, helpful, practical nature, of much use in the world, strong and capable for those who are weaker than yourself. You will have some tendency to extravagance and loss of money, but this may be forced upon you by circumstances and may not be your fault altogether. There is some likelihood of money by marriage or legacy ; but you may lose money through your marriage or business partner when you are under bad directions.

**78.** VENUS IN SAGITTARIUS. This gives imagination and love of the beautiful and sublime. You ought to have real taste for beauty, harmony, and elegance, and might cultivate this in various directions, through the fine arts, music, poetry, or literature. You love beauty in form, ornaments, beautiful clothing and pictures, and you might make money at any occupation in which these tastes can be turned to account. Your affections are active, romantic, and generous, but you are a little liable to fickleness, lacking in caution, and prone to impulse. There is some likelihood of two love affairs or marriages. This gives a good deal of devotion to the nature, which may attract you to a person, a cause, or to religion. You may travel a little, especially in connection with your occupation or after marriage. There is a little danger of love of show, ostentation, conventionality, and ceremony.

**79.** VENUS IN CAPRICORN. This indicates that although you have an affectionate nature you have also a good deal of prudence, tact, and self-control, and are not likely to let your feelings run away with you. You have faithfulness and constancy ; and when a person has once won your approval, whether in love or friendship, you do not easily change or forget. This position sometimes delays marriage or interposes some obstacle ; and, if you are under bad directions this may be caused by money matters, worldly position, occupation, or a parent ; but when you are under good directions you may benefit considerably from all these sources. You have practical financial ability and could easily learn to manage money matters, investments, or business. You are likely to rise in life, with care, and you will win the approval of elders and superiors, and may gain popularity and the friendship of people in good standing.

**80.** VENUS IN AQUARIUS. This influence should contribute to your popularity and social success, and should bring you many friends and acquaintances, some of whom may be in a good position in life and able to benefit you socially if not in occupation or financial matters. It is favourable for love and marriage, but it is liable to cause delay or disappointment, chiefly when you are under bad directions ; and at such times you may suffer through false friends. This also gives you faithfulness and constancy in affection and friendship, and bestows fondness for children and pleasure through them. It refines the mind and gives some imagination and taste for music or the fine arts. You should have some ability in money and business matters and might gain through investment or speculation.

**81.** VENUS IN PISCES. This position gives you a sympathetic and charitable nature, with a fellow feeling for those who need help, whether through suffering or poverty. You are cheerful, good-natured, and easy-going, sometimes a little indolent and lacking in energy. You should have a good imagination, an intuitive and sensitive mind, and a sociable disposition. This gives good taste and an appreciation of the beautiful in painting, music, in the decoration of rooms, in clothes or ornaments ; and you might have success at an occupation dealing with one of these lines. There is some little love of show, ostentation, form and ceremony. You are a little given to fickleness in matters of affection and feeling, and may have two love affairs, two marriages, or even two occupations. While under bad directions you will be liable to lose money through fraud or otherwise, or some trouble turning upon money may occur. This position sometimes gives a secret engagement or marriage.

# CHAPTER VIII,

## THE POSITION IN THE SIGNS OF MARS AS RULER.

**82.** MARS IN ARIES. This is a strong and fortunate position for Mars, as it strengthens all the best side of the planet and impresses its influence deeply upon your character. It gives you energy, positiveness, decision, and enterprise. You are self-reliant, courageous, and adventurous; but you are a little liable at times to carry these qualities too far and to prove lacking in coolness and restraint. You can face danger and hold your own, but you are rather imprudent and combative; you are easily offended and are quick to resent a slight, whether real or fancied. You will yourself be the direct cause of many of the misfortunes from which you will suffer. It gives good vitality and strength but danger of fever, infectious complaints, wounds, accidents, surgical operations. It is fortunate for any occupation of the nature of Mars, such as soldier, sailor, engineer, surgeon.

**83.** MARS IN TAURUS. This gives you much firmness and determination. When you have once decided on a given course of action it is difficult for you to change; you go steadily on your way and are not to be turned aside. You have patience, persistence, and strength, but you can show both obstinacy and anger when provoked. It gives you some practical ability, the power of working on and accomplishing much by strength of will and perseverance; and you should have the ability to earn money by the exercise of these qualities; but there is some likelihood of loss of money, free expenditure, undue generosity, or rash enterprises in business matters. It favours marriage to a slight extent but there is some risk of jealousy or inharmony. You may gain by legacy, partnership, or marriage. There is liability to affections of the throat. Under bad directions you will meet with enmity, rivalry and opposition.

**84.** MARS IN GEMINI. The forcefulness of Mars in this case expresses itself through the thought rather than the desires; mentally rather than passionally. It should help to make you quick-witted prompt in thought, apt in word, and decisive in speech.  It tends to give mental courage and resource, with some amount of mental combativeness and positiveness; inclination to irony, wit, sarcasm, or satire.  You should have critical ability, and could gain skill in writing, speaking, debating, and argument; but at times you will be apt to offend other people a little by opposition or plainness of speech or writing, and may get a few enemies in this way.  You scatter your energies a little by attending to too many things, and you would gain by concentrating on one thing only.  This position is liable to cause death of, or estrangement from a brother or sister; trouble through letters, literary or educational matters; and accidents or death while on a journey or outside the house.  The lungs may be affected.

**85.**   MARS IN CANCER.  This position gives an independent spirit and some inclination to rebel against rules, regulations, superiors, and the exercise of authority.  You may suffer at times at the hands of superiors and perhaps experience something akin to injustice, unfairness, or tyranny; or, on the other hand, you may be troubled with insubordination or disobedience from servants or employees.  There is liability to some trouble through a parent, probably the mother; disagreement with, estrangement from, or early death of such.  But the position is favourable for inheritance from a parent, and gain through house or land property or an occupation connected with land.  There is some inclination for travelling, especially by water, but liability to trouble or accidents while travelling, also to danger from burning, scalding, or fire in the house.  The stomach and digestion may suffer.

**86.**   MARS IN LEO.  This is a strong position for Mars, giving some success through matters governed by the planet.  It makes you energetic, active, and independent, and contributes strength of will and character.  It indicates that you are sincere, honourable, open, candid, and generous; it fits you for a position of responsibility where you would have to control others, to manage, order, and command.  It brings you recognition and respect from superiors and those in authority, and possibly may lift you up in life and give honour or preferment.  It is apt to make you a little too positive or militant in manner, so that when you are under bad directions you may make enemies and meet with opposition and contention.  This increases the fire and vitality of the body but gives a little liability to fevers, accidents, and high temperature.  You may suffer from social opposition or from family disputes; there is danger of too much impulsiveness or rashness in love matters; and there may be death of a child. The heart or back may be affected, but no serious evil need be feared as Mars is strong here.

**87.** MARS IN VIRGO. You will make a practical, energetic, and capable worker, but you will succeed better in the employ of another or when working under a superior than you will when independent. You have some amount of ambition, but you will have better luck as a servant, manager, or agent than as a master or head. Your nature has more caution and reserve about it than is usual with Mars, and you can plan and exercise shrewdness and diplomacy. You have inventive and constructive ability. When under bad directions you may suffer through servants or subordinates, by enmity, treachery, or dishonesty; also through false friends. You may lose friends or servants by death. This gives some ability for scientific work, for intellectual or literary pursuits, especially if put to practical use. You can carry out work that is planned or suggested to you by another; and you can manage and pay attention to details and be careful and precise. There is some liability to disorder of liver, bowels, or digestion.

**88.** MARS IN LIBRA. This kind of influence may vary a good deal according to whether you are under good or bad directions. Its good effect is to attract you strongly to other people, either in partnership, friendship, association of some sort, or in marriage. You are very devoted to such persons and you would make an ardent and enthusiastic friend or lover, as you are eager and somewhat passionate in your attachments, and this may result in an early or hasty marriage. The marriage or other partner will probably be of the martial type, positive, active and rather masterful. There may be gain by marriage, partnership, or legacy; and there is good working or earning capacity in association with others. When under bad directions there is danger of disagreement with others, disputes, friction, incompatibility of temper; enemies arise, and rivalry or jealousy is provoked; and there may be breaking of ties, and separation from or death of the marriage or business partner. The kidneys or groins are liable to be affected or you may suffer through the action or negligence of other people.

**89.** MARS IN SCORPIO. This is a very strong position for Mars, and it tends to make you positive, firm, determined, and strong willed. You are ambitious, and your mind is very set on any object that attracts you, or any idea that appeals to you; and you give your whole self, for the time being, to the task of acquiring the object or pursuing the idea. You can show great devotion to a person or a cause and make great sacrifices for it. You are swayed a good deal by pleasures, feelings, and moods, but you can also be very steadfast, rigid, and unchanging. You have good practical executive ability, and can work hard when you like, and you are fitted for any occupation of Mars, such as soldier, surgeon, chemist, engineer, etc. This position increases the vital energies but gives liability to accidents, fever, high temperature, and infectious disease. You have a strong sense of dignity and some pride, and will be a little apt to offend people at times or take offence yourself rather readily, and so suffer through enmity, rivalry, jealousy, opposition. There may be gain of money through legacy, marriage, partnership or association with others, but there is some tendency to extravagance.

**90.** MARS IN SAGITTARIUS. This gives you fire and energy, which may operate as much mentally as emotionally, and take the form of impulse, ardour, and enthusiasm. At times this may carry you away, and you may follow an idea or a desire too far, or go to too great extremes in the pursuit of an object. You need restraint, moderation, and prudence. You have the courage of your ideas and opinions, which are not always those of the people around ; but your natural tendency is to go your own way at all costs. In religion, this position makes one who is either a little unorthodox or who is very active, devoted, and perhaps a little militant in manner. You are a quick and active worker but liable to change, or to take up too many subjects, or to scatter your energies too much. It favours travel, and change of opinion, occupation, and abode ; also outdoor life, riding, walking or athletics. There may be danger while travelling, and disagreement with brothers and sisters or separation. A law suit is possible and quarrels or disputes are probable.

**91.** MARS IN CAPRICORN. This gives you ambition, determination, and ability to make your way in the world and carve out your own career. You have a good deal of practical executive ability, can work hard and capably and accomplish much. You have a sense of authority, are able to direct and control others, and are fitted for some post of responsibility. It tends to lift you up in the world, to give you some degree of prominence or mastery over others, even if only in a small way ; but it also tends slightly to isolate you and to make you more feared or respected than loved. Mars is strong in Capricorn and gives fitness for occupations signified by this planet, such as soldier, sailor, surgeon,

chemist, engineer, also parliamentary or official state and municipal positions.    When under bad directions,you may incur enmity, criticism, rivalry,
especially from superiors or public persons ; and it is also unfortunate for
the father, giving some danger of separation, disagreement, or his death.
There is some tendency to rheumatic or allied disorders.

**92.**  MARS IN AQUARIUS.    This produces a mind that is both quickly
moving and firm, swift in action but unyielding and somewhat
contentious.    You have much nervous force and capacity for work, but
also, so far as this position is concerned, a good deal of impulse that is
apt to work rather erratically.    It tends to make you prompt and decisive
both in speech and action, but sometimes a little brusque and abrupt.
When under good directions you are very devoted to those friends or
causes that you value, and you may gain both pleasure and profit through
them and rise in life.    But under bad directions you will suffer much
through friends or associates, may lose them by death or separation
or be alienated by difference in views.    There is danger from false friends
and of quarrels with friends.    You need to cultivate coolness and
prudence, and learn to give way gracefully to others.    There is some
liability to nervous breakdown through overwork.

**93.**  MARS IN PISCES.    In this position Mars shows less of its fire
and impulsiveness than it does in most of the signs, and it is
accompanied by a good deal of reserve.    You have power and capactiy
but you do not show your whole nature on the surface.    You do not rush
into action without thought as people under this planet often do ; neither
does this give you the iron will and unyielding spirit of some of the signs.
You know how to bide your time ; how to choose suitable moments for
action ; how to wait with some degree of patience, diplomacy, and subtlety
to achieve your end ; and you can accomplish much in this way.    But
under bad directions you will be liable to incur secret enmity and to suffer
from opposition, criticism, or hostility, generally more or less unexpected
or hidden ; you will lose money through mistakes of judgment, or take
some false step that will hamper or hinder you, bring unpopularity upon
you, or cause something in the nature of a downfall.    You should beware
of giving way to vacillation, indecision, or irresolution.

# CHAPTER IX.

## THE POSITION IN THE SIGNS OF JUPITER AS RULER.

**94.** JUPITER IN ARIES. This position increases the warmth, dignity, generosity, and sincerity of your nature, and is fairly fortunate in general. The social instincts are increased, and it contributes to benevolence, fellow-feeling, and popularity. It is favourable for success in any of the pursuits signified by Jupiter, and tends to develope in the disposition the qualities of this planet. Religion, the law, medicine, and occupations connected with these are brought to the front. There is some likelihood of travelling or voyaging; there may be a change of occupation, or two different pursuits or hobbies may be followed. It inclines to the higher cultivation of the mind through philosophy or religion with some people; while with others it may give liking for amusements, society, open air pursuits, horses and travelling. It is a good position for those who have to do with the sick or poor, for physicians, nurses, and for the philanthropic. It gives some amount of pride and formality.

**95.** JUPITER IN TAURUS. This gives a sense of beauty and harmony in nature or art, and some taste for music, painting, and ornament. You have an affectionate and sociable nature, but with some touch of reserve and dignity, and liking for ceremony and etiquette. You appreciate comfort, luxury, and ease. You might gain through subjects connected with religion, medicine, or the higher cultivation of the mind. You have something of the devotional and religious spirit in you, which this position tends to make constant and not liable to change, as it appeals to you more through intuition and inward feeling than reason. There is some inclination for travelling, but it will generally be for some definite purpose, such as the occupation or health. The position is fortunate for money matters or legacies, and property in house or land; but under bad directions there may be some loss.

**96.** JUPITER IN GEMINI. This improves the intellect and gives it harmony and refinement, and is favourable for education, cultivation, and good judgment. It gives you good sense and ability to advise,

45

guide, or train others sensibly. You will learn by experience and will possess tact and common sense. You will be fond of travelling and are likely to move about frequently, even if only short distances. You are fond of change mentally, and may occupy yourself with more subjects than one, or pass from one to another frequently. It inclines you to take a critical view of religion, or to view it from the intellectual or philosophical side. The position is good for marriage and for getting on well with brothers, sisters, and relatives; but when you are under bad directions you may be troubled through these channels and loss or separation may follow, but this need not be serious.

**97.** JUPITER IN CANCER. This strengthens the imagination and intuition, and gives you some taste for art. It is fortunate for family life, gives peace and harmony in the home, constitutes a tie between yourself and your parents, and brings happiness and prosperity. You may have a legacy from a parent, probably the mother, or her side of the family. You may travel a little and there is a possibility of a voyage, or you may follow some occupation that entails travelling. You might benefit through houses or land or occupations connected with them. You have taste in furniture and house decoration and like beauty and elegance in the home; and you could understand architecture and gain skill at it. It will attract you somewhat to the psychic or occult side of things, or perhaps give you ability to develope some psychic faculty. It inclines somewhat to the devotional side of religion as well as to mysticism.

**98.** JUPITER IN LEO. This makes you high-minded, honourable, and good-natured. It gives you a strong sense of dignity and fits you for positions of honour and responsibility. You are likely to gain the esteem of superiors and would do well as a head or chief over others. You will very likely rise in life and win respect and esteem, perhaps gain power and reputation. This should bring you many friends and acquaintances, some popularity and social success. You have a sense of your own worth and do not undervalue yourself; you appreciate display, show, ceremonial, good taste, and sometimes show some amount of ostentation, but you do not offend anyone by it because you are generous and magnanimous. You have deep feelings and a strong love nature. This position increases the vitality and bodily vigour.

**99.** JUPITER IN VIRGO. Jupiter is not strong in this sign, and its fiery side does not show out well here. The position is somewhat good for business and commercial matters, for success through servants

and employees, especially where many are employed or associated ; and
you might gain through partnership. But when under bad directions you
may have trouble or financial loss through these channels. You have a
sense of order, method, and arrangement, but this position sometimes
goes with indifference to personal appearance, carelessness or indolence.
You are more intellectual and philosophical than devotional, are critical
and analytical, and should have ability for science or for teaching. The
position is not very good for digestion, is liable to affect the liver or
bowels ; and at some time in your life you may be hampered in some
way through a rather lingering complaint. There may be travel through
business or on account of someone else. When under bad directions you
may suffer from fraud, treachery or deceit.

**100.** JUPITER IN LIBRA. This increases the social side of your
nature, and brings out those qualities that contribute to friendship,
companionship, and popularity through association with others. You
should therefore have many friends and be a person well known and
esteemed in your own circle, and you may perhaps attract public notice
and gain some degree of prominence beyond the ordinary. It is also
fortunate for marriage and partnership, and for joining societies,
associations, companies or large groups of people whether in business or
otherwise. It favours travelling and voyages. It increases imagination
of the intellectual type, and may give some religious feeling of a mystical
or imaginative kind ; also taste for art, poetry or music. When you are
under bad directions it may cause some inharmony or incompatibility in
marriage, and something similar in matters of friendship and partnership
which may show as falseness, treachery, or secrecy.

**101.** JUPITER IN SCORPIO. This gives warmth, enthusiasm, and
ardour to the nature, and increases the feelings and emotions.
The positive side of these is prominent, so that you will have resource,
and strength of will, fitting you to be of considerable practical use in the
world. It gives some financial ability and good fortune in money matters,
investments, and speculations, with possibility of money through marriage,
partnership or legacy. There will be some inclination to the mystical or
occult in religion, and either some touch of unorthodoxy or else a positive
and slightly militant disposition. You have some little pride and sense of
dignity, and this is apt to be rather easily wounded, although you have
much good nature and generosity. You might have pleasure or profit by
travelling and occupations connected with the water or liquids, also

through things having to do with religion or philosophy and the higher education; but under bad directions you may have trouble or loss through any of these subjects.

**102.** JUPITER IN SAGITTARIUS. This position is a strong and favourable one for Jupiter and brings out all its active characteristics beneficially. It is good for the higher side both of the intellect and the feelings, for religion, philosophy, law, medicine; and for the philanthropic and social instincts, giving benevolence, compassion, generosity, good sense, and humour. You have some love of beauty and harmony, which could find an outlet through music or art. You have some sense of personal dignity and prefer to conform to the manners and customs of good society, but you have also much toleration and good nature and can readily be brought to forgive those who offend you. The position is favourable for travelling and voyages. It also tends to bring peace in home and family life. It contributes to vitality and bodily health.

**103.** JUPITER IN CAPRICORN. This increases the strength of will and also the ability for practical work in the world. You probably have a good deal of ambition and love of power, in small things or in large; and to some extent you are fitted to manage, arrange, and organise things and persons, to occupy some prominent or responsible position, to be at the head of things. This gives a good deal of financial and commercial ability, adaptation to business life and some good fortune therein. But you might also gain through professional pursuits, through travelling; and it is good for those who hold a public or semi-public position or office, for money gained through these channels and for money or legacy from the father, brother or sister, and for working in connection with them. You are likely to travel and may go a voyage. The position tends to thoughtfulness and gravity, as well as frugality and economy.

**104.** JUPITER IN AQUARIUS. This position will bring you many friends and acquaintances, some amount of social popularity and success, and the good will of those amongst whom you move. It is fortunate within the family circle as well as in the world, and gives pleasure through brothers and sisters. It inclines to associating with other people in various ways, joining religious bodies, belonging to societies, associations, brotherhoods, or companies, whether in social or business matters. There are strength of will, firmness and independence; some dignity and self-reliance, and ability to command, control, or manage others. It gives you some business ability and some success in money matters. It is sometimes accompanied by an attraction to occultism or mysticism, or else to some mystical or out-of-the-way form of religion.

**105.** JUPITER IN PISCES. This gives you a good-natured easy-going disposition, well disposed to others and inclined to be charitable and benevolent. It is a good position for a medical man, or nurse, also for those who have to do with the sick or poor either from the point of view of practical help, of medicine or of religion. It is favourable for religion, sometimes of a mystical or occult kind, but sometimes quite orthodox and very devout. It gives a good deal of imagination and sense of beauty in form or harmony, which may attract you to music, art, or poetry. You like neatness, beauty, and luxury in the home ; and this position tends to preserve peace and harmony in home life as well as bringing you friends and some amount of social popularity.

# CHAPTER X.

## The Position in the Signs of SATURN as Ruler.

**106.** SATURN IN ARIES at birth will bring you more or less to the front, according to your environment. You are ambitious, diplomatic and distrusting, fond of power, and can exercise some authority, are also able to manage others, organise and plan. You are very confident and assured, but sometimes manifest austerity, gloominess, and love of retirement. It gives self-satisfaction and irritability, or bad temper when provoked. Your fate in life, especially your public career, is made largely by your own choosing, and thus your misfortunes will often be of your own making. If you can make truth and toleration your virtues, you will gain great power and success ; but avoid intolerance and impatience.

**107.** SATURN IN TAURUS at your birth tends to make you firm, persistent and strong-willed in pursuing your purpose. It gives you a slow but quiet and kind nature, yet with a temper easily angered. It is not good for monetary matters in a general sense, for money will come slowly or tend to waste away ; though you may gain (or, when Saturn is afflicted, *lose*) money through some public venture, stocks, shares, investments, banks and companies, or speculation in these things ; there is moreover some possibility of your gaining through elderly persons. You can be careful and economical in money matters and the greatest success is promised by thrift and perseverance.

**108.** SATURN IN GEMINI at your birth threatens you with trouble in early life, also difficulties connected with education, clerical or literary work, your brethren, and short journeys. You may however, by patience, and industry acquire much intellectual ability. Strength of character and subtlety of purpose, depth of thought and ability for scientific research may be cultivated to advantage. At some time of life, when Saturn is well aspected, you will gain success through matters of an intellectual nature, or through your family ; but when Saturn is afflicted, troubles will come from this source. Avoid irritability and bitterness in feeling.

50

**109.** SATURN IN CANCER at your birth is unfavourable for holding possessions or position, and for success or honour, as it brings trouble in business or profession, threatening downfall, loss of repute and financial loss (especially when Saturn afflicts the Moon, Venus, or Jupiter) ; it conduces to mediumship or occultism of some kind. Guard against notions and impressions, and separate your imagination from fancy. You are much affected by others and they may drain your vitality ; therefore be careful with whom you associate. Strengthen your will, and never encourage discontent or resentment. You will seek to avoid responsibility, which you will not find desirable. Your occupation is likely to be an unpopular one.

**110.** SATURN IN LEO at your birth will help you on in life, giving you power, authority or responsibility, and in a measure you will stand outside the crowd. It slightly diminishes your circulation and vitality, and may affect the heart. It will bring favours from superiors and those in the higher ranks of life. You are rather firm and self-contained. Troubles may arise through love-affairs or your passions, unless you can practise chastity without incurring coldness. Your principal experiences will come through your feelings ; and if you can control passion, and slay the lion of anger, you will avoid much of your fate.

**111.** SATURN IN VIRGO at birth gives an orderly, critical and analytical mind of a serious cast, tending to make you original and able to deal with profound subjects ; this might not show to advantage during early life, however. This serious tendency may increase at times to gloom, when you may be far too diffident and reserved. There is the possibility of disappointment or reversal in your occupation, and your ambition may be thwarted, or you may be kept back by unpopular occupation, or ill-health, or some cause coming from your elders. The occult significance of this position is 'discrimination,' by which you may gain wisdom, and improve your lower nature.

**112.** SATURN IN LIBRA at your birth is rather fortunate, this being the sign of Saturn's exaltation. It is generally favourable for all matters connected with partnerships, especially with those older than yourself, bringing you some gain by partnerships, companies, or association with others. This position tends to make you rather exacting where justice is concerned, but as you expand and develope, it will widen your sympathies, and make you more considerate, religious and mystical. Under evil "Directions" it reverses friendships, causing some opposition, jealousy, selfishness, etc. This being the sign of the balance you will have the choice of two courses of action, at some period of your life, which will very considerably influence your future.

**113.** SATURN IN SCORPIO at the time of your birth increases your will, and force of character, also your love of power and authority, creating within you a dislike of opposition and restraint. It gives you a forceful, strong, and even turbulent disposition, unless it is counteracted by good influences. Its tendency is rather critical. It imperils your honour and repute and may cause you some unpopularity. Downfall and collapse are at times threatened. It is not favourable for occultism, but it will give you some power in all things secret, hidden, occult and mystical. You will tend to become very reserved, and self-controlled, and you should avoid pride and jealousy, these being the two chief dangers in your life.

**114.** SATURN IN SAGITTARIUS at birth will give you a philosophical type of mind, thus making you interested in science, philosophy or religion, and as you progress your thinking will be more original, clear, and philosophical, signs of advancement being that you will embrace new views as gravely as you may have viewed those which you at one time thought to be the ultimate. Your mind will be an enquiring one, and were you to give your mind to religion you could become a great divine, or if to philosophy, a great philosopher, if to travelling a great explorer; and if to finance a great financier. But concentration MUST be practised, ere you can achieve any of the virtues promised by this position. It will, however, make you earnest and sincere.

**115.** SATURN IN CAPRICORN at your birth will tend to lift you up, giving you power, mastery, independence, ambition, and at times loneliness and isolation, but its influence will be modified, according to your sphere of life. This position sometimes gives fortune in occupation or in financial affairs, with ultimate reversal or collapse under bad " Directions." When Saturn is afflicted you will be gloomy, serious, and melancholy. It strengthens your personality, bringing ambition, love of power, and, unless Jupiter, Venus or the Sun prevent, some indifference to the interests of others. You should also have a strong individuality and the power to raise yourself to a good position in life by self-control and diplomacy.

**116.** SATURN IN AQUARIUS at your birth controls the fate considerably, acting as a brake or limiter of your impulses. It gives power and some good fortune connected with associations, companies, and groups of persons, this being a good position for the occult and mystical. It gives a judgment of human nature, although at times you may be mistaken in your friends, and suffer from deceit, etc., against which you should guard. You would do well in connection with some popular movements, and matters where money is concerned, or by investment in stocks and shares. The occult significance promises you progress according to your power and ability to respond to the vibrations of Aquarius.

**117.** SATURN IN PISCES at your birth is unfavourable for occupations, public position, reputation, and popularity; you may incur opprobrium, or disrepute, deserved or not. Superiors, authorities and those in position are apt to be unsympathetic, for you have critics, enemies, and also false friends. You will be liable to attacks from inferiors, but when Saturn is well aspected benefit will come to you if in any way concerned with hospitals, charitable institutions, asylums, private occupations, secret societies, or unpopular pursuits. Temperance, tolerance and firmness will benefit you greatly, and help you to overcome the misfortunes indicated above. Strengthen your will, and avoid as far as possible making errors in your judgment.

# CHAPTER XI.

## THE HOUSE-POSITION OF THE PLANET URANUS.

IT will be easily understood from what has been said in **Chapter II.,** p. 13, that Uranus can seldom or never be regarded as the Ruling Planet in any horoscope. Indeed in many cases, perhaps most, it will be found to exercise little or no effect. Where it does, it is the position by house rather than that by sign which is most marked. For example, Uranus in Cancer in the third house will show its effect more as regards speech and writing and other third house and mental matters than as regards the feelings and desires, signified by Cancer. That is to say in other words that its position by house generally overpowers its position by sign. In this chapter, therefore, the influence of Uranus in the twelve houses is given rather than that in the signs, as likely to be of more use to the student, quite apart from the fact that both Uranus and Neptune (in regard to which similar remarks will apply) both move so slowly as to remain about seven and fourteen years, respectively, in one sign ; thus affecting all persons, born during that time, more or less in a similar manner. Probably the *sign-positions* of these two occult and mysterious planets are more concerned with the particular classes of egos coming into manifestation from time to time, and the general Karma of such classes, than with the special temperament of individuals. This however is only a speculation.

**118.** URANUS IN THE FIRST HOUSE. This position confers on you original thoughts, and an uncommon and somewhat bohemian character : you may display a certain inventive genius and will in any case be inclined to strike out an entirely new line for yourself. It will bring some reversal of fortune, strange and peculiar events, lifting you high up at one time and then casting you down again. It will bring you danger of estrangement from those nearest to you, and will break many social ties abruptly and suddenly. You are inclined to be somewhat

See note on page 58.

abrupt and at times too plain-spoken ; occasionally too you are self-opinionated and irritable.   You should restrain also a certain tendency to be erratic.   You are metaphysically inclined, and love the profound and wonderful.   You will make some attainments in occultism or the higher thought.

**119.** URANUS IN THE SECOND HOUSE.   This will cause you some restlessness of disposition and many changes of fortune.   Sudden gain and sudden losses will make your financial affairs more or less uncertain at all times.   You may gain a large fortune through some speculation or invention, and suddenly lose it all.   You would gain by railway shares, also by investments in inventions, by unique and extraordinary ventures or large liability companies ; but you will need to be guarded, as you may lose as much as you gain.   There is no certainty with Uranus in regard to finance, though good aspects are generally beneficial.   The operation of this influence in the mental plane will cause you to have many profound thoughts during life, and you may become deeply interested in astrology.

**120.** URANUS IN THE THIRD HOUSE.   This will make your mind somewhat peculiar, eccentric, inventive and curious.   It gives you ability to study deep and profound subjects, and you are generally inventive and ingenious in your methods.   This position causes you to receive many strange letters, also to have an extensive and varied correspondence, probably with those who study metaphysics or are engaged in occult pursuits.   You will have a very great amount of correspondence (much at times and little at others), and there is some liability of complications through letters or sudden receipt of news.   You will be fond of travel ; will have difficulties with your kindred, and will hold strange or peculiar views and hence are liable to be severely criticised by others.

**121.** URANUS IN THE FOURTH HOUSE.   This will affect your home life, and bring you many changes of a very unexpected and probably abrupt nature.   You will be liable to strange experiences in your residence, in the house you were born or even the town or country in which you reside.   You are liable to disputes or strange scenes with your parents or with fellow residents.   You must be very careful as life advances to avoid strange and incurable diseases.   You should always seek to have harmonious conditions near you, and should be careful with

See note on page 58.

whom you associate ; especially in old age. Your end will probably be rather sudden and quite unexpected.

**122.** URANUS IN THE FIFTH HOUSE. This position will give you very strange love-affairs, bringing you many very romantic and peculiar adventures in this connection ; and you should be very careful in choosing your acquaintances of the opposite sex, or your friendships may be abused. It will bring you estrangement from those you love : yet you may be drawn into very peculiar pleasures and strange experiences concerning so-called pleasure. You should be guarded in your speculations as you would have very sudden losses and sudden gains. Your children would cause you much trouble and would be reared with difficulty ; but should they survive they will either leave you entirely or bring you either discredit or anxiety by their strange and peculiar behaviour.

**123.** URANUS IN THE SIXTH HOUSE at your birth. This is not good for your health. It will bring you some nervous disorders, and may also bring some strange or incurable complaint that it would be difficult to eradicate, in fact, the tendency of any ill-health would be towards incurable diseases. You must, however, be careful to avoid hypochondria or nervous disorders, which would give you much misery and unnecessary suffering of a mental kind. You should be guarded in your dealings with servants and inferiors, as you would have much worry and anxiety and possibly sudden loss connected with them. They would bring you discomfort and annoyance, and would be unable to minister in any way to your comfort or happiness. You are liable to sudden and strange accidents.

**124.** URANUS IN THE SEVENTH HOUSE at your birth. This causes very strange and peculiar events in connection with marriage, or partnerships. Either your partner will have undergone some strange and remarkable experiences, or you will have formed some impulsive attachment which is likely to bring many complications. You will be in danger of separation, either by estrangement, divorce, or sudden loss of your partner. You should not take steps to come before the public unless you are very well equipped, and well able to hold your own, as you would meet with much persistent opposition. You should exercise care

See note on page 58.

in all dealings with strangers and all eccentric and peculiar persons would be best avoided. This position inclines to platonic unions.

**125.** URANUS IN THE EIGHTH HOUSE. This position has a peculiar and occult significance : and it should cause you to take a very profound and sincere interest in all things that relate to other planes of existence beside this physical earth. It causes you to have at times very clear dreams, and it interests you considerably in after-death states. From a physical standpoint it will give you money in a peculiar and unexpected manner by will or legacy, or by marriage or co-workers, or in some exceptional way. It is not altogether favourable for the nature of one's death, as it shows a very abrupt and sudden end. But much will depend upon the aspects to Uranus at birth, and those received by this planet as your horoscope progresses : hence no definite or precise information can ever be given with regard to this position.

**126.** URANUS IN THE NINTH HOUSE. This position is a good testimony for all matters concerned with metaphysics, astrology, occultism, or for imaginative work. It inclines towards originality and invention, and favours dealing in curios and antiques, or the study thereof. It gives you a prophetic tendency, and it also causes you to have strange dreams, dreams which sometimes come to you as warnings or even as revelations. You are liable to accidents (or good fortune, according to the aspects of Uranus) while travelling, especially on long railway journeys, or abroad. You will incline to reform in religious and scientific matters.

**127.** URANUS IN THE TENTH HOUSE is a position which gives you sudden changes in your position of a quite unexpected character. Now up, and now down, you sometimes enjoy great credit and at other times suffer from ill-repute. Your employers pass through peculiar difficulties, and you become involved with them in some manner. You have a tendency all your life to follow some very original avocation, and do well in pursuits of an eccentric or uncommon nature. Your life will be full of romance and peculiar episodes, many of which are associated with your calling. You should avoid all dealings with public bodies and public questions as far as possible, unless the aspects to Uranus are favourable.

See note on page 58.

**128.** URANUS IN THE ELEVENTH HOUSE will bring you your truest friends from those inclined towards occult or metaphysical studies. It brings the friendship of original thinkers, inventors and eccentric characters. Some of your acquaintances may be decidedly bohemian in temperament or even (when Uranus is badly aspected, and when under any affliction) adventurers. You will have hopes and wishes very different to those of most people, and you will love the weird, profound and wonderful. It will bring the friendship of those who have romantic love-affairs, and you will hear some very strange stories from your friends. Your friends will be those of advanced thought, and original methods and directly or indirectly such will help you.

**129.** URANUS IN THE TWELFTH HOUSE is an unfortunate position, as it may bring you exile or estrangement either from your country, or else from your friends or relatives. You would do well to avoid eccentric people, and to have no dealings with those who are not perfectly straightforward. This position will possibly bring you some romantic and disastrous adventures with strangers, or perhaps in connection with other persons with whom you may be acquainted : and you should be very careful to guard against treachery. Be prepared for sudden surprises in connection with all things of a secret nature.

---

NOTE.—Unless there is some *strong aspect* between Uranus and one or the nearer planets, it is not likely to exercise much influence whatever its position.

# CHAPTER XII

## THE HOUSE-POSITION OF THE PLANET NEPTUNE.

THE remarks upon the planet Neptune on p. 14 of Chapter II. should be well studied before giving any attention to the meaning of its house-position as here briefly outlined. The opening paragraph of Chapter XI. should also be read in this connection. Much less is known about the nature of Neptune than of Uranus, and the following observations should therefore be regarded as somewhat tentative, and taken as hints rather than definite pronouncements.

**130.** NEPTUNE IN THE FIRST HOUSE at the time of your birth, will affect your life in an uncommon manner. You will be mediumistic and romantic, or psychically inclined. Some very strange experiences and also some remarkable episodes will occur in your life. It is only the very few who can in any way respond to the subtle spiritual vibrations of the planet Neptune, and they are the souls that live the purest lives. You must be on your guard against hypnotic suggestion, and should be very choice in your associates and acquaintances. You will in all probability, have some very remarkable dreams, which you should endeavour to remember. You will not escape being very mediumistic at times.

**131.** NEPTUNE IN THE SECOND HOUSE will give you strange experiences with regard to financial affairs. It may give you some ability to sing or study music, and will incline your thoughts to the mystical side of life. It will, however, be a weak influence unless powerfully aspected by other planets, especially the luminaries. It gives some taste for the weird and eerie.

**132.** NEPTUNE IN THE THIRD HOUSE will cause strange events in your family history; one of your relatives, probably a brother or sister, will be of a strange and uncommon character. Your mind will be

---

See note on page 61.

subject to peculiar fancies or inspirations; remarkable experiences may come to you while travelling. It would be well to act very discreetly with regard to correspondence. Strive to develope a positive attitude of mind, and do not neglect to cultivate the scientific as well as the artistic side of your mind.

**133.** NEPTUNE IN THE FOURTH HOUSE will bring peculiar episodes at the close of life. It may affect domestic affairs by bringing uncommon occurrences, or you may have family ties of an exceptional character. This position tends to render you mediumistic. Take note of the psychic conditions of the houses in which you may be called upon to live.

**134.** NEPTUNE IN THE FIFTH HOUSE warns you against strange magnetisms. It may bring you peculiar children, or very strange pleasures either mystical or otherwise. Strive to cultivate the spiritual side of your nature, and remember that the purely sensuous appreciation of beauty also has its dangers.

**135.** NEPTUNE IN THE SIXTH HOUSE threatens you with uncommon ailments. You are liable to catch complaints from others and suffer through impure magnetism. You are liable to suffer from the fraudulent action of servants or inferiors.

**136.** NEPTUNE IN THE SEVENTH HOUSE denotes strange relationships with the opposite sex, and a very peculiar or uncommon marriage. Beware of being too easily swayed by others, and always see that your intellect approves the choice of your feelings.

**137.** NEPTUNE IN THE EIGHTH HOUSE does not appear to be an important influence, and nothing definite is known concerning it. It has probably some connection with the state of consciousness during sleep.

**138.** NEPTUNE IN THE NINTH HOUSE promises very remarkable dreams and sometimes visions, and a mystical outlook on life.

**139.** NEPTUNE IN THE TENTH HOUSE seems to produce peculiar avocations, and uncommon pursuits. It may bring unexpected honours or discredits.

See note on page 61.

**140.** NEPTUNE IN THE ELEVENTH HOUSE denotes strange friendships and very peculiar associations. It inclines to clear vision, or clairvoyance.

**141.** NEPTUNE IN THE TWELFTH HOUSE denotes powerful enemies, and much treachery through seeming friendship. It gives psychic tendencies.

NOTE.—Unless there is some *strong aspect* between Neptune and one of the nearer planets, it is not likely to exercise much influence whatever its position.

§ 2.—*Individuality*

## CHAPTER XIII.

### INDIVIDUAL CHARACTERISTICS.

THE Individual Characteristics are symbolised by the position of THE SUN. The Sun is the source of the "vital force" in the Solar System, and is specialised in the Sign through which its rays are passing month by month, this force or influence being again modified by the solar aspects, and in a somewhat lesser degree by the other planetary positions also. Any Aspects to the Sun (pars. 202 to 225) should therefore be considered, jointly with its sign-position, under this head; unless the Rising Sign happens to be Leo, in which case the solar aspects will already have received consideration in Section 1 under the heading of Aspects to the Ruler.

The Sun is the significator of the individuality, the fixed basis of the nature, and its position has an important modifying influence upon the type of character indicated by the rising sign. In the personality the Sun chiefly rules the vital force.

A full description of the Individual Characteristics has already been published in *Astrology for All*, pages 13 to 47, and the following therefore must be looked upon only as abbreviated descriptions condensed within the limits suitable to our present purpose.

**142.** SUN IN ARIES. The "vital principle" of the Sun's ray in this sign endowed you with a fiery, untameable and aspiring spirit It gives a strong character, making you energetic, enthusiastic, somewhat wilful and at times impulsive and rash. You are independent, fond of liberty and responsibility : you love approval, and desire to be appreciated, working well under encouragement, but you will refuse to be over-driven. You are naturally very magnanimous, also generous and loyal to all your friends. You are idealistic, intuitive and prophetic, at times liable to go to extremes and over-estimate : but you will be a born pioneer, possessing splendid foresight, rapid perceptive judgment, loyalty, vigour and heroism, and will always delight in leading others.

**143.** SUN IN TAURUS. The "vital principle" of the Sun's ray in this sign will make you determined, persistent, patient and enduring, executive, practical, rather conservative, and at times a little dogmatic and obstinate. There is a tendency for you to become more authoritative, quiet, reserved, firm and inflexible as your life advances. Beneath all your firmness will be a warm heart, and you will ever be well disposed and generously minded. Your internal character will be rather dignified, cautious and careful, but although you will be slow in coming to decision, your judgment will be practical and solid. Internally the negative principle will be well developed, making you affectionate, kind and sympathetic.

**144.** SUN IN GEMINI. The vitalising principle of the solar rays in this sign will make you quick-witted, mentally impulsive, and inclined to be imperative. You will be intellectual, interested in literature, science or art, and also somewhat ambitious and aspiring. You should cultivate concentration if you would become clever, for you have latent ability in connection with literature or public speaking. There will be restlessness in your internal character, which will lead to nervousness and irritability, and when not guarded against, there will be a tendency for you to become volatile, indecisive and unreliable. It will be well for your comfort and happiness in life, if you learn to avoid worry and restlessness. A study of thought control would enable you to turn much of your intellectual ability to good account.

**145.** SUN IN CANCER. The "vital principle" of the Sun's ray passing through this sign will make you fond of your home and family; inclined to make strong ties, with sensitive feelings regarding them. You will be rather retiring, shy and reserved, and not much inclined to push yourself forward. This position will make you love the memories of the past, antiquities, ancient customs, and incline you to romance. You will be economical and very persistent, able to hold on where others lacking your tenacity would let go. Any over-sensitiveness will injure you, keeping you back in life, also any extremes where sensation is concerned will be injurious to you in many ways. Endeavour to distinguish between your own and the feelings of others.

**146.** SUN IN LEO. The "vital principle" of the solar force passing through this sign will make you generous, warm-hearted and will give you a loving nature. You will have deep emotions and a firm will, but when uncontrolled, the desires will be impulsive and the feelings easily affected. You should try and strengthen your will and live in the higher side of your nature if you would realise its nobility and magnanimity. You will be internally generous, sincere, earnest, persevering and much inclined to self-perfection. This sign will give you affection, unselfishness, ambition, pride and love of power. Its dangers are cowardice, prevarication, love of pomp and show and a hasty temper. You are a lover of justice, also of the natural pleasures of life, but should avoid all excess of feeling and emotion.

**147.** SUN IN VIRGO. The "vital principle" of the Sun's ray passing through this sign will give you an industrious character, and make you practical, philosophical, constructive and discriminative. It will endow you with criticism, self-protection, caution, diplomacy and ingenuity; but there will be much sensitiveness in your nature, a retiring, quiet and thoughtful attitude resulting. The more you encourage discrimination, the wiser you will become, for your inherent quality is discrimination, but you should avoid too much reserve or indecisiveness, or you may find yourself becoming too cold and unsympathetic on the one hand, or too vacillating on the other. You are active and businesslike in character, inclined to be fully alive to your own interests, and will know just how far it will be wise to exert yourself along practical lines.

**148.** SUN IN LIBRA. The "vital" or solar influence in this sign denotes balance, justice, equilibrium, impartiality. Your internal nature will be just, and inwardly you will love harmony and order. This position gives you the power to compare, and thus enables you to give an all-round and dispassionate judgment, yet makes you very sensitive as well, for you feel all the surrounding vibrations very keenly. But you have a kind and amiable nature, are always courteous and obliging, and your inner character will be equable, pure, perceptive, and docile, ever seeking to *learn* from what you observe. As your intuition expands with increased purity of life, your will grows stronger and you will learn much through comparison, through perception, and through your sensitive feelings.

**149.** SUN IN SCORPIO. This is a fixed and watery sign, and the "vital principle" of the Solar influence passing through this sign will make you a firm and powerful character, arising from the silent force within, giving you also occult leanings. You possess magnetic power, critical perception and ability to judge keenly, but when not fully under control your character will be rather exacting, jealous and proud. You will have strong likes and dislikes, and can be very reserved and dignified, though when vexed you are apt to be sharp and sarcastic if not actually cruel. You will, however, have much self-control, determination, tenacity and secretiveness, and as life advances there will come a stronger desire to investigate the occult and mystical. Avoid pride, cultivate sympathy, and endeavour to see things from others' standpoints as well as your own.

**150.** SUN IN SAGITTARIUS. The "vital principle" of the Sun's ray passing through this sign at your birth denotes that you are intuitive, prophetic, self-reliant, bright, hopeful and happy in disposition, though somewhat restless and over-active, and at times far too candid, out-spoken and assertive. If you are not careful you will say and express more than is wise. In your internal nature you have a religious spirit and you naturally possess much real devotion and affection. You will be very frank, honest, generous and loyal to those to whom you are attached, and will ever seek to become philosophical, but you should add some scientific knowledge as a solid basis to all your thoughts and actions.

**151.** SUN IN CAPRICORN. The "vital principle" of the Sun's ray passing through this sign will make you an ambitious, persistent industrious, and persevering character, possessing independence, self-reliance, determination, thrift and prudence, with the ability to acquire wealth and possessions. Your character will tend to become more patient, enduring and economical; you will respect age and ancient customs, possess a strong individuality, and have a love of the mystical. This sign will increase your ideality, and give you a love of beauty. It will also give you a love of justice, chastity and perfection, and you will surely succeed through your sterling traits of character. This sign gives you the ability and power to undertake responsibilities, and also tends to steady the whole character, and make it trustworthy and reliable.

**152.** SUN IN AQUARIUS. The "vital principle" operating through this sign will make you patient, cautious, faithful and determined, intuitive and refined. There is much in this sign that cannot be lived until the mind is withdrawn from the animal conditions, it being one of the distinctly human signs; yet even those who are unable to live up to it fully, intuitively feel that there is a lofty standard to be reached. You possess a kind, humane, honest, quiet and equable nature, and as life advances will become a good reader of character and judge of human nature, as you will be dispassionate in your judgment, since emotion will not often sway you.    You can easily make yourself at home with strangers.

**153.**    SUN IN PISCES.    The "vital principle" of the Sun's ray passing through this sign tends to make you trustful, honest and humane, having much sympathy in your nature especially for dumb animals.    You feel deeply, and also very keenly, though your emotions may be very rarely expressed ; moreover you have a desire to be at peace with all. You possess but little ambition, and are rather lacking in self-reliance ; a little more will and assertiveness should be shown at times.    This sign somewhat inclines you towards mediumship, but makes you sociable, good-humoured, sincere and inclined to be religious.    Being very sympathetic you will always delight in hospitable and social undertakings. You will do well not to pay undue attention to details.

## CHAPTER XIV.

### PERSONAL CHARACTERISTICS.

THE personal characteristics are symbolised by the position of THE MOON in each of the twelve signs. It is the ' sensitive spot,' so to speak, of the horoscope. It is the magnetic vortex into which are collected the various influences of the planets, and there changed into *personal characteristics.*

A full description of these characteristics will be found in *Astrology for All,* pp. 63 to 70. Those here given are more or less condensed. It should always be remembered that the aspects formed by the Moon are quite as important as her sign-position, if not more so. The lunar aspects will be given in due course ; an aspect to the Moon accentuates, neutralises, or modifies, the tendencies shown by the sign-position, according to the nature of the aspect. Any Aspects to the Moon (pars. 226 to 246) should therefore be considered, jointly with its sign- and house-position, under this head ; unless the Rising Sign happens to be Cancer, in which case the lunar aspects will already have received consideration in Section 1 under the heading of Aspects to the Ruler.

The Moon is the significator of the personality and of the more changeable and fluctuating moods and feelings. It has some influence upon the bodily form and appearance. It somewhat modifies the indications of the rising sign, especially in all matters that are naturally ruled by the Moon.

**154.** MOON IN ARIES. This will give your personal character a martial and rather aggressive tendency. It will increase your personal independence and make you very self-reliant, rebelling against authority, and wishing to lead or control and be at the head of things. It will give you a keen intellectual nature, making you sharp, shrewd and observant.   You will be aspiring, very assertive, and fully conscious of your own ability : but unless you cultivate control, will be irritable and hasty in temper, insisting upon having your own way at all costs.   It will be well for you to study tolerance and to avoid over-doing things : also to guard against impulsive speech and hasty action.

**155.**   MOON IN TAURUS.   This indicates a reserved, persistent, and determined personality ; it will give you some amount of ambition, acquisitiveness, and the ability to persevere in spite of obstacles, and a desire to uphold ancient customs.   The Moon is exalted in the sign Taurus and greatly increases the love nature, giving you patience, and endurance, and also, if not controlled, some pride.   But the virtues of this position are firmness, stability, and generosity.   You will be very intuitive, and also feel very deeply at times.   There will be a tendency for you to be firm and somewhat obstinate ; but your disposition will be good, kind and sociable.

**156.**   MOON IN GEMINI.   This will considerably strengthen your intellect, giving you a love of books and scientific or literary pursuits, and thus you may greatly improve your personal character.   It will incline you to be active in mind and body, and will also sharpen your wits, giving you the ability to follow more than one occupation at a time and also to adapt yourself to new surroundings.   You should avoid going to extremes, however ; for at times you may be impulsively generous, while at others you may be parsimonious and thus miss opportunities.   If you avoid superficiality, you may become very clever, having both insight and capacity.   This position will cause you to have dual experiences in the course of your life.

**157.**   MOON IN CANCER.   This denotes a personality much attached to home life and family ties.   This position of the Moon will much increase the emotional nature, making you extremely sensitive.   It will expand your sympathies and accentuate all your feelings.   You will possess a lively imagination, but you should avoid becoming fanciful. Your memory will be very good if cultivated, and towards the close of your life you will become much interested in psychic matters.   You like to be appreciated, and feel things that are said of you very keenly.   You will be fond of change, yet inclined to be careful and economical.   This position gives a great deal of receptivity, therefore it is essential that you mix and associate only with pure-minded and cheerful persons, or you may find yourself liable to " moods," often undesirable ones.

**158.** MOON IN LEO. The influence of this position on your personal character, is such as to lift you upward in life, and make you fond of responsibility and management. You will be nobly ambitious, very persevering, warm-hearted, kind, affectionate, generous, honourable, and very straightforward in all your dealings, always preferring candour to being secretive and insincere. You have a generous love nature, and will be faithful in all your affections, but are rather susceptible in affairs of the heart. You possess a poetical soul, and love music, the fine arts, and all things harmonious. You are intuitive and your imagination is very fertile and will be helpful to you. If once pride and self-will have been overcome, you will have few failings.

**159.** MOON IN VIRGO. This gives you good intellectual powers and the capacity to follow intellectual pursuits : it also gives you a good memory, enabling you to learn readily. It tends to make you trustworthy in all your undertakings for others. This very useful position will make you quiet, easy-going, and not over ambitious : although you will be somewhat critical and keen in business matters. Your personality will be humane and refined, not over-assertive, eager to follow hygienic studies, and to adopt all practical measures for improvement. You may become very discriminative as life advances : for this is the quality you are to realise, when you have passed through sufficient experience.

**160.** MOON IN LIBRA. This position confers upon you personally a refined character. It will make you love ease and pleasure, the arts, and social gatherings. You will always be kindly, genial, affable, and courteous, and will try to preserve a happy disposition. You will like approval, and life will be sweet to you when you are appreciated, but not so when you remain unnoticed. You will be just as well as generous, and love order and refinement. You have good powers of imitation and perception, and love of comparison. Always endeavour to be even-tempered, and try to keep the "Balance." It will not be well to carry comparison too far, and activity may at times be beneficial. You have some artistic tastes.

**161.** MOON IN SCORPIO. This will make you firm, determined, self-reliant ; well able to stand alone in life, and to fight your own battles. At times you will be abrupt or too plain spoken, so that you should always be careful in speech not to wound others, as whenever you are annoyed your words are apt to be sharp and sometimes unkind. I judge that you will love mysticism and secret subjects; you will therefore have the ability to study occultism or to investigate psychic matters. You will not be easily influenced, and interference will make you rather obstinate. You will have an energetic nature, and capacity for hard work. Avoid too much secrecy, and do not allow yourself to become intolerant; or you will find yourself more selfish than is good for you. This influence gives you quite enough dignity and firmness to enable you always to hold your own.

**162.** MOON IN SAGITTARIUS. This position will make you quick, active and restless, and at times rather rebellious and unsettled, but it will also make your disposition very sincere and honourable, and give you a tendency to be religious, and good-humoured. There will be a strong religious vein running through you, and you will be very sincere in your beliefs, even although they may happen to be unorthodox. You will be quite open to investigate mysticism, psychism and occultism, and it would not be difficult for you to teach others also, for you will have a very philosophical and prophetic tendency. You should avoid extremes and over-exertion. You may expect some dual experiences during life, two things often happening at the same time, or two ideas possessing you at the same moment.

**163.** MOON IN CAPRICORN. This is a position which indicates that you will have a desire for fame, and an ambitious personality. As a rule, those born with this position either attain wide popularity or become very well known in the circle in which they move. It gives that kind of character which brings one prominently before others. It also gives chastity, prudence, economy, and generally, owing to the acquisitive faculties being well developed, a desire to get the best of a bargain. You will never have too much self-esteem, although you may be approbative and sensitive. At some time of your life your personal character will be such as to court responsibility, as this position gives a love of leadership and a great desire to be at the head of things.

**164.** MOON IN AQUARIUS. This will endow you with a unique personality, inclining you to all things occult and adding a touch of the eccentric or uncommon to your nature. You will become an excellent character reader if you study human nature, for you have a natural gift for it; and you may develop a great love for mysticism and occultism. You are very refined in your tastes, intuitive, with broad and humanitarian sympathies, sociable and independent, yet loving appreciation.  This position inclines you personally to science, combined with philosophy and literary pursuits.  You are very sensitive to the mental conditions of other persons.  In connection with associations and societies you would do well.

**165.** MOON IN PISCES.  This will give you a quiet, retiring, and at times irresolute personality.  You must therefore try not to be easily discouraged, for you will meet with obstacles in life, and they should tend to make you less negative and receptive.  You will have a tendency to be mediumistic and silently emotional, and you may become very psychic and too easily influenced.  Avoid depression, and cultivate all the hope you can, never fearing that you may grow too decisive: firmness and independence are good for you, as you will not abuse them.  You will love all that has to do with feeling and hospitality, and if you try to analyse your own impressions you will often know the conditions of those around you.  You will be fond of mystical subjects, and the romantic and emotional side of life.

# CHAPTER XV.

## THE MOON'S HOUSE-POSITION.

THE House-Position of the Moon is most important in every horoscope, quite apart from its influence upon the personal characteristics as indicated by its Sign-postion already described. It shows the direction which those activities indicated by the personal disposition are likely to take. The following paragraphs give a description of the Moon's influence in each of the twelve houses.

**166.** THE MOON IN THE ASCENDANT at your birth shows a love of fame, activity and change. You will seek to be at the head of things mentally, or take a prominent part in all that concerns you. It makes you very ambitious, aspiring, and also ingenious, fond of planning and taking up original and novel ventures. It gives you an imaginative brain, loving change, novelty and adventure. This position brings popularity, but also opposition and liability to scandal through and from inferiors and the public. It will bring you into some fame, or public recognition through your own merit or ability. You will do well with common things, such as novelties and public commodities, or those things that appeal to the public taste and fancy.

**167.** THE MOON IN THE SECOND HOUSE of your nativity will cause finance to fluctuate. Success in life will come through dealing in public commodities, or in connection with liquids, or concerns where there is a quick and rapid turnover. It generally indicates receptivity where money is concerned, and the public mind is generally felt in regard to financial movements. All matters public or commercial should be attractive to you; and you are fitted to hold public office. It promises success through travel, but your fortunes are liable to many changes; therefore your efforts should be directed to a fluctuating business or a profession in which water or movement plays a prominent part. Your mind is ingenious, active, and full of imagination or romance.

**168.** THE MOON IN THE THIRD HOUSE of your nativity will bring you many adventures in life, with constant change and travelling.

This is not a good position for constancy or concentration, except when in a fixed sign, the mind being too changeable and fond of activity. It gives you a love of curiosities and a liking for many uncommon pursuits, with an aptitude for living by your wits even, if necessary. You have a love of knowledge, much curiosity, and the ability to take up many subjects. You are fond of your relatives and all matters to do with brethren and sisters will have prominence in your life. Your mind at times will be full of desire, and anything monotonous will easily tire you. Intellectual pursuits will provide the best vehicle for your energies.

**169.** THE MOON IN THE FOURTH HOUSE at the time of your birth is important, and it will cause you to be far more active, and your life more eventful, at the close than at the beginning. At the close of life you will incline toward mysticism and occult things, taking a very deep interest in all psychic matters, your mind growing more receptive, and probably at times rather mediumistic. It will cause many changes, and will break or make ties when you least desire it. It tends towards increased economy in domestic affairs and interest in home life. You will probably inherit or benefit financially through this position.

**170.** THE MOON IN THE FIFTH HOUSE shows that you will gain by experiences connected with pleasure or sensation, and out of sensational matters, probably directly connected with the feelings, will come an exceptional experience probably needed to free you from the meshes of the senses. You will be fortunate in connection with schools, or matters to do with children, amusement, etc., and at times with all matters connected with speculative affairs. It makes you very ardent in all matters of the heart, for you put much feeling into all that gives pleasure to yourself and others; there is however a tendency to be fickle in love affairs and you will come in contact with those who are not so constant in their affections It will bring you much romance.

**171.** THE MOON IN THE SIXTH HOUSE shows that your chief experience will come through psychic things. You are trustworthy in carrying out any special work committed to your charge, but you can do better under the guidance of a stronger influence than your own. It will keep you back in life, and will prevent you from being fully appreciated. At times you are irresolute and wavering, and will lose opportunities in consequence. Your health will suffer through this position and fail you when required, probably through over-work or worry, as this will affect the mind and react on the body. You will gain more through common pursuits than by those of a prominent, or very high class character. Many joys and sorrows will come through inferiors.

**172.** THE MOON IN THE SEVENTH HOUSE will bring you into intimate relation with the public, and you will be popular in your own sphere, though at times you may have to contend with some public opposition. You will come into contact with those who travel much, and make acquaintance with some who lead Bohemian or roving lives. Your chances of success in law will fluctuate, at times going well, at other times adversely, according to the aspects. Another life will surely be mixed up with your own, causing you anxiety as well as pleasure and happiness, for your fortunes will always be strangely bound up with those of another, either in marriage, partnerships, or where there is more than a single and separate interest.

**173.** THE MOON IN THE EIGHTH HOUSE shows gain through partners and co-workers, a probability of money through inheritance, wills or legacies, and when your marriage partner comes under good influences, gain also thereby. This is not the best place for the Moon, but it is good for occult and mystical affairs. A trance or an uncommon death is possible. This position favours mediumship, mesmerism, and all secret or strange psychic affairs. Danger will attend all long voyages, and care should be taken to start under good aspects; you would in all probability be a victim in any public calamity and one of those drawn irresistibly towards any national disaster.

**174.** THE MOON IN THE NINTH HOUSE shows travel to foreign lands, giving gain thereby. Your mind is good and prone to investigate metaphysical subjects, taking a deep interest in all philosophy and occultism. It inclines you to the mystical and the occult, and also causes you to investigate and explore all new domains before definitely accepting them, and makes you sincere when you believe anything concerned with the soul or the higher mind. It makes you able to teach others, inclining you to be prophetic, speaking inspirationally or through intuition. Always listen to the dictates of your Higher Self, your soul being ever ready to seek for the inner truth that is always within and not without you.

**175.** THE MOON IN THE TENTH HOUSE at the time of your birth gives you some desire to lead a public life and obtain recognition. It will raise you into good positions, which will at times be difficult to maintain, there being liability to change. It awakens all latent ambition and stimulates business instincts. You will not be entirely happy unless you hold a prominent position in whatever sphere you move, therefore you will surely rise in life. This position nearly always brings fame, sometimes notoriety ; therefore you should guard against scandal, slander and treachery, using care in dealings with inferiors or those jealous of your position.

**176.** THE MOON IN THE ELEVENTH HOUSE of your nativity tends to bring you several friends and acquaintances, some reliable and others quite the reverse. You will gain through societies, associations and through utilitarian affairs. You will be sociable and easy to understand and attract. You have very strong fancies and desires, loving the occult and mystical, possessing ability for astrology, and kindred subjects. If you can control your senses you will become an excellent judge of character ; therefore try to study and cultivate this useful art. It gives a refined influence to the nativity, being very favourable for receptivity to the conditions of others, also bringing help and favours from the public generally.

**177.** THE MOON IN THE TWELFTH HOUSE at the time of your birth will bring many secret affairs into your life, inclining you towards mediumship and psychic phenomena. You will be drawn into romance, or be very strongly influenced by it, and all that is weird and mystical will possess fascination for you. Be always guarded against false accusation and treachery, or anything that may cause you to run the risk of losing your liberty, for you will make some enemies during the course of your life. You will take some long voyages when directions indicate or favour them. It is not a favourable position for the Moon, except for things that do not give prominence to your personality.

## 4.—*Mentality.*

## CHAPTER XVI.

### MENTAL QUALIFICATIONS.

THE position of the planet MERCURY in each horoscope denotes the mind, and hence the mental qualifications. This position is modified by aspects, more especially any aspect to the Moon, which affects the lucidity and clearness of the capacity for mental expression. Further, since Mercury is also related to the nervous system, and the Moon to the brain in a general sense, good or bad aspects between these two planets will have a bearing upon the general nervous condition, whether serene and well regulated, or hypersensitive, fidgetty, irritable, etc.*

Any Aspects to Mercury (pars. 247 to 264) should therefore be considered, jointly with its sign- and house-position, under this head; unless the Rising Sign happens to be Virgo or Gemini, in which case the said aspects will already have received consideration in Section 1 under the heading of Aspects to the Ruler.

**178.** MERCURY IN ARIES. Your mental faculties will be quickened. You will be quick to perceive and observe, possessing a fertile and inventive brain, good at originating designs and quick in all mental work. You have active mental combativeness, and your mind will always be alert and aspiring. Avoid anxiety and mental excitement, for this will result in brain trouble, neuralgia, or severe headaches. You can appreciate all intellectual pursuits, and respect persons who are mentally clever. Study moderation in expression, concentration, and continuity of ideas. If you can do this your success is assured, for you have the ability to lead mentally, and most people will look up to you, believing in your intelligence.

**179.** MERCURY IN TAURUS indicates that you are slow to make up your mind, but that it is immovable when once it is made up.

---

* Uranus has some influence on the nervous system, and afflictions between Uranus and Mercury (more especially the square aspect) are generally accompanied by a disturbed and somewhat hysterical nervous temperament.

You can, however, exercise much patience and perseverance in all mental pursuits, and it makes you disposed to be sociable, friendly and affectionate. It also inclines you towards religion, and gives you a taste for art, music or poetry. You can exercise much endurance in all you undertake mentally, and I judge that you possess good memory. This position of Mercury in a fixed sign, make you just, constant, firm, industrious, strict, sincere, and uncompromising, but you must guard against a danger of becoming mentally obstinate.

**180.** MERCURY IN GEMINI. This will bring to the front all "mercurial" affairs, giving you the ability to write, and study. You would however, learn more by travelling, than by studying or reading, for Mercury in Gemini is rather against concentration ; the mind having a difficulty to fix itself on one subject at a time ; therefore, travel is the best means for the expansion of your mind. Mentally, you will be variable, and able to engage in two distinct pursuits or studies, which adds considerably to your versatility. Your mind is active and alert, and you could become a good conversationalist, speaker, or entertainer, having a ready wit and a more or less dexterous facility of expression.

**181.** MERCURY IN CANCER will cause you to be active and somewhat changeable. You will also be very ingenious, and inquisitive, grasping many subjects, and taking a wide, comprehensive view of things. Cultivate your memory, and make your mind strong, and alert. You will act wisely to investigate occult subjects, as you could easily become psychic or a "true-dreamer," and manifest occult gifts of some kind. You possess intuition, tact, talent : and although ambitious, you tend to draw friends from those who rank lower than yourself, and sometimes also from persons engaged in investigating mystical subjects. You are fond of the water and may gain through travelling by it.

**182.** MERCURY IN LEO. This position considerably strengthens the rational mind ; it makes you very strong-willed and positive, yet kind hearted, generous, and at times easy going. This position will enable you to hold some post of responsibility, giving you the ability to manage and control others. You have keen appreciation of mental harmony, while there is a wisdom possessed by you that comes from the heart more than from the head : so that this position makes you mentally intuitive. You should exercise care to avoid over-work, or brain-fag, as you are inclined to be too thorough and too determined where mental work is concerned. You would however, always use your mind advantageously in pursuits connected with the command, control, or management of others.   You have the autocratic type of mind.

**183.**   MERCURY IN VIRGO.   Your mind will be active and comprehensive.   You learn readily and love scientific investigation ; you have a very good memory, and can turn all your studies to good account.   You would be practical in any capacity, but you are apt to have too many things on hand at a time.   This position is somewhat opposed to public success, although much may be done quietly in a sphere where you have not to take the lead ; teaching, literary-work, book-keeping, agencies, etc., would be successful pursuits for your mind.   If you can avoid being drawn to a lower mental level by others, you will attain to real ability and rise through merit as life advances.

**184.**   MERCURY IN LIBRA makes your mind well balanced and refined, and indicates that you have ability for reading, writing and study, and an eloquent tongue.   It favours studying with others, but does not indicate great depth or much staying power ; but it is good for comparison and judgment, though unless the other planets denote energy, there is not much inclination to work or study hard with the mind.   Your mind is affable, imitative, artistic, neat and orderly, and your disposition humane, just and persuasive.   Your intuition is good, and you appreciate art. You have poetical ability, and with suitable training would become proficient in oratory or literature.

**185.**   MERCURY IN SCORPIO will incline you to be somewhat positive, obstinate and difficult to convince.   But you may be moved to much enthusiasm by any cause you espouse, and to great resentment or hatred by a real or fancied wrong.   You are shrewd and active in mind, somewhat sarcastic, and may have a ready flow of language.   You love secrecy, and will never be short of tact and diplomacy, as you possess a mind capable of understanding mysteries.   This position will also give you some manual dexterity, and make you ingenious and fertile of resource, with the ability to invent or discover.   You could pursue a train of thought with much concentration.

**186.**   MERCURY IN SAGITTARIUS.   This will give you a just, straight-forward, and generous mind.   In religion or philosophy you will be very earnest, although at times liable to change.   You will be able to study more than one subject at a time, but will not possess much continuity.   Religion, philosophy and science will always interest you, and you love reading or writing on all deep and thoughtful subjects.

When you speak it is to the point, and your words will often bear prophetic significance. This position of Mercury gives diplomacy, but your tact would be more useful in any subordinate position in life than where you had full responsibility.

**187.** MERCURY IN CAPRICORN will make your mind subtle and cautious, diplomatic and profound. This position makes the mind really clever, and gives you the power to keep your own counsel and use tact in argument. It will bring you honour and recognition in all mental pursuits. You will rise in life through ambition, aided by tact and resourcefulness, and you need never fear to undertake responsibility and organisation. You have a systematic and orderly mind, enabling you to work methodically. You will be thorough in all your mental work. You will have the ability to study astrology and kindred subjects. It will always be to your advantage to cultivate straightforwardness in thought.

**188.** MERCURY IN AQUARIUS adds to the strength of your intellect, giving you a good memory, and a strong and comprehensive mind. It increases any tendency to mental culture or science, literature or religion, but you are inclined to have fixed opinions, being averse to change, and not very easily influenced. You are capable of clear mental work, can be original and with good education could do great things. Mercury is very strong in this sign, giving a power of concentration which may be beneficially cultivated. It also strengthens the intuition, and gives some ability to study and judge human nature. You can entertain others, and would have much social success if you gave your mind to the entertaining or the instruction of others.

**189.** MERCURY IN PISCES. Your mind will be very receptive, inclined to be somewhat mediumistic, able to sense things without being able to give an explanation as to how the knowledge was obtained, in fact a mind that can act diplomatically, quietly and withal in a systematic manner. This is a position which gives ability for speaking, singing or writing, but the common and everyday affairs of life will be more advantageous to you than the peculiar or uncommon. There is a love of spiritualism and mysticism, and the mind is able to dip into spiritual mysteries, and discover some of the secrets of the soul. There is, however, at times, a tendency, to be rather too indifferent mentally, and not sufficiently active in mind. You should guard against mental superficialities.

# CHAPTER XVII.

## MERCURY'S HOUSE-POSITION.

MERCURY is the chief ruler of the nervous system and of the intellect. Its position by sign (Chap. XVI.) indicates the type of intellect, while its position by house, now to be described, shows the direction in which the intellect will seek expression, or in other words the most suitable direction in which to turn for healthy and beneficial mental exercise.

**190.** MERCURY IN THE FIRST HOUSE. This will accentuate the mental characteristics, making you quick witted, sharp and keen, gifted in writing and in speaking, quick at retort and repartee, and also liable to a little exaggeration at times, and to some sarcasm. It will make you mentally enthusiastic, and when you are under the influence of much feeling, you will be rather excitable. You are clever and possess a subtle wit, and an excellent power of adaptability to circumstances; but you should avoid restlessness and inquisitiveness, and exercise control over your thoughts. This influence will tend to make you a prolific writer, with a very fertile mind that is quite original and inventive.

**191.** MERCURY IN THE SECOND HOUSE. This is favourable for gaining by correspondence, letters and writing, also for financial success in literary pursuits, and in professional and artistic affairs generally. Although a good position for Mercury on the whole, and when under favourable directions you would be successful as regards travel and short journeys, it is on the other hand not very favourable when afflicted. You have mental abilities for finance and would gain either by trading, or through scientific pursuits, lectures, etc. But you should guard against theft and fraud, as at some time of your life you may be the victim of sharp practice.

**192.** MERCURY IN THE THIRD HOUSE considerably accentuates your mental ability. It tends to quicken your mind, making you studious and capable of embracing many subjects. At the same time it will enable you to readily change from one subject to another, making you versatile, and competent to deal with Mercurial subjects.   It will give you a taste for reading, make you very fond of curiosities and give you the ability to study astrology and kindred subjects.   It is one of the strongest positions for Mercury, giving clearness of intellect and penetrative thought.   To appreciate this the power of concentration must have been cultivated.

**193.**   MERCURY IN THE FOURTH HOUSE of your nativity will considerably modify this planet's general influence.   It will bring many changes, especially in business, and you may frequently change your place of residence.   You would do better by travelling than by settling down.   This position will bring you in touch with occultism or bring you work in connection with the occult.   It will be well to be careful of what you read as the mind acts on the body very quickly in your case.   You should love the water, and your mind would expand while travelling.   You can improve your mental powers by constancy and concentration.

**194.**   MERCURY IN THE FIFTH HOUSE will make your mind somewhat easy going, fond of pleasure and at times inclined to self-indulgence.   It makes you fond of children, music, poetry, singing and the drama.   You should not over-study or you will affect the heart.   Your mind is loving and affectionate, but you should guard against inconstancy and excess in pleasure.   You must never be carried away by speculation, or a gambling spirit may be encouraged.   You should be good at mimicry and there is some latent ability for acting.   Children born to you would be intellectual and very clever.

**195.**   MERCURY IN THE SIXTH HOUSE favours the study of hygiene and medicine.   It warns you against over-study or over-worry as this would affect your health.   If you worry you will have many petty annoyances, and this will give a tendency to acute nervous troubles or dyspepsia.   You may have much trouble through inferiors at times when Mercury is afflicted.   You have some capacity for occultism, but fame should never be sought, and all should be done unnoticed or you might become unpopular.   You should be content to engage your mind in comparatively obscure and unknown subjects.   This position gives great danger of loss through servants or inferiors at some time of life.

**196.**   MERCURY IN THE SEVENTH HOUSE will tend to keep your mind exercised on matters pertaining to partnerships, marriage and things concerning others more than yourself.   Be careful to avoid wrangling or disputes, or you may find yourself involved in much disputation and may be drawn into litigation over what may appear to be trifles. This position is not good for argument as your opponents would probably be too strong for you. It threatens loss and brings worries and anxieties, and if you allow yourself to be imposed upon you may suffer from vexation. Your partners would be clever and quick-witted, but sharper than yourself.

**197.** MERCURY IN THE EIGHTH HOUSE will make your mind more positive and it will be difficult for you to be convinced against your will. It inclines your mind to mysticism and occultism, and there is a tendency to look below the surface for the cause of things. It gives you an enquiring mind, making you at times anxious regarding the solvings of problems, and concerned as to a future life, until the truth is known concerning the after-death state. Your mind is likely to be over-anxious in this position and your ingenuity and resourcefulness increased, Do not wear yourself out by over mental activity, anxiety or worry.

**198.** MERCURY IN THE NINTH HOUSE. This position will give you a splendid mind for science or philosophy, and discrimination in regard to religion. It will help you in literary pursuits and give you a general all-round knowledge of many subjects ; your mind will always be active and fond of knowledge. You would do well abroad or by taking long journeys. You will succeed much better if you practise concentration and do not allow your thoughts to wander, or take up too many subjects at a time. You have the ability to study astrology. occultism, and all subjects of a metaphysical nature.

**199.** MERCURY IN THE TENTH HOUSE will keep your mind exercised in matters to do with employments or position in life. It gives you an ambitious and somewhat restless mind but inclines towards literature or Mercurial pursuits. It is good for commercial affairs, also for recognition from those who have influence in the literary world. You should gain through commission work, agencies and such details as come under the influence of Mercury. It increases diplomacy and ambition and gives success in government employments, such as the civil service. You may rise in life through your mental abilities, but do not become over-anxious.

**200.** MERCURY IN THE ELEVENTH HOUSE strengthens the intellect, giving a firmer, stronger and more comprehensive mind. It gives scientific and literary ability and increases the power of concentration, enabling you to fix your ideas.   It strengthens the whole mind, and according to your education will make it original and expansive. The intuition is improved and there is some latent tendency towards mysticism, or a religion which appeals to the head as well as to the heart. If you cultivate character reading you may become an excellent exponent of that art.   You will be much attached to your friends, but some of them may deceive you, or involve you in trouble and anxiety.

**201.** MERCURY IN THE TWELFTH HOUSE will tend to keep you back in life and not allow you to exercise your mind as fully as you should.   You may suffer from secret enmity or slander, deserved or not.   You will be in some temporary danger of mental affection at some time of life and it would be well not to let yourself be drawn into any unwise scheme, especially where writings are concerned.   Be careful not to put your hand to papers unthinkingly, and never let your mind be overtaxed or worried as it would affect the brain.   You might easily over-ride enmity by being careful in speech and action.

# CHAPTER XVIII.

## THE POSITIONS AND ASPECTS OF THE SUN, MOON AND PLANETS.

APART altogether from the influence of the Sign-Positions and House-Positions of planets, their aspects to each other and to the luminaries (Sun and Moon), and the mutual aspect of the two latter, have a most important bearing upon the reading of a horoscope. It is a safe thing to say that a Nativity in which there are not one or two significant strong aspects—whether benefic or malefic need not concern us for the moment,—is a very weak one.

Aspects are roughly classed as " benefic " and "malefic," as shown in the table on p. 62 of *Astrology for All*, but it should not be hastily supposed by the beginner that " bad " aspects are necessarily to be turned from with loathing. On the contrary, there are few strong characters whose horoscopes do not show one or more 'afflictions' of this kind. Perhaps "comfortable" and "uncomfortable," though hardly dignified words, might be usefully substituted for 'good' and 'bad' in this connection. For the benefic aspects tend towards a harmonious expression of the qualities ruled by the planets concerned; whereas the malefic aspects, while affecting the very same qualities, tend to a manifestation that is abrupt, awkward, excessive or violent, in other words either under- or over-done.

For instance, an aspect between Mercury and Saturn disposes the mind to seriousness; if a benefic aspect, towards study and contemplation, with a calm and reflective outlook on life : if on the other hand an affliction, then the tendency will be rather towards gloom and suspiciousness in ordinary matters, hypercriticalness and carping, the mind being rather over-disposed to look upon the "dark side " of things. But it is the same forces that are being dealt with, and for those who learn to "rule their stars " a 'bad' aspect controlled is found to furnish a reservoir of power which would perhaps hardly be voluntarily exchanged for the most favourable and harmonious 'good' aspect. A good aspect may oftentimes be likened to the model boy at school, who gives no

84

trouble but excels at his work and becomes a useful member of society, while the bad aspect is like the young rascal who is the despair of his teachers, rebellious and naughty, and yet perhaps with the seeds of greatness within him which time will bring to fruit. It is not the good or bad aspects, so much as the use made of them, that marks the strong soul.

With these few preliminary remarks we may turn to a consideration of the general effects of each aspect, as found working in the majority of horoscopes.

### ASPECTS TO THE SUN.

**202.** The luminaries in CONJUNCTION is not a favourable position, excepting for those who have made great attainments, and are merging the personality into the individuality, but it marks a stage wherein both the individuality and the personality will take their many experiences coloured by the different aspects that the luminaries meet in your nativity. It has a tendency to limit your experiences in certain directions, but in the event of the individuality becoming stronger than the personality, the influence will not be quite so injurious, but should the personality assert itself too freely the influence cannot be good, as the animal soul would absorb too much of the solar vitality without that freedom of expression indicated when the Moon is free from the Sun.

**203.** The BENEFIC aspect of the Sun with the Moon improves your nativity. This will bring you success in many ways, and help you to the attainment of many of your desires and wishes, you will be rightly ambitious and aspiring, while prosperity will attend any efforts that you will make to earn success in life. You will obtain acknowledgment, and recognition in the sphere in which you move, in accordance with the use you make of your own abilities. This influence will also greatly improve your disposition, and will add to your vitality. You will obtain success in all affairs that may relate to the heart; for, in affection, you will be extremely sympathetic and sincere.

**204.** The Sun and Moon in ADVERSE aspect at your nativity is not fortunate, as it will bring obstacles into your life, and cause delays and hindrances to your hopes, wishes, and desires. It is not good for vitality or health, which may at times suffer. You would do well not to look for popularity, as it will tend in some way to react upon you. Use all care in safeguarding your honour, avoiding every action that would be likely to injure your credit in any way : in this respect you should exercise caution and diplomacy in all dealings with your superiors or with those in authority. Preserve your eyesight.

**205.** The Sun in CONJUNCTION with the Mercurial planet is a doubtful position, and it is only those who are more *individual* than *personal* who can answer to its vibration : it then gives much mental ability, with clear thinking of a high order. But when the personal side of the nature predominates, this position is powerless to act. To make this position active and profitable all personal bias must be eliminated, and the wisdom of the soul allowed to transcend the intellect. For it is a position that favours the subjective consciousness, or intelligence, more than the concrete or objective display of knowledge. With the majority this position remains a mere latent possibility, until the soul is developed.

**206.** Owing to the small size of Mercury's orbit the Sun can only form with this planet a *weak* BENEFIC aspect which is unimportant, and **207.** also a weak ADVERSE aspect which is of very little importance.

**208.** The Sun in CONJUNCTION with the beautiful planet Venus will awaken all joyous and blissful vibrations in you, so that all other aspects and positions of an adverse nature will be very greatly modified. To awaken this influence to the full, however, it will be necessary to live more to the individual side of the nature than the personal. It is a position that touches the more momentous affairs of life and brings matters connected with pleasure, joy or success into activity. The artistic side of your nature may be stimulated and cultivated to advantage, and you may associate with others with full confidence that much joy and happiness will follow. It is a very fortunate influence.

**209.** The Sun at your birth was in somewhat BENEFIC aspect to the planet Venus, which although it will not have a very strong influence on your outward circumstances yet renders your inner nature more harmonious, and more inclined towards gentle and peaceable methods than would otherwise be the case. It shows you to be internally loving and harmonious, willing to see the best in others and always endeavouring, so far as you can, to address yourself to that higher portion of their nature. There is always a certain love of art, or of artistic and elegant surroundings, connected with this influence, and it has a generally refining influence on the mind and on the Individual part of your self.

**210.** The Sun at your birth formed an aspect with Venus which was ADVERSE in its nature, and this will prevent an easy flow of the virtues and benefits which Venus usually bestows when unafflicted at birth. It will cause you to have some disappointments in connection with your feelings, and at certain periods of your life monetary troubles and also some social difficulties will make your environment not altogether as easy as it would have been had the Sun been free from this affliction. However, it is not altogether a disastrous aspect in its nature, though it does not give that contentment or ease of mind so essential to success and prosperity. Be very guarded in all your dealings with persons who are likely to in any way affect your feelings and emotions : as there is a liability for you to be disappointed and thwarted in your hopes and wishes, particularly where your feelings are in any way at the mercy of others.

**211.** With the Sun, and the planet Mars, in CONJUNCTION there will be a struggle between your will and desires during this life, the Sun representing the will, and Mars the desires. This will be felt through passion or anger, arising from over-abundant vitality at times, and periodic heats causing a very feverish condition of the blood, exciting you to impulsiveness, or excess of feeling; and, while it will give you courage and some strength, it is not a desirable conjunction unless great self-control is exercised, much depending upon yourself whether WILL or desire gain the mastery. The dominating and ruling element is strong in you, and this will give you much force of character, and the power to command or control others.

**212.** The Sun and the planet Mars in BENEFIC aspect, is remarkably good for your health and vitality generally. It will give you courage, and a strong constitution. Your will power and desire nature are blended, which will enable you to force your way in life with an intensity of purpose, energy, and perseverance that will seldom, if ever, be thwarted. You can control and command others, you will generally carry your point through energy and strength of will more than through tact and diplomacy. You may accomplish great things if you let your individual nature act more often than the personal desires and wishes. This very powerful influence often gives too much life, and it is necessary to either have plenty of exercise, or live an active life to distribute it through the system evenly.

**213.** The Sun in ADVERSE aspect with Mars shows that there exists some amount of conflict between your individual will and your desire nature, and between these two influences you will suffer. You should therefore try to strengthen your individual will, not allowing yourself to be carried away by desires that you cannot attain.  I think you would do well to avoid excitement of all kinds, and it may be necessary at certain periods of your life to guard against accidents. Before undergoing operations of any kind you should deliberate very carefully, and you should also guard against fire and fire-arms.  You are constitutionally liable to feverish complaints, and are apt to be too hasty in general.

**214.**  The Sun in CONJUNCTION with the benefic planet Jupiter will bring you into touch with those vibrations that will awaken the individual side of your nature, and allow you to live to the noblest side of your being.  You will prosper through this position and find many opportunities to progress, both mentally, morally, and also physically.  The social element will bring you into touch with those who hold good and permanent positions in life, and the help of others will be at hand whenever it may be desired.  New undertakings prosper, and the constructive ability is strengthened.  The life forces will abound, and you will have as much vitality as you can well use up.  It will therefore be necessary to live temperately.  This position strengthens the moral tone, also expands the feelings, sympathies and emotions.

**215.**  The Sun was in a BENEFIC aspect with the planet Jupiter at your nativity.  This will bring some very good fortune into your life, and will in all probability elevate you to a high position or greatly improve your social status as your life advances.  You will possess the true religious spirit, and a genuine good feeling, making you benevolent and sympathetic to all those with whom you come in contact.  You will meet with the success in life that you deserve, and nearly all your undertakings will turn out very satisfactorily.  You will be of a hopeful and cheerful disposition under your difficulties, and will generally see your way to adjust your circumstances quickly and with ease.  Health, finance and love affairs are all strengthened under this benefic aspect.

**216.**  The Sun in ADVERSE aspect with the planet Jupiter is not favourable, although Jupiter is the most fortunate of the planets. This aspect will cause some delay in the good promised you by those affairs governed by Jupiter, and also some trouble arising out of all those things from which you would expect benefit to accrue.  You must be careful in your dealings with religious people, also in your dealings or correspondence with those persons whom you love.  This influence is not good for your health so far as the blood is concerned, and it would be as well if you used some care in diet, for your liver will not always be in good working order, and this will affect your life and spirits, and make you at times melancholy and despondent. This aspect hinders your social advancement.

**217.** The Sun in CONJUNCTION with the ponderous planet Saturn will give you some measure of power in life, but, at the same time, you may be raised into power only to be brought to a fall, unless you can keep a humble spirit, and not aim too high ; for this position is one of the most critical, giving great responsibility and power, in some directions, but with the liability to assume rather more than is at all times wise. You will have many and various opportunities to study the virtues of thrift, economy, patience, and perseverance. The steadying and restraining qualities are in evidence in your individual nature. You are cautious, and at times rather fearful, and should never allow yourself to become too reserved or despondent, or you may through this lose opportunities.

**218.** The Sun in a BENEFIC aspect with the planet Saturn is a fortunate influence. It will tend to make you steady, patient, persevering, prudent, and honest, and possessing these traits of character you will command respect, and will be able to hold some very responsible posts in life if you care to seek them. Persons older than yourself will benefit you, and those who hold very important positions in life will befriend you if you require their help. Your moral nature will be strengthened more and more as you progress in life, and you will become more and more conscientious. Moreover, your health will improve as life advances and if abstemious, you will probably live to a very considerable age.

**219.** The Sun in ADVERSE aspect with the planet Saturn is a very unfortunate position, somewhat weakening your individual character, and bringing many sorrows into your life. You will in some manner be limited and cramped, and unable to achieve your ambitions, either through the interference of your elders or through lack of due opportunity : delays and hindrances will upset your plans and thwart your progress. Your health will also be affected at times, owing to the imperfect circulation of your blood, therefore avoid cold as much as possible. By improving your moral nature you will improve your general and financial condition. Exterminate selfishness, jealousy and enmity.

**220.** The Sun in CONJUNCTION with the planet Uranus adds a certain amount of originality to your horoscope, this position making your individuality somewhat unique and exceptional. You will at some time of life be called upon to play a prominent part in all matters with which you have concern, when the inventive faculties will be fully exercised, and all your ingenuity taxed to the full. But you will be able to grapple with any difficulty that comes into your life if you only free yourself entirely from bias and limitations; for your constructive ability is remarkable, and you may either invent or create both physically and mentally.

**221.** The BENEFIC aspect of the Sun with the planet Uranus is an influence very favourable to all those who can fully respond to this high vibration, for it bestows considerable inventive genius and much originality, making the individual character self-reliant and resourceful. Hence you will have an independent spirit, and love to carry out your own plans, which you will usually see clearly and accurately. You have decided magnetic power and can exercise over others a certain fascination which will make it easy for you to influence them. You will tend to become very broad-minded, philosophical, unconventional, liberal and free, and you will be sympathetically inclined towards all occult subjects.

**222.** The Sun in ADVERSE aspect with the planet Uranus at your birth is unfortunate and disastrous. You will have some very strange experiences, and may be estranged from, or lose those you love, and thus experience sorrow. You should do all you possibly can to think carefully before you act, and never allow yourself to be carried away by impulse, or the fascination of others. Try to know your friends before you trust them, and never allow strangers to influence you. Unexpected and unforeseen events will come into your life, upsetting all your plans and arrangements.

**223.** The Sun at your birth was in CONJUNCTION with the weird and little known planet Neptune. This will render your life different in many ways to that of most people, and will bring many strange experiences to you, depending in their nature upon how far you can respond to the spirit of Universal Love which this mighty planet represents. You will indulge in dreams on a lofty scale and will treasure secret schemes either for your own benefit or that of other people. The conjunction of the planet Nepune with the Sun frequently confers upon those born under this influence a peculiar and subtle charm of manner which renders them strangely attractive to others. You should beware of surrendering your own individuality to others, and should be careful to avoid all dubious experiments with drugs, anæsthetics or hypnotism.

**224.** The Sun was in a BENEFIC aspect with Neptune, indicating that the influence of this mystical planet is beneficial to your spiritual growth, and probably you will find your greatest expansion of consciousness will arise out of experiences which you would have a great difficulty in adequately describing to others. The real paradoxes of life will be always more or less present to your consciousness, and certain truths that can only be expressed in the form of a paradox will always have a special meaning and reality for you, if you can rise to the highest side of this influence. You will be, in the general sense of the word, lucky (though you may not consider yourself so), and you will be much liked by other people as a rule. You should, however, beware lest the sensuous side of life dominate you.

**225.** The Sun was in AFFLICTION with the planet Neptune at your birth. This will render you liable at all times to deceitfulness and treachery from those about you, or from strangers. You are likely to be called upon to forego many things upon which you may have set your heart, and grievous disappointments are likely to befall you. You should regard this as resulting from your having disturbed the harmony of nature by violating the law of love, or compassion, so that these losses you are called upon to endure furnish the only means of restoring the lost equilibrium, or harmony. In this way you will come under the higher influence of this aspect, which will enable you to raise your consciousness to a higher level so as to sense the divine life permeating the whole of Nature.

## ASPECTS TO THE MOON.

**226.** The Moon in CONJUNCTION with the planet Mercury will give you a splendid intellect, and endow you with quick, and accurate perception. The animal and the rational mind are both blended, but the rational will always cause you to lean more to the human side of life than to the animal. The more you allow reason to guide you, the more you will realise life and its purpose, and this is one of the necessary things for students to accomplish. You may cultivate truth and honesty to advantage; for, by so doing, you will awaken the mind to its highest perception. Thus you will quicken the mind and gather knowledge, at a much more rapid rate than by allowing the usual glamour of Mercury to fascinate you with the fragments so highly prized by smaller minds.

**227.** The Moon and Mercury were in BENEFIC aspect at your birth. This aspect will endow you with the best mental abilities and make your brain acute and active. You will succeed in life through your wit and quickness of perception. You possess the ability to make money and should do well with papers and writings. This aspect will enable you to appreciate life and make the best of it, as you are intelligent and able to think for yourself. You should cultivate your intuition, also your fine memory, which is a feature of this aspect when it is active and not latent. You have the ability to speak or write and can very easily express your thoughts and ideas.

**228.** The Moon and Mercury were in ADVERSE aspect at your birth. This aspect is rather unfortunate for your progress through life. But it will sharpen your wit, and make you very cute, but, at the same time, somewhat sarcastic when put out or in any way upset. Your nervous system will not always be in good order, and this may cause you to be a little erratic and changeable. You will incur criticism, and your opinions will be often at variance with those of others. Be very careful when signing papers, for you will be liable to make mistakes in connection with letters and correspondence. Avoid going to extremes, and see that your expressions are clear, and always accurate.

**229.** The Moon in CONJUNCTION with the pleasure-loving Venus will give you a good environment whilst you allow this vibration to be the one most in evidence. You will be fond of refined and probably artistic pursuits, and should be fortunate and successful in the majority of the undertakings that may engage your attention. You have a loving disposition, and also a very pleasing personality. The personal or external side of your life will be the best, and is in many respects very different from the internal or individual side, so that you will learn in this life more through pleasure and social life than by going inward to the mind or the purely intellectual side of development. You should have an easy passage through life.

**230.** The Moon and the planet Venus were in BENEFIC aspect at your birth, which is most favourable, promising you a successful journey through life, and very good opportunities for success. You will be refined and artistic, will possess good taste, and a keen appreciation of all that is good and beautiful. You will be loving and will thus attract those who will bring some happiness into your life, and become a social success. You will never be short of friends nor will you ever be poor while this good aspect asserts its influence over you. The opposite sex will be drawn to and benefit you in many ways. You will be musical, and fond of singing.

**231.** The Moon and Venus are in ADVERSE aspect, bringing sorrow and disappointment, especially in your domestic affairs. Your feelings will be affected, and you will be in danger of acting carelessly, and may expect disappointments, and also disagreement with the opposite sex. Any matters having to do with pleasure are better avoided, for little happiness or pleasure is indicated. You will do well to practise restraint, avoiding excess of feeling, grief, or sorrow. This aspect usually causes some extravagance, or excess in some way, and also sometimes affects the health; but it is, however, an influence that can be overcome by care, and by avoiding conflict with the feminine sex generally.

**232.** The Moon in CONJUNCTION with the fiery and forceful planet Mars will cause you to commit impulsive acts, and to resent all control and authority. In fact it is a very rebellious and unfortunate position for the Moon. You will see life through red glasses, and have such a strong personal bias, that you may become very intolerant, hasty and rash (unless you impose a check upon your out-going energies) and thus bring trouble on yourself, through your strong feelings and emotions. Guard your speech, and do not let your fearlessness carry you too far. It has been found true by long experience that "discretion is the better part of valour," and you will never lose by pondering well over the above-quoted statement. Your independence and forcefulness will bring you misfortune; therefore do not allow feeling to over-ride your reason.

**233.** The Moon and the planet Mars were in BENEFIC aspect at your birth. This aspect will make you fearless, enterprising, and courageous. You can exhibit much pluck and endurance, being resolute and full of that confidence in yourself which will enable you to deal successfully with others. You are fully competent to undertake anything upon which you set your mind. It is a very hopeful aspect, provided you are not too free and generous, as you may then tend to become rather prodigal or too extravagant. This influence will strengthen and tone up your constitution, enabling you to resist disease. It will also make you bright and cheerful, improving your disposition.

**284.** The Moon and the planet Mars were in ADVERSE aspect at the time of your birth. This is a very unfortunate aspect, tending to make you rather unfortunate in life and at times this result will be brought about by impulse and your own rash actions. You should never rush out too quickly nor say more than you really mean, as you will find yourself given to exaggeration and to enlarging upon circumstances. You have some very strong likes and dislikes, and will often be resentful, and say and do things you are sure later on to regret. Avoid being careless and reckless and do not let yourself be carried away by passion or anger. You will gain by practising self-control.

**285.** The Moon in CONJUNCTION with the benefic planet Jupiter will make your life fortunate, peaceful and successful ; whatever difficulties you may have to contend with in life, you will eventually attain to success. You have some splendid social qualities, latent or active, and much hope to carry you through all your undertakings. You have sufficient dignity and power, enabling you to occupy a prominent position, and you will, eventually, attract some recognition. You will obtain much personal success in life, and your environment will be such as to maintain it. Persons born under this conjunction generally gravitate to good circumstances, and surroundings, all of which go to make the life progress favourably. You are well disposed and this will win you the aid of powerful friends.

**236.** The Moon and the planet Jupiter were in BENEFIC aspect at the time of your birth, one of the most favourable aspects that can occur in any nativity. It will bring prosperity into your life, and also some social advancement. This aspect denotes a splendid vitality as it fertilises both the mind and body. You are mentally honest and intuitive and progressive, with a religious spirit, and will become more and more just and sympathetic as your life advances. You possess a very hopeful disposition, and this will be the means of your attracting those persons who will be beneficial to you and your interests.

**237.** The Moon and the planet Jupiter were in ADVERSE aspect at the time of your birth. This aspect will not allow the benefic planet Jupiter to bestow upon you all the blessing for which it is noted. In some manner it will tend to waste your substance, and, either through some extravagance or carelessness, you will have financial loss or difficulty in obtaining as much money as you would like to possess. You will need to be very careful in all your dealings with others, for there is some danger of your being the victim of fraud, or of suffering through the accusation of others; therefore always deal with others in the most straightforward manner possible, avoiding association with those whom you cannot trust. Temperance in all things is advisable.

**238.** The CONJUNCTION of the Moon with the planet Saturn will, in many respects, restrict and hamper your progress in life. Your early environment has not given you the social and personal advantages required, to in any way allow you to make much impression upon surroundings. This position is generally very unfortunate, but it is usually so owing to the reserve and fear which it gives to personalities under its influence. You must avoid becoming too critical and sceptical, or you will attract an atmosphere round you that will be repellant and thus cause others to mistrust you and also to suspect your motives. You are not in any way demonstrative, but you can be faithful and sincere, just, and fond of responsibility.

**239.** The Moon and the planet Saturn at the time of your birth were in BENEFIC aspect. The saturnine virtues are purity, truth, and sincerity, and this aspect will therefore aid you to become prudent, thrifty, faithful and reliable in character. You possess the capacity for organisation and can hold responsible posts in life. You will be successful in your dealings with elderly persons, and all your actions will be justly tempered, systematic and orderly. This aspect gives much patience and a contemplative spirit, and by the practise of meditation you can attain to great things. You have good tact and forethought, and I judge that you will become very serious and steady.

**240.** The Moon and the planet Saturn in ADVERSE aspect, astrologically considered, is generally the worst aspect that can occur in a nativity, and being the aspect of fate, as a rule it brings misfortune and sorrow into the life. You will do well to exterminate all the selfishness from your nature, avoiding discontent, as this aspect limits and binds those who come under its influence. Therefore the best way to counteract its force for evil is to sacrifice the lower nature as quickly as possible. Your life will be thwarted by others, especially elders, and superiors. Your health too will be against you, but this will arise from despondency or very poor circulation. Cultivate HOPE.

**241.** The Moon in CONJUNCTION with the mystic planet Uranus wil cause you, at some period of your life, to make very important changes of a somewhat sudden and unforeseen character. You will have a chequered career, and this will be owing to a peculiar disposition, which is indicated by the nature of Uranus. Your very powerful magnetism will affect others, and, at times, to your disadvantage. You are apt to be rather abrupt, and also irritable. Never allow any eccentricities to stand in the way of your progress, for although you have inventive or uncommon abilities, you may lose in personal disposition much that would carry you further forward in evolution. This position gives a touch of genius to those who are free from all prejudices and personal bias, but not otherwise.

**242.** The Moon and the planet Uranus were in BENEFIC aspect at your birth, and this will give you much love of all occult matters, especially astrology and kindred subjects. You are original in all your ideas and should have some inventiveness or constructiveness. You have magnetic and healing power, and if you practise or try to cultivate concentration you may accomplish much with your life. You will break away from all convention when your higher mind begins to awake and to shake off the fetters that limit the mind to the brain and surrounding conditions. You are quite able to strike out new paths for yourself, and your character is in many respects unique.

**243.** The Moon and the planet Uranus were in ADVERSE aspect at the time of your birth. This is an unfortunate aspect, leading you into some sudden troubles or difficulties. You will do well to be careful in all your dealings with strangers, and should avoid all chance acquaintanceships. The opposite sex will exercise some fascination over you, and there is a possibility of one in particular causing you much sorrow and trouble. This aspect gives a liability to accidents, or, very strange and unlooked-for experiences. You will always be liable to do things that you may afterwards regret. There is some tendency towards eccentricity, and you will be considered a crank in your peculiar way, as you will have some extreme and uncommon ideas at times.

**244.** The Moon at your birth was in CONJUNCTION with the weird and mysterious planet Neptune, and your life is likely to be full of strange and peculiar experiences, especially at those times when other planets progress to aspects of Neptune. You should distinguish between sensation or impulse, and thought or deliberate desire, or you may find yourself hurried into actions which you will afterwards regret. This is a very curious position, and you will need to study your whole nature more carefully than most people do, if you wish to make the best use of your real power; yet you must not expect the generality of people to understand you or sympathise with you fully. You should have some artistic ability, for you certainly have a very keen appreciation of the sensuous side of art. Your psychic nature is very sensitive.

**245.** The Moon at your birth was in BENEFIC aspect to the planet Neptune, rendering you able to receive some of the favourable rays of this remote and mysterious planet, and translate them into ideas and emotions through the physical brain. This is a beneficial influence, enlarging the sympathies, increasing the affections, and adding a certain artistic element to the nature, with sometimes a kind of inspirational poetic faculty. In any case it gives a roundness to the character, and lends an added charm to the personality, making one more or less hail-fellow-well-met with all, without in any way detracting from all necessary reserve. Those in trouble or afflicted, whether mentally or physically, will always meet with sympathy from you. The sensuous side of art will always appeal to you strongly, and you will have a vivid sense of physical beauty.

**246.** The Moon at your birth was in ADVERSE aspect to the planet Neptune, an unfortunate position in many respects, indicating many disappointments and peculiar or involved conditions which tend to hamper your freedom of action. You should be very careful to avoid yielding up your will to others, for this influence renders you somewhat liable to be psychologised by others and made subject to their will, and you should not allow yourself to be hypnotised under any circumstances. You are also likely to be peculiarly susceptible to the action of all drugs, especially narcotic drugs, and you should beware of ever experimenting therewith. The moral side of the nature is rather apt to be weakened by this aspect, which enhances the power of the feelings over the mind, rendering them at the same time more subtle and more exacting.

## ASPECTS TO MERCURY.

**247.** Mercury in CONJUNCTION with Venus is a very good position, refining the mental qualities and causing your mind to be sympathetic, artistic and poetical : you are thus able to appreciate all matters connected with art.    Possessing a good eye for colour, and loving all things beautiful, you naturally incline to painting, music, poetry or singing, everything in fact that is likely to give pleasure to yourself and others.    Science is not likely to attract you, but you delight in reading, especially the lighter form of literature, though your mind will not be very concentrative or studious.    You will be well-disposed and affable in disposition, ever choosing the social and pleasurable side of life, not the laborious.

**248.**    Mercury and the planet Venus were in BENEFIC aspect at your nativity.    This very greatly improves the vibrations of Mercury, making the mind soft and gentle, inclined towards the fine arts, reading and poetry.    Your mind will be merry and cheerful, and more or less light-hearted and free.    You will have the ability and desire to become musical, and should know how to entertain others and also how to give them pleasure.    You will be disinclined to look for evil, and you will be more often sinned against than sinning.    You will not, however, care for much exertion mentally or be inclined to undertake responsibility.    The artistic faculties will be well developed.

**249.**    The planets Mercury and Venus in ADVERSE aspect at your birth is an influence unfavourable for the higher uses of the mind, for the mental processes will not have the co-operation of that strange faculty known as the intuition, the internal perception or sensing of truth and beauty.    This is not an influence that militates particularly against success in practical life, but it prevents the highest development of the artistic faculties.    Its disadvantages are chiefly to be appreciated indirectly by comparison with the conjunction of these two humane and beautiful planets, and the charm of manner and delicacy of feeling which they confer.    So that the unfavourable aspect is rather an absence of advantages than a positive disadvantage.

**250.**    The CONJUNCTION of Mercury with the planet Mars is a powerful position, imparting much energy to your mind, making you very active and energetic mentally.    This position will sharpen the wit and make you quick to perceive.    You will take expansive views of life, but from a material more than ideal standpoint, being able to come in touch with the world's thought, especially in matters of enterprise, and business-like affairs.    But you must guard against impulse, there being a tendency for your mind to rush out too quickly towards objects.    Nevertheless, it is a favourable position, making the mind sharp, shrewd, keen and active. Do not over-estimate or exaggerate, for there is danger of your magnifying things too much, and thus becoming too hopeful.

**251.** Mercury and the planet Mars were in BENEFIC aspect at your nativity. This will considerably energise your mind, making you acute, sharp, and active. You possess much mental force, and could turn your abilities to good account in almost any direction you wish, provided you cultivate concentration. You are witty, bright, and cheerful, and if inclined you could be somewhat sarcastic and satirical; but you generally try to abstain from hurting others with your wit. You are doubtless clever at drawing, sketching, and designing, for you have splendid mechanical ability, also manual dexterity, making you good at conjuring and also the technique of music. Moreover, your objective consciousness is very extensive, keen and alert.

**252.** Mercury, and the planet Mars were in ADVERSE aspect at your nativity. This is by no means a favourable aspect for your mind, as it tends to make you impulsive, and over energetic. You have a great deal of active or latent sarcasm in your nature, with a quick wit, and a very subtle mind. However, you have intellectual ingenuity, and ability to follow scientific pursuits. You are very courageous, but somewhat too venturesome at times.

In speech you are apt to be hasty and it would be well for you to be discreet both when writing or speaking, for you are apt to say more than you mean, and inclined to assert your opinions too freely.

**253.** The planet Mercury, in CONJUNCTION with the benefic Jupiter, will endow you with a very joyous and hopeful mental attitude, causing you to see the bright and happy side of life whenever you let your mind assert itself. But you should take care that you never allow the influence of others to destroy that intuitive portion of your mind which knows, in a manner peculiar to yourself. You have a devout, and in many respects religious mind, and if you have entirely risen superior to the narrow, limited and orthodox side of religious thought, you will be able to obtain a great amount of benefit and help spiritually by the practice of meditation and contemplation. You will be fortunate in more senses than one, but it will be owing chiefly to the sound state of your mind that you will be able to achieve your greatest fortune and success in life.

**254.** Mercury and the planet Jupiter were in BENEFIC aspect at your nativity, one of the best aspects in regard to the mind that can occur in a horoscope.  You are endowed with excellent judgment **and** possess a broad mind, one that is philosophical, intuitive and harmonious. You are tolerant of the views of others, and you love everything that is straightforward and conscientious.  You have the true religious spirit in you, and it only requires right environment for you to allow it to expand, and your imagination to carry you into the subjective or inner world : for you have the power to mentally realise that "The Kingdom of Heaven is within you," also that true peace comes from within.

**255.** Mercury and the planet Jupiter were in ADVERSE aspect at your nativity.  This is not a good aspect for the mind, and indicates that you are liable to make many errors of judgment throughout your life.  You will not have much success in connection with matters related to religion, and it will be very difficult to convince you on any point you do not see clearly, this position making you rather sceptical.  You should endeavour not to create any false impressions about yourself by your attitude toward others, and it would be as well to be tolerant also of the opinions of others.  You are liable to suffer from scandal, at some period of your life.  Be very careful in legal and literary affairs.

**256.** The planet Mercury in CONJUNCTION with the planet Saturn is a favourable position.  It will give you a rather subtle mind, and cause you to look upon life with a grave, and at times serious aspect. You will always be thoughtful, concentrative, and much inclined to ponder, study and brood, over all that comes under your notice, and when the other conditions in your horoscope allow this to act fully you will be very serious, and may at times despond.  This aspect practically gives you two Saturnine influences in your horoscope, the planet Mercury absorbing the influence of whatever planet it may happen to be in conjunction with.  You will be very fond of metaphysics and the occcult generally.  Avoid becoming too critical and exacting, or you will lose many opportunities to progress.

**257.** The planets Mercury and Saturn were in BENEFIC aspect at the time of your birth, and this influence will fit you to hold responsible posts in life, endowing you with a prudent and thoughtful mind, and giving you depth of thought and the ability to study metaphysical subjects.  Memory and reasoning power are good, and all occult and mystical subjects should be pleasant to you, while you may cultivate concentration without danger.  Recognition may be gained through writing, speaking, etc., and through your philosophic attitude towards life. You will have a certain unobtrusive power over others and will tend to be serious and faithful in all your attachments.

**258.** Mercury and the planet Saturn were in ADVERSE aspect at the time of your birth. This will make the life rather unfortunate, especially if you worry. It is an aspect that causes hindrances and delays and also the adverse attitude of others to you, and especially those who are older than yourself. You will experience disappointments in life, therefore never seek to get into responsible posts, for you may be severely criticised, and suffer loss of credit, etc., through false reports about you. You must be very careful with regard to what papers you sign, also cautious in speech. You are somewhat unforgiving, and inclined to be rather severe on wrong-doers. Avoid worry.

**259.** Mercury was in CONJUNCTION with the mystical planet Uranus at your birth, a favourable position for all forms of original thinking, for inventive and ingenious schemes, and for all that pertains to new thought, and what is termed originality. You must however avoid becoming what the world terms a " crank," or you will find yourself out of touch with others and liable to be misunderstood. You will at times have too much nervous energy, making you irritable and erratic, and perhaps too regardless of the feelings and opinions of others. This position inclines towards an abrupt and independent manner, unless you can control your mind, which will at times prove too sudden in its changes for your good.

**260.** Mercury and the planet Uranus were in BENEFIC aspect at your birth, which is one of the best aspects that Mercury can have, for those who are making intellectual and spiritual progress, since it bestows an occult and original turn of mind and fits one to study astrology and the deepest metaphysical subjects. You are inventive, have a wide mental outlook, and as life advances you will grow more deeply interested in the higher thought. The analytical faculty is strong, but you are intuitive and possess an inner perception that enables you to understand your surroundings quickly. This is a good aspect for travelling, or making new acquaintances.

**261.** Mercury and the planet Uranus were in ADVERSE aspect at the time of your birth, an unfortunate aspect, making the mind rather critical and at times erratic. You should be careful in your dealings with strangers, and also with regard to the papers you sign. You will be criticised and find others against you when you least expect it, but this may arise from your own attitude also, for you are somewhat inclined to be sarcastic, and may even take distorted views of things. This arises from the condition of your nervous system, which will be out of gear occasionally. You have much of the reformer's spirit in you, but it would be as well not to be too hasty in the methods you adopt.

**262.** The planets Mercury and Neptune were in CONJUNCTION at your birth, an uncommon and peculiar position, which will have a great effect upon your mind, rendering you internally very strongly disposed towards mystical beliefs and uncommon modes of thought not generally accepted or even approved of by the majority of people. In fact, it gives a distinctly " æsthetic " tendency to all who are born under this position. There will always be a certain love of paradoxical forms of stating truth. You are rather liable to come under the domination of a stronger mind, and should strenuously cultivate independence of thought, training yourself to exact method of thought by the study of either science or formal logic. Otherwise, the intuition and poetical conceptions of your mind are likely to become mere vague and unpractical dreams.

**263.** The BENEFIC aspect between the planets Mercury and Neptune is favourable for your mind, rendering you very susceptible to the charms of music and poetry, and all elevating emotions, and adding a somewhat mystical colouring to your mental make-up. Romantic experiences that will come into your life will have a very great influence upon your mind. Your mental sympathies will be broad, and you will have many friends in the world of thought, especially among the mystical and devotional school of writers. You should endeavour to live out in practical life some of the lofty ideals you treasure in your mind, for there is a tendency with this influence to allow them to remain ideals forever unrealised. This is decidedly an artistic influence in every way, giving great skill in the weaving of plots or originating of designs. The sea will have a special charm for you.

**264.** The planets Mercury and Neptune were in ADVERSE aspect at your birth. This is an unfavourable influence mentally, rendering concentration difficult and opening the mind to vague and unpractical imaginations, visionary and utopian ideas that are unlikely to reach fulfilment, even where they are otherwise free from reproach. In fact this is a very deceptive and untrustworthy influence, and you should do all you can to overcome its baleful effect by definitely training the mind to exact and precise thought by means of scientific study or otherwise.

If the lower effect is thus overcome, this aspect may be made beneficial to you, since it always gives some poetical or musical tendencies, for the mind is rendered very sensitive to subtle emotional impulses. Giving way to the sensuous side of life would have a very bad effect upon your mind.

## ASPECTS TO VENUS.

**265.** The planets Venus and Mars in CONJUNCTION will cause you to have very exceptional and powerful likes and dislikes, and it is quite possible that love at first sight will affect your emotional nature and stir up the feelings. You are somewhat impulsive, where feeling is concerned ; and although very generous, light hearted and free, at the same time, you are likely to make mistakes in regard to your own feelings. Never be rash or impetuous in your affections and ever reflect before committing yourself in speech or action in your dealings with the opposite sex. This position will make you light-hearted, merry and cheerful ; and will ever keep you up, however trying your circumstances may be. Avoid impulsive action.

**266.** Venus in BENEFIC aspect with Mars is a fortunate aspect in many respects, especially for emotional affairs, and all the events in life that are connected with feeling. You will be ardent in your affections and likely to gain through, or by, those to whom you may be attached. You are inclined to be free and liberal with your money, and social matters generally will have much attraction for you. You will be rather fortunate in financial matters and will either gain by will, or legacy, or through your associations with others. It favours love affairs and is also generally beneficial in marriage, unions, or partnerships.

**267.** Venus and the planet Mars were in an ADVERSE aspect in your nativity. Although this is an unfortunate aspect it will in many ways stimulate your feelings, making your emotional nature very keen and active. It is rather an improvident aspect, tending to make you over generous and impulsive, and through this you may lose financially, and through excess of feeling may in some way be imposed upon. You should be guarded in all your dealings with the opposite sex and never let yourself be drawn into any scheme or plan that might be misconstrued. This aspect is not favourable for love, or marriage, denoting dangers from quarrels and jealousy. It spoils financial prospects.

**268.** The planet Venus in CONJUNCTION with the benefic planet Jupiter is a very favourable and harmonious position, it brings success in life at certain times when the luminaries are favourably aspected to this part of your nativity. This position alone is not very powerful, so that more of its real influence will be felt under good directions, for then the nativity will have progressed to the necessary position, to make the influence of these two benefic planets active ; but until then they may remain latent. It is a good and propitious position for social affairs and in some respects favourable for financial undertakings, but as I have said above a very great deal depends upon the future Directions.

**269.** The planets Venus and Jupiter were in BENEFIC aspect at the time of your birth. This aspect will bring you some gain, either through religious persons, or by will or legacy. It is one of the most harmonious and peaceful aspects, greatly improving the nativity by holding other aspects of an adverse nature in check. You would gain by travel under this aspect and your love affairs will tend to run smoothly, so that marriage should be happy and prosperous. Much sorrow that would in the ordinary way fall on you will be averted by this benefic influence, and a certain amount of philosophy is promised by this aspect, which will be of great help to you.

**270.** The planets Venus and Jupiter were in ADVERSE aspect at the time of your birth. This position is in general unimportant, though it denotes some losses through carelessness in monetary affairs, but only to those who are naturally improvident and extravagant. You will do well to use care in all relationships with females in connection with religious matters, for differences of opinion and unpleasantness are likely to arise through religious controversy. This aspect tends to bring deceit into your life, and your best course would therefore be to act with perfect straightforwardness in your dealings with others, more especially in all family or domestic affairs.

**271.** The CONJUNCTION of Venus and Saturn is a peculiar, and a somewhat unique position, and very difficult to interpret, owing to the fact that but few are able to respond to the vibrations caused by this position. It should make you exceedingly fond of the mystical, and all things that are ancient and antiquated, old and antique. You respect ancient customs, and tend to be somewhat conservative, and possess a peculiar kind of intuition, which makes you appear to be shrewd and very far seeing.  It should make you rather thrifty, and a keen judge of financial matters, stimulating your economy, prudence and chastity, but it will bring you disappointments and sorrow in matters of feeling.

**272.** Venus and the planet Saturn were in BENEFIC aspect at your nativity.  This is a very high vibration for the planet Venus, the purifying and steadying influence received from Saturn tending to make permanent many of the harmonious virtues denoted by Saturn.  It will make you a steady character, giving you a love of thrift and wise economy, allowing you to accumulate wealth if you should ever desire to do so.  You have tact, and good abilities, also the power to conserve your energies.  You are a very faithful friend, and would be most sincere in all your attachments, thus attracting towards you those whom you can love with sincerity, and who will reciprocate your love.

**273.** Venus and the planet Saturn were in ADVERSE aspect at the time of your birth, and this will bring much disappointment and sorrow into your life.  You will have some financial losses, or difficulty in ever obtaining the amount of money you desire.  It is not a favourable aspect in money in many ways, and any expectations that you may have will not be fully realised.  Be careful in your business transactions with others and see that your moral standard is the highest you can reach.  Never lend money without good security, or sign legal papers.  This aspect has an unfavourable influence on all matters connected with love and the affections, causing disappointment, grief and delay.

**274.** The planet Venus in CONJUNCTION with the mystic Uranus will bring either romance or a pleasant change of an unexpected nature into the life.  This position has a tendency to in some way weaken the deeper side of the feeling and emotional nature.  It causes attachments of an uncommon type to arise, and seems to be a purifier of the love or soul principle, but only those who have cast off the animal instincts can possibly respond to these very keen vibrations.  But it is a condition that must awaken all that is latent in the Soul.  If unable to respond, it must pass you by, waiting for a more fitting occasion.  On the material plane this position gives sudden and unexpected wealth, legacies, windfalls, etc.

**275.** Venus and the mystical planet Uranus were in BENEFIC aspect at your nativity.  This influence is very favourable for all matters coming into your life that are in any way original, and free from convention.  You hold some rather advanced views, and particularly is this the case in all those matters which affect the heart, and feelings. There is a touch of romance in you which will work itself out when you meet with those whose magnetism is strong enough to play upon your emotions, and affect those vibrations connected with the love life. You will have sudden financial gains, and may also have some very unexpected travels, removals or changes coming into your life.

**276.** Venus and the mystical planet Uranus were in ADVERSE aspect at the time of birth. This is not a fortunate influence for love-affairs. You will be fascinated or in some way affected by the magnetism of those of the opposite sex who may be attracted to you. Sudden and unexpected disappointments are threatened you, also sudden financial losses, which you should guard against by avoiding risky speculation. You cannot be too careful in all dealings with strangers, also in all affairs connected with love and marriage. There is some danger threatened you through jealousy and treachery. This aspect causes separations, divorce and many estrangements from friends and loved ones.

**277.** The CONJUNCTION of the planets Venus and Neptune is on the whole good, adding something of a mystical touch to the mind and elevating and broadening the sympathies and affections, that is, where the lower side of the Venus nature is not brought into play. For the influence of Neptune, where it is *not* elevating, is of the most baleful kind, it is therefore necessary that you should purify your emotional nature by every means in your power, seeking ever the highest and most unselfish type of love which Neptune truly represents. For when the lower side of the nature is lived in, this position renders possible very great degradation, proportionate to the elevation that may be achieved if the higher influence is consistently sought. Neptune is in this respect the planet of *renunciation*.

**278.** The BENEFIC aspect between the planets Venus and Neptune broadens your sympathies and refines your love nature, rendering you deeply sensitive to the beauty of nature, and easily won over to lofty ideals of life and conduct. It will, however, be much more difficult to live out these ideals in practical life, for you have some tendency to remain a dreamer of beautiful dreams, and you should endeavour to realise in some practical form, the beautiful ideas with which you feel yourself filled. This might take the thought of either decorative or pictorial art, music, drama, or the more practical fields of work, such as nursing, etc., according to the general tendencies of the horoscope. You will always love the sea, though you may not, perhaps, be a good sailor.

**279.** The ADVERSE aspect between the planets Venus and Neptune is very serious and unfortunate, affecting the whole of the emotional life, these two planets representing personal and universal love respectively ; and the conflict between the two means that you need to purify your love nature from the selfish element, seeking to make that which is personal universal. There is a dangerous side to this aspect, and that is the tendency it brings to fall completely under the sway of the senses. You yourself will know if there is any fear of this in your own case, but if so you should battle against it with all the strength of your nature, for, when evil, the effect of Neptune is most insidious. Avoid all narcotic drugs as you would the plague.

## ASPECTS TO MARS.

**280.** The planets Mars and Jupiter in CONJUNCTION is not good for Jupiter. In many respects it may be considered a good position so far as Mars is concerned, but as Jupiter is robbed of all his virtue, by this counterfeit of the spirit Mars, it will make you liable to prodigality and over-generosity. Troubles and loss will arise from either waste or extravagance. Avoid law and any expenditure exceeding receipts, and certainly impulse and the display of prodigious energy, or enthusiasm ; for this position will make you somewhat over-zealous, and inclined to extremes in feeling. You cannot live too temperately, and should avoid disputes over religion and legal affairs. It will also affect the state of your blood.

**281.** The planets Mars and Jupiter were in BENEFIC aspect at your birth. This position causes some extravagance, with a tendency to be over-generous and liberal, and therefore it will not always be beneficial to you where money is concerned. You have some pride and dignity in your nature, also self-reliance ; in many respects you are a pioneer, putting great energy and enthusiasm into all you do. You are enterprising, courageous, and very fortunate in many ways through your strong and venturesome spirit ; but recklessness and over liberality should always be avoided. You love freedom, independence, strength and justice, and will never allow yourself to be imposed upon.

**282.** The planets Jupiter and Mars were in ADVERSE aspect at your birth. This is in many respects a very unfortunate aspect. It denotes financial loss, either through extravagance, or prodigality of some kind.  You are inclined to be far too generous, and if you came into much wealth would be more likely to become a spendthrift than a miser. You should always avoid litigation, or you would be involved in the loss of heavy sums of money, and in all probability find that legal affairs were disastrous for you in all respects.  Still, you are very enthusiastic in whatever you espouse and will throw much energy into all you undertake. See that your blood is pure, or the health will suffer.

**283.**  The CONJUNCTION of the two so-called malefic planets Saturn and Mars is generally considered a very evil position; but as the true astrology teaches that there is no real evil, but only that which is relative, it is within your power to make this a good position and this you may do by allowing your ambition to conquer your senses, but beware of escape from one danger to fall into another, for the mind is much more dangerous to cope with than the senses.  It will give you a strong and very powerful will, and a fearlessness that will be favourable if selfishness is kept out of it.  You will be able to hold very unique and also responsible posts, where skill and courage are necessary, but do not become over-ambitious.

**284.**  The planets Mars and Saturn were in BENEFIC aspect at the time of your birth.  This aspect will cause you to be ambitious and make you persevering and eager to excel in whatever enterprise you undertake.  You are brave, courageous and fearless with regard to danger, and you not only possess force of character but tactfulness also. There is much of the hero spirit in you and you love to be at the head of things and would make a very capable leader.  This aspect promises you success, especially in the direction of improving and strengthening your character, and by this you will have success in life, and win the admiration of those who are able to help you.  It indicates that the desires and the lower or personal mind are working in harmony, and it is therefore a splendid aspect for the achievement of your wishes.  Do not let it make you selfish, however.

**285.**  Mars was in ADVERSE aspect with Saturn at your birth, a very unfavourable aspect to those who have not learnt to practise full self-control.  At times the aspect will tend to make you express much more than is wise, and you will not only use sarcastic, and very bitter speech, but you will incline to use words that are not over choice, especially if you are seriously annoyed.  You have much courage, but will be rather reckless where danger is concerned. You have the making of the " Hero " in you, but I fear that you are apt to risk your life upon the impulse of the moment, when under any great enthusiasm. You have a very strong desire nature, and when roused to anger, will be violent.

**286.** The CONJUNCTION of the planets Mars and Uranus will give you plenty of energy but also a rather irritable temperament. Your nervous system will at times be over-charged with life or magnetism and this will make you too active and probably excitable and far too energetic for your own good. It will give you a love of all mystical subjects, especially astrology, and the metaphysical side of things. Be always on your guard against sudden impulse, rash tendencies, or violent expressions and actions ; for this is the position that carries one away ; either by enthusiasm, strange, and unaccountable mental conditions, or blind impulses. It is one of the most dangerous aspects when the soul is in any way unbalanced ; therefore, act discreetly.

**287.** The planets Mars and Uranus were in BENEFIC aspect at the time of your birth. This a wonderful aspect to those who can respond to the vibrations of the mystical planet Uranus. It gives much real energy, mental and physical. It stimulates thoughts of originality and therefore makes of those who can respond, geniuses in some direction. It favours inventors and those who can invent and construct. It is an aspect that gives confidence and self-reliance, making those under its influence reformers, fond of all progress and advancement. You are in all ways broad-minded, liberal, and fearless of public opinion, and may even become an enthusiast in metaphysics, philosophy, or astrology.

**288.** Mars and the mystical planet Uranus were in ADVERSE aspect at the time of birth. This influence tends to make you some- what erratic or eccentric. You are enthusiastic and at times irritable, inclining to be over energetic, also too forceful. All this arises from an overwrought condition of the nervous system, which Uranus governs. You should endeavour to be more calm, not so rashly inclined, and should never allow yourself to become excited. This aspect is likely to bring you legal troubles and dangers in connection with the opposite sex. It is unfortunate, owing to the fact that most events during your life will tend to be sudden and unexpected. Avoid entering into disputes and guard against exposing yourself to any undue liability to accidents.

**289.** The CONJUNCTION of the planets Mars and Neptune is a very peculiar and remarkable one, giving you an extraordinary fund of energy, boundless resources, and a capacity to enter upon tremendous enterprises. It is not altogether a favourable position, nevertheless, for there is a tendency for any born under this influence to become " top-heavy," to undertake more than he can or will perform and to over-estimate his own importance. Nevertheless, the position in itself is good, and if the right attitude of mind is maintained, and due regard is always paid to the rights and opinions of others, this influence is a tremendous power for accomplishment, and hence for *good.* You will need to beware of becoming a " crank," and you should be very careful that your big ideas do not run away with you. Attendance at spiritualistic circles, etc., would not have a very beneficial effect upon you.

**290.** Mars and the planet Neptune were in BENEFIC aspect at your birth, a favourable influence, adding to your general executive capacity, and rendering you something of a general favourite with your fellows, since the personal magnetism which it supplies is abundant and agreeable. This aspect gives great breadth of scope to the ambitions, and renders you capable of planning great things. Whether you can fully carry out the great schemes will depend largely upon the aspects of the Sun, Moon and Mercury, and also upon your natural determination and fixity. For there is a certain amount of changeableness in this aspect. It gives a very keen sense of colour, and in good combination with good general aspects to the Moon or Mercury gives special ability in painting.

**291.** The ADVERSE aspect between the planets Mars and Neptune is decidedly unfavourable, rendering you prone to intemperate enthusiasms of various kinds, and driving you at times into company you would be wiser to avoid. You should strive to overcome any tendency to go to excess in any special direction, whether mentally or emotionally, or in your physical habits—in short, *all* forms of intemperance should be eschewed. You are liable at some time of your life to come into violent conflict with the lower classes, and you should beware of nursing a prejudice against them. If the intemperate tendencies spoken of are controlled this aspect becomes of great benefit, adding a great deal of physical energy and enabling you to cope with large demands upon your capacity. Avoid all narcotic drugs, and do not go in for sensational experiments.

## ASPECTS TO JUPITER.

**292.** The CONJUNCTION of the planets Saturn and Jupiter may be said to be a favourable condition for Saturn, but not for Jupiter. Saturn being a negative planet is more likely to absorb the influence of Jupiter, which is a positive planet. Its effect upon your life will be good, if you can cultivate hope and allow the joyous side of your nature full play; but if you become too careful and economical it will warp your nature and cause you to become over-ambitious and near sighted where your real interests are concerned. If religion should in any way affect your life, see that you are real and sincere in all that you are supposed to believe, for there is some danger of self-deception from this position.

**293.** The ponderous planets Jupiter and Saturn in BENEFIC aspect, at the time of your birth, is a very fortunate position for these very important planets, and the nature of their vibration will be such as to assist you under any trying circumstances that you may have to pass through. It benefits your financial prospects, and mitigates any other influence that is not favourable in this respect, and makes your path through life much smoother. You have, deep within you, the true religious spirit, and also a reverence for that which you know is your superior. You can be original, also very charitable and benevolent, and you will never come to want, or suffer great misery. Happiness will come to you as life advances.

**294.** Jupiter in ADVERSE aspect with Saturn is not a favourable aspect, excepting that Saturn gains in influence by partaking of some of Jupiter's ray. Its effect upon your life will be to cause you to despond at a period when probably your liver is upset or chilled. It is not a good aspect for your financial affairs. At times you will have losses; it would, therefore, be as well never to lend money without security, or to be a responsible party to engagements involving financial risk. Mentally it would be well to ever act in a perfectly straightforward manner, there being a liability to false and libellous accusations at some period of life. Be careful in dealing with religious people.

**295.** The CONJUNCTION of Jupiter with the mystical planet Uranus will affect you only in that way, or rather direction in which you have any latent genius, for Uranus cannot benefit Jupiter except by awakening whatever there may be latent in the nature, and Jupiter's conjunction can only cause a temperate medium for the vibration of Uranus to come through to you.  To those who are musical or artistic the influence is most favourable as its nature is such as to touch the higher part of the nature more than the lower or more materialistic.  To those who are religious and philosophical in thought it allows the spiritual vibrations to be felt, but it is a purely subjective influence and is thus more evil than good to the unawakened who could not appreciate the vibration coming through.

**296.** Jupiter and the planet Uranus were in BENEFIC aspect at your birth.  This is an important aspect to those who are advancing in thought, and those who are original, or inclined towards the metaphysical and occult.  This aspect, in a general sense, will bring you some sudden and unexpected gains, either by will, or legacies.  You will either invent something, or strike out in an entirely new direction, and thus become fortunate, but in all you do to gain through this influence an element of the unexpected must enter ; but its tendency is more toward originality in the thought sphere, and to the overcoming of the conventional and orthodox.  It adds a great deal of enthusiasm to all your undertakings.

**297.** The benefic planet Jupiter in ADVERSE aspect with the mystical planet Uranus, is in nowise a fortunate vibration, for it spoils the good promised by Jupiter, and tends to rob you of the joys and blessings which the benefic Jupiter gives.  You will have very sudden and unexpected losses throughout your life, and will be in danger of litigations and costly disputes.  It will be well for you to avoid strangers, and have very little to do with public companies or associations and societies.  You will have some sudden change of opinion which may affect you subjectively or objectively.  Unnecessary travelling should be avoided as far as possible : or great care taken to avoid accidents.

**298.** The planets Jupiter and Neptune are in CONJUNCTION, a strange and unusual influence which when prominent in a horoscope usually brings peculiar religious tendencies, the religious nature perhaps being a little over-developed.  Indeed, " megalomania " has by some been thought to be the outcome of this position, and you would be wise to strengthen the purely mental and scientific part of your nature, as well as the common-sense side, in order to conteract the excessive sensibility of your sympathies, and the desire that you feel to go out in love towards all. Over-exuberance might be said to be the keynote of this position and therefore you should take pains to keep your winged Pegasus within bounds. Nevertheless, the enthusiasm and breadth of view bestowed by this influence is in itself a splendid thing, and if you use due moderation you can become of great service to your fellows. Remember, however, that there are other points of views than your own ; and do not be tempted to assume undue authority over others.

**299.** The BENEFIC aspect of Jupiter to the planet Neptune is a very fortunate position, both for your worldly prosperity and also for your spiritual welfare, if you are able to take advantage of it in this direction. Beneficial influences will flow towards you, and you may make what use of them you will—spiritual or temporal. There is some tendency to extravagance, however, in this influence, and you should seek to correct this by disciplining yourself in other lines of thought, such as science, or mathematics, in order that the sensuous and emotional nature (which is likely to be very strong) may not assume too great a sway. Financial schemes are likely to bulk largely in your life, directly or indirectly. You should take care to practise what are termed the sterner virtues, also simplicity and frugality.

**300.** The ADVERSE aspect between the planets Jupiter and Neptune is not altogether a favourable position and seems to indicate that some of the faculties represented by Jupiter, such as superstition, self-esteem and personal pride, need to be spiritualised and transmuted into higher attributes of the soul, such as charity, compassion and true reverence. Hence the restricting and hampering effect of Neptune's affliction should result in the purification of your nature. You will have many strange experiences during your life, especially those that affect the higher side of your consciousness, and if you were able to recollect your dreams you would no doubt find you had been taught much by them. You should beware of being led away by intemperate enthusiasms of any kind, and you should strive to cultivate the exact and precise virtues, such as scrupulous accuracy in speech, promptness in payment, etc., for you have some tendency to be careless in such matters.

## ASPECTS TO SATURN.

**301.** The CONJUNCTION of the planets Saturn and Uranus at your birth, is a position that will have comparatively little outward effect upon your life, in all probability, its influence working chiefly upon the plane of thought.  Hence it will result rather in a modification of your mental outlook than in any marked personal qualities.  You will have a strong leaning towards the occult life in some shape (though as yet this inclination may be latent), and all kinds of out-of-the-way studies and pursuits will attract you to a remarkable degree.  There is likely to be some amount of acquisitiveness shown, possibly more in regard to knowledge than wealth, and great organising power displayed in connection therewith.  With this position a remarkable degree of concentration of purpose is attainable.

**302.** The ponderous and mystical planets Saturn and Uranus, in BENEFIC aspect at the time of your birth, is a vibration that you may not in any way be able to reach in the life of this present incarnation.  It is an aspect that endows those capable of responding to its high keynote, with clairvoyance, or the psychic faculty known as clairaudience, but the clearer and more refined your thinking and feeling become, the nearer will you be towards awakening your psychic faculties.  You may study concentration to advantage and should also keep your mind free from those objective conditions that bind the soul, as much as possible, if you would realise all that this great vibration signifies.

**303.** The ADVERSE aspect between the planets Saturn and Uranus, the most distant planet of our system (except the remote and little-understood Neptune), is not likely to affect you very seriously as regards ordinary everyday life since its influence tends to operate chiefly upon the mental plane.  There will always be a strong taste for the out-of-the-way and uncommon, and a somewhat peculiar habit of mind having strange tastes and unorthodox opinions.  At some period of your life you are likely to meet with some experience which will tend to upset all your previous ideas, and which may prove a turning point in your career; whether for good or ill, will depend upon the use you have made of your abilities and of the inner strength, or character, which you may have developed.

**304.** The CONJUNCTION of the planets Saturn and Neptune is a very strange and uncommon position, and its influence is very difficult to describe.  It is quite possible that you may remain almost entirely unaffected by this vibration, but *per se* its influence is to unite the mental with the spiritual nature, which may result either in the elevation of the former or the degradation of the latter, according to the progress made by the soul in its evolution.  Most probably the effects of this position will be experienced in the form of severe limitations of personal liberty, either through the influence of some enemy or through other circumstances over which you have no control, which will thus have the effect of throwing you in upon yourself and making you reflect deeply.

**305.** The planets Saturn and Neptune were in BENEFIC aspect at your birth, indicating an ability for concentrating the efforts in one special direction with very great persistence ; in fact, this aspect of itself bestows a wonderful power of perseverance in spite of obstacles and defeats, where its influence is fully utilised. There will always be a certain liking in your nature for the strange and the uncommon, and you will be capable of pursuing your own way quite contentedly, whether it is approved of by others or not. It brings some tendency towards hardness into the nature, and you should strive to expand your sympathies and seek to develop your love for others, in order to counteract this. Music will always have a strange effect upon your inner nature.

**306.** The ADVERSE aspect between the planets Saturn and Neptune is an uncommon and strange position that is likely to bring you into remarkable situations at some time or other during your life. It is a very lofty vibration, to the true nature of which present day humanity cannot hope fully to respond, and much of its influence may pass over your head, so to speak. It is not altogether favourable, and appears to indicate that there is some "kink," as it were, in the inner nature that time and circumstances may declare, or which, perhaps, may never come to fruition in this life but remain entirely unsuspected. You should always guard against the subtler forms of selfishness, which are especially likely to beset you. The cultivation of the psychic faculties would not be good for you. There is always some melancholy tendency associated with this position.

## ASPECTS BETWEEN URANUS AND NEPTUNE.

**307.** The CONJUNCTION of the distant, ponderous and mystical planets Uranus and Neptune is a position that can occur but once in a century, although owing to the position of the Earth in its orbit varying throughout the year, the aspect will become complete and then be re-formed several times during two or three years ; (this also applies to the opposition). The nature of this aspect is in the main similar to the benefic aspect described below, but is of an even more powerful character.

Nevertheless, unless very strongly placed by house-position (see Ch. XI.) this conjunction will not show out very markedly in the nature unless there are aspects to it received from other planets such as Saturn, Mars or Mercury.

**308.** The BENEFIC aspect between the two most distant planets of our system, Neptune and Uranus, is an influence that will have little actual bearing upon your outer life, its effects being more directed upon the inner nature or character.   It indicates that the subjective and the objective elements of the nature are in a harmoniously balanced condition, and that consequently the outer life is the less likely to be disturbed by sudden outpourings of energy initiated from within.   While this may be looked upon as a very fortunate position in itself, you should not count too much upon it in the sense in which the word fortunate is ordinarily used, since this influence is too far removed from our physical life to have much direct effect upon it, and consequently the aspects of the other planets, in your nativity, will be relatively much more powerful.

**308a.** The ADVERSE aspect between the two outermost planets of our system, Uranus and Neptune, at your birth is an influence which will have but little direct effect upon your outer life.   But in regard to your inner nature this aspect indicates that there is going on within you a certain amount of struggle between the subjective and objective elements in your nature, and this is likely at certain times to lead you to very sudden and unexpected changes in your thought, and perhaps in your habits as well.   This struggle will always be going on, more or less, and may therefore reflect itself to a certain extent in the outer life, for you will always be placed in positions where you are forced to choose between a temporal and a spiritual gain.

§ 5.—*The Houses of the Horoscope.*

## CHAPTER XIX.

### FINANCE.

THE general financial fortunes are judged from the chief planet occupying the Second House, or, if no planet be there, by the ruler of the sign on its cusp.

An alternative method, where there is no planet in the Second House, is to judge by the quality of the sign occupying it or on its cusp, as given in paragraphs 318-320 ; or by the angular position of Venus or Jupiter. Which of these latter methods is to be employed must be decided by the student's own judgment, but if in any doubt use 318-320. To give a full and accurate judgment of the financial character of a horoscope requires much experience, as well as considerable powers of judgment, but the general tendencies as regards money matters can easily be seen in this way.

**309.** THE SUN, at the time of your nativity, governed matters connected with finance. This promises you gain through matters in which Government is directly, or indirectly concerned, fitting you to hold any important post, either under government, or for some leading firm. The financial prospects are hopeful ; you will eventually gain through superiors, and may obtain favours that will benefit you financially. At some period of your life, you will gain by speculation, or through judicious investment. All financial plans and projects, with which you are in any way concerned, should be on a large scale. The influence favours a fixed income, but it is advisable to watch expenditure.

**310.** THE MOON governing the second mansion of your nativity is an indication that you will have fluctuations in monetary affairs, your finance waxing and waning like the moon. It is therefore evident that if occupation is necessary, pursuits where a rapid turnover is the main feature are best in every way for you. Success by investing in public companies and associations is shewn, but particular attention should be given to all businesses concerned with public commodities, or those catering for the general public in some form or other. You can be easily impressed with regard to the public's wants and requirements.

**311.** MERCURY governs the house of finance in your nativity, and thus promises gain through literary matters, agencies, papers, etc. ; in short, all stationery occupation in which the mind is more employed than the body. You have good business abilities, and you are inventive as well as rather acquisitive where money is concerned, but you should guard against fraud and theft, and also be cautious in signing all financial documents. You would do well in all professions where a quick and rapid movement is required, and journalism or businesses and professions connected with printing, commission, agencies, etc., would furnish the most remunerative mode of income for you.

**312.** VENUS governing the second house of your nativity is very favourable in regard to your financial affairs, and shews that you will have a great deal of success in all monetary concerns. Matters governed by the planet Venus will bring you fortune and prosperity. Venus favours music, singing, and the fine arts, and all those things which minister to the pleasure and happiness of others. You will always be more or less fortunate in your dealings of a financial nature, and you will either gain by legacy, or through your profession, business, or partner ; in fact, it does not matter in which direction you turn your attention for gain, you will always be more or less successful.

**313.** MARS governing your house of wealth, though favourable in many ways is at the same time unfortunate, owing to the nature of Mars, which has always more or less a wasteful tendency. You will gain through others in some way, either by will, legacy or inheritance, also through partners and co-workers: but you must expect losses, either through your own or another's extravagance. You are apt to be very reckless at times about monetary affairs, and should never lend money without security, or you will lose it. You can be practical where money is concerned, except where your feelings sway you, and you should prosper on the whole, for you have the ability to make money quickly, and in earning money you will find much joy and pleasure.

**314.** JUPITER governs the second house of your horoscope, bringing you good fortune in matters connected with finance. You will never be poor and may through right action accumulate wealth.

Jupiter being the most beneficent of planets promises the best of fortune in connection with those things he presides over or governs financially. You may gain through foreign affairs or by travel; also in pursuits connected with the land, food, clothing and those things needful for the comforts of others. Under any favourable "directions" to the benefic Jupiter you would have very great success in life, gaining by legacies or gifts, and by or through pleasure and wealthy persons.

**315.** SATURN governing the second house of your natal figure is not a very favourable significator as it causes delays and hindrances to progress and financial advancement. Gain however is promised by industry, slow plodding perservance, and by carefulness, thrift and economy. Through purity of motive you may acquire wealth in time, and by careful investment in land or property, and all things that are solid and concrete, you may have more than ordinary success. It is not a favourable signification for those who are not born into a good environment, as it denotes more labour and real hard work than good fortune in financial matters. You are, however, very just in your monetary affairs.

**316.** URANUS governing the second house of your nativity denotes some very great and sudden changes in your fortunes. You will have some peculiar and remarkable experiences in your financial affairs, and you should be very careful in matters of a speculative or uncertain nature. This is a favourable position for those who deal in curiosities, and all antique furniture, or old books and curios, etc. It is also favourable, and unfavourable, for railway affairs; therefore, care will be necessary in all matters of this nature, sudden loss and sudden gain being promised, with much uncertainty as to result; indeed all your monetary affairs tend to uncertainty.

**317.** NEPTUNE governing your second house will tend to bring you financial loss, either by the fraudulent conduct of others, or by investing in companies or affairs that will turn out disastrously; therefore it will be well for you to be careful in dealing with others. You must guard against signing papers likely to bring upon you financial loss and difficulties. Financial benefits accruing to you will come about in most peculiar ways, either by a vision or dream, or contact with peculiar persons, and you may gain from some totally unexpected source and come into money by the most odd and eccentric means, or else by following some occupation of an uncommon nature.

**313.** A CARDINAL SIGN ruling the financial house of your nativity ambition with regard to financial success in life is shown, you will expend much energy in acquiring wealth, and will accumulate more by your own activity and industry than by any other means.   You are thus capable of rising to high positions in life, whenever there is a financial incentive to go onward.   Changes are good for you where finance is at all concerned, and there is a certain amount of speculative enterprise about you which enables you to foresee quickly where most money may be made, and the kind of investments and undertakings likely to prove profitable.   Acquisitiveness is well developed.

**319.** A FIXED SIGN occupying the cusp of the second house of your nativity indicates a tendency for your income to remain fixed, and not to fluctuate as is the case when the other signs occupy the second. Investments will be better for you than speculative affairs, although when under good " directions " you would have some success in specula- tion, but you are more likely to be satisfied with a fixed income than to entertain risks or incur liabilities that would seriously affect your income. There is some indication of your being indifferent where money matters are concerned and you would be more contented than most persons if you were assured a fixed and steady income in preference to uncertainty and doubt with regard to finance.

**320.** A MUTABLE SIGN ruling the financial house of your nativity, monetary affairs are likely to fluctuate more or less through your life.   You will have more than one way of acquiring an income though this is not the best of influences to govern financial prospects.   You will make money best by everyday, unimportant undertakings, either business or professional, but in all probability you will lose financial opportunities either by indecision or by entering upon some occupation for which you are not quite adapted.   Your mind will in some way be much exercised with regard to your financial affairs, and you will worry and become over-anxious with regard to your money-matters.   Speaking generally, you will gain most when you do not seek to come too prominently to the front, and by occupations or investments of an indifferent, obscure or common-place nature.

**321.** THE ANGULAR POSITION OF VENUS in your nativity will always benefit you in your financial affairs and you will never really want and become impoverished excepting when the ' directions " in your natal figure are exceptionally adverse, but this is no reason why you should not have fortune and also success in life, so far as your monetary prospects are concerned.    Venus in an angle gives money by marriage, or through friends, also through profession, and the female sex in a general way.    This influence causes those who have it in their horoscopes to be, what is called " lucky " ; therefore you will be successful in all monetary affairs, and finance generally.

**322.**    THE ANGULAR POSITION OF JUPITER is a sure indication of success in all matters connected with finance, and as the angles represent things that are made manifest, at some period of your life, you will be able to accumulate wealth, or come into possessions, either by lawful right, or by inheritance.    There will, of course, be some periods when your financial affairs may not be so good as at other times, but as a general rule, throughout the whole course of your life, you will have nothing whatever to fear so far as finance is concerned.    This planet gives the greatest fortune during the middle portion of the life.    In all monetary affairs, Thursday is probably your best and most fortunate day.

# CHAPTER XX.

## Travel, etc.

THE Third House in a general sense indicates travel; it also affects the mind and shews its capacity, etc; it also shows the natives relatives, especially brethren and sisters and the influence they will have upon his or her life.

Where there is no planet in the Third House, either the planet ruling the sign occupying the house, or the quality of the sign itself (332-334) should be considered. [Compare second paragraph of Chapter XIX.]

**323.** THE SUN governing the third house of your nativity is rather favourable for any travelling that you may take during life, but in a general sense it does not indicate much moving about. You may come into contact with or meet persons of high and noble birth while taking journeys, as the Sun signifies all things connected with rank and high estate. All your travels should have some high mission connected with them, or you may have some commission to perform that necessitates your moving from place to place occasionally. You have a very high spirit and agree well with your brethren, and benefit by or through them in some manner. The mind is broad and generally impartial and there is agreement with relatives.

**324.** THE MOON has influence over your third house and travelling; this luminary controlling your journeys, travels and changes. You will be very fond of travelling, and you will journey and travel about a great deal either from choice, or compulsion, and for many reasons, there being a tendency to be moved about from town to town, or between business and home, both long and short distances being easily covered. Most of your mental experience this earthlife will come through travelling, and you much prefer change and movement to any monotony. You will come into *touch* with the general public whilst travelling, and should be very receptive to the conditions of others.

**325.** MERCURY governs the third house of your nativity. This is an indication of much activity in all matters connected with travel, and you will take many journeys, and do a great deal of moving about during your life-time. You have a great love of travelling and sight-seeing and may be engaged in some pursuit that necessitates a constant changing and moving about on your part. You will gain information, and especially more experience; also obtain many benefits in this direction. This influence is good for your mental and physical activities; but it is against the acquirement of concentration to enable you to become permanently successful, your mind being rather over active at times; therefore you should endeavour to cultivate concentration.

**326.** VENUS having rule over the third house of your nativity, makes travel, changes, and removals pleasant and profitable. You should not only gain by travelling, but will also find your chief enjoyment and your greatest pleasure in the journeys you will take during your life. This position of Venus very greatly improves your mind, and it denotes that you are artistic, and love the beautiful, especially in Nature. You will agree with relatives and brethren generally, either gaining through them, or being also of some mutual benefit to them, directly or indirectly. You will at some time of your life travel for pleasure, or profit, this position of Venus being very favourable.

**327.** MARS ruling your third house is not good for travelling on any journeys that may be taken for business or pleasure. It threatens some accidents, or severe trials through circumstances that may arise whilst travelling. In a general sense this planet has not a good influence, causing the mind to be at most times very hasty and impulsive, and thus it is likely that you may directly, or indirectly cause accidents to happen. This influence also denotes trouble by, or through relatives; brethren causing you annoyance, and making disputes. You should always be guarded in your speech and correspondence. This position will give you plenty of mental courage when necessary to use it.

**328.** JUPITER ruling the third house of your nativity is very fortunate for all matters connected with travel, especially upon what are comparative short journeys in our time. It will bring you in contact with very helpful and beneficial influences, and, when travelling for either pleasure or gain, you will have success and profit. This division of the heavens is also concerned with brethren and the state of the brain mind. With Jupiter the most benefic planet placed in the third, all these matters will be in a way peaceful and successful. Your kindred will be well disposed, your mind religious, and your mental condition generally harmonious. You may practice meditation with advantage.

**329.** SATURN governing the third house of your nativity will cause hindrance and delay in connection with your travelling and any journeys that you may undertake. You will do well to prepare for disappointments in connection with travel. You will gain many experiences that will come through sorrow or grief in connection with travel. This influence is against your agreement with relatives or brethren, and it is probable that you will be estranged from them or suffer through their actions, their attitude towards you at times being cold and distant. You will have a love of the occult and mystical, and should seek to dip into those matters that favour psychic things ; it gives you the ability to study astrology and kindred subjects thoroughly.

**330.** URANUS in the third house is not altogether a favourable aspect for travelling, for it is an indication of some sudden and unexpected journeys through life. You will love to be travelling and roaming about, and you will find it difficult to settle down permanently in one place for very long. Your mind will be quite original and in no way conventional. It indicates that you will have friction with your relatives, or someone connected with you by family ties will be eccentric and uncommon. You will be very fond of astrology and metaphysical subjects. It will be as well for you to guard against accidents while travelling or rambling.

**331.** NEPTUNE occupying the third house of your nativity shows that you will meet with some extraordinary experiences during travel. You may meet with very peculiar misadventures. This is not altogether a good or hopeful position moreover, so far as your relatives are concerned, for some of them may be in some manner strange characters, either of a very good or very bad type, but very difficult to understand. Enough is not known about the influence of Neptune to be positive as to how his vibrations will act in any nativity. With some, his nature is decidedly evil, and only those who are at all spiritually advanced can feel his influence in connection with the third house affairs.

**332.** CARDINAL SIGNS occupy the houses of travel, therefore there is no doubt that you will do much travelling during the course of your journey through life, for the Cardinal signs not only give a love of change, and moving about, but also the opportunities to travel. Under certain "directions" you will be forced to make changes and undertake journeys and these will prove more or less profitable in accordance with the nature of the influence that may be operating at the time. You will act wisely by endeavouring to discover the position and aspects of the Moon before you start upon any important journeys, for much will depend upon the lunar orb and also her conditions as to the happiness you will meet with whilst travelling.

**333.** FIXED SIGNS govern the houses of travel at the time of birth, and this is an indication of either very little travel coming into your life, or a disinclination to move far from your native place. Therefore all travel may be more or less compulsory, or the result of circumstances over which you have no control, which may be seen from a study of that part of the horoscope dealing with the future, and called "Directions." There are times when it would be best for you to avoid travel, or to take journeys purposely, it being evident that your experience is to be gained from a fixed and stationary position. There will of course be times when to travel may be absolutely necessary, and this will be marked in the "Directions."

**334.** MUTABLE SIGNS having rule over your travel you will be quite indifferent as to travelling, but circumstances will decide this matter for you, and all your journeys and even removals will be produced from outside causes more than through your own initiative. The mutable influences with regard to travel are marked by *indecision*. It is thus difficult to arrive at any definite and clear idea as to when you will travel, or if any journeys will be undertaken by you ; but there does seem more indication of long than short journeys, the common or mutable signs being more connected with foreign lands than the native place of birth.

# CHAPTER XXI.

## ENVIRONMENT.

THE Fourth House is concerned with the end or resting-place of things, and therefore governs home, also the close of life. It affects all home and domestic affairs and indicates the general state of the environment, and more especially the surroundings towards the *latter* part of life.

**335.** THE SUN, having rule over the fourth house of your nativity, promises a somewhat glorious ending to your career. You will either come into contact with powerful people who will assist you, or your life will be made more sunny through conditions that you yourself have set in motion. However, the close of life is shown to be better than the early part, and you will, individually, be benefited and reap the fruit of what you have sown in your earlier years. This influence of the Sun manifests according to the sign into which its ray passed at your birth, more at the finish of what you undertake than at the beginning, and shews that your ventures will have a satisfactory termination.

**336.** THE MOON governing the fourth house of your nativity will bring many changes toward the close of life, and indicates a tendency for things to fluctuate, in a general sense, so that whatever your undertakings will be, always expect uncertainty towards the finish. You will have domestic cares and worries at the end of your existence, and will probably be rather unsettled, and not fixed in your post or conditions. Changes and fluctuations are strongly marked, but they will be changes necessary for you to obtain many of those realisations that will help forward your occult growth. You are fond of the mystical and all things concerning the other worlds.

**337.** MERCURY governs your fourth house, and denotes that you will probably have some mental worry at the close of your life. You should be very careful in dealing with sharp-witted and very clever persons as years advance; and it would also be well to use discrimination in regard to any papers you may have to sign at any period. The end of all the affairs with which you have anything to do will require the exercise of your mental abilities, but your mind should ever be keen and alert, and well able to cope with any difficulties with which you may have to deal. Probably you will be interested in or concerned with young life as you advance in years.

**338.** VENUS having the principal influence over the fourth house promises you a very peaceful and happy period towards the close of your existence, in so far as worldly goods and comfort is concerned. You will find yourself in better circumstances and with more harmonious surroundings at the close of your life, than formerly, and may be surrounded by those who will be much attached to you, and willing to make your life all that you could desire at its close. This influence also brings matters in which you may at any time be interested, to a very satisfactory issue, especially whenever the planet Venus is well aspected by " directions " or meets the good aspects of other planets.

**339.** MARS governing the fourth house of your nativity promises you some disputes and difficulties in connection with domestic affairs and warns you to be careful of troubles, which at certain periods of your life will arise out of turbulence, or inharmony. It is not a good influence for the environment into which you may be thrown. This is not at all good for the parents, or those who may have any authority or control over you, and rather favours removal from residences than remaining too long in one place.

**340.** JUPITER having influence over the fourth house of your nativity promises you a good environment at the close of your life; in fact, the end of your life is the best, and a good termination to your existence is very plainly marked. It will be much better for you to remain in, or near your native land and home, than to reside in a foreign country, or to travel from your home for success. You will gain in all those transactions that have to do with social or home affairs and domestic life generally. This influence shows some good coming to you from parents, and promises you inheritance. Every year of your life should be more and more prosperous, and comfort secure at the end.

**341.** SATURN governing the fourth house of your nativity warns you to guard against over-carefulness, there being an inclination for you to be acquisitive, and also anxious to acquire wealth, more particularly as your life advances. You will not be over generous with this influence, and may become rather reserved and more secluded as life progresses; and towards its close you are liable to be left alone, and not surrounded with those to whom you are most attached.   This influence always favours economy, and will enable you to save money and accumulate better than any other influence in the horoscope, and there is no need to advise you to take care for old age as you are inclined to be quite careful enough in that direction.

**342.**   URANUS having rule over the fourth house of your nativity indicates that the latter portion of your life is to be somewhat peculiar and eccentric.   You will take up studies towards the close of life of which in the earlier part you had little if any idea.   This position of the planet Uranus is not altogether favourable, as it indicates some sudden surprises and unexpected events in the closing years of life, and you may come into some environment that you will not be able to respond to unless you have made great progress in occult matters.   You have some ability to study astrology and kindred subjects.

**343.**   NEPTUNE was in the fourth house of your nativity.   This is an indication of some peculiar experiences towards the close of your life.   It is difficult to speak with any degree of certainty or definiteness in regard to this planet as but little is known of its vibration; but in a general sense some peculiar experiences on mediumistic or spiritualistic lines will most probably come to you, and you may live in a house that is haunted, or where there are some very peculiar phenomena, or else be drawn to those places where influences that are out of the common are at work.   Therefore you will do no harm by changing your residence from time to time.

# CHAPTER XXII.

## ENTERPRISE.

THE Fifth House is one that indicates all speculative things where there is scope for individual effort and initiative, it is therefore known as the house of enterprise. It is the house of the *heart*, and therefore signifies those things into which the heart enters largely—love-affairs, pleasure-seeking, speculations and all forms of enterprise, children, and the artistic creative capacity.

**344.** THE SUN has influence over the fifth house of your horoscope and this is very favourable for matters of an enterprising nature in a general sense, but much will depend upon the solar aspects with regard to the success that you will have in your enterprise. You have speculative instinct and should be able to invest money to your advantage, but it should be in big concerns or with a considerable amount of capital to be what you would desire. In many respects you have the capacity to take kindly to pleasure, and should be able to take all your enjoyments in a right royal fashion, as you love to do things on a very grand scale. You would gain by children.

**345.** THE MOON having rule over the fifth house of your horoscope indicates a great amount of enterprising spirit, but it is of a somewhat fluctuating character. In all of your investments and matters of a very enterprising and speculative nature, deal with those concerns that affect the general public, or have the good of the populace as their concern. This influence is rather inclined to favour gambling, and those matters that are risky, and common, or what may be termed " chance," wherein the element of uncertainty prevails, so that many of your enterprises will be of a fluctuating kind, with little or no permanency attached to them. You will be deeply concerned regarding children at some period of life.

**346.** MERCURY having rule over the fifth house of your horoscope indicates much mental enterprise. It favours quick and rapid action with regard to speculative matters, but it warns you against signing or accepting any papers and documents with which you are not thoroughly acquainted.    You will have much correspondence with regard to love affairs, and some romance will come in your way, either through much reading, or through activity of your mind.    You will do well to live purely, and to avoid any of those speculations that may be turned into gambling.    All your investments should be with those concerns that have a rapid turnover.    You should have much to do with young children.

**347.**    VENUS having rule over the fifth house of your nativity, promises you success in all monetary affairs connected with investment, and also speculation.    You will invest your money to advantage, and in all matters connected with pleasure you are shown to have gain.    This is a fortunate and in a general sense very favourable house, and being under the influence of Venus, love and pleasure should bring you happiness; your capacity for enjoyment and pleasure is very great, and few can enjoy as sincerely as you.    This influence promises a fruitful and also happy union with one of the opposite sex, also happiness from children and their affairs.    Avoid excesses in pleasure.

**348.**    MARS having rule over the fifth house of your nativity, denotes much energy and an enterprising spirit, and if you avoid impulse in matters of speculation, also with regard to certain investments, you may apply your energy to advantage in speculative matters, but you should carefully avoid gambling or any risky enterprises where you have to rely upon the honesty of others.    You are somewhat free in matters connected with pleasure, and ardent in your affections, with a tendency to involve yourself with the opposite sex if you are not cautious in dealing with them.    This influence indicates some pain or some trouble through children, and warns you against all rash conduct in your enterprises.

**349.**    JUPITER having control over the fifth house of your nativity, promises you fortune and success through speculation, investments and enterprises, apart from the actual labour to acquire wealth. Under any favourable " directions," you should be very successful in speculation, and by judicious investment may, eventually, amass wealth in various ways.    You should have much social joy and pleasure in your life, and children will bring you gain, and also happiness.    The fifth house is the house of pleasure, and being under the influence of Jupiter, all matters that bring success and enjoyment into your life should go well and all social matters be satisfactory.

**350.** SATURN governing your fifth house, indicates that you should use great care in regard to any matter concerning investment and speculation. You would do best to favour old established concerns, not by investing in new ventures. This position, however, is not good for matters of the heart, and will affect all affairs connected with emotion and children, and disappointments are also threatened causing delays and hindrances to all enterprising and speculative matters. You will find that age is more favourable and helpful to you than is youth, and your affections may be absorbed by persons older than yourself, especially by those of the opposite sex.

**351.** URANUS has much influence over your fifth house, and thus al affairs of an enterprising and speculative nature will be affected by this Uranian influence. Sudden and unexpected events are indicated, and although it is probable that you may gain by matters connected with railways, yet you run risks in speculative matters. You will have some romance enter your life, and some strange experiences may come to you through the opposite sex. Children will be wayward and cause you anxiety, and many excitements will come into your life owing to this Uranian influence. You will incline to original thought upon love matters, and will also magnetically affect others.

**352.** NEPTUNE governs the fifth house of your nativity. This in many ways is rather a peculiar influence. So far as speculation and investment is concerned you cannot be too careful, for you are likely to come in contact with frauds and shams of various kinds. In matters of the heart your enterprise will be affected according to the purity of your life. But as nothing in any definite sense is yet known about the planet Neptune, we cannot say just how its influence in this position will turn out. When you can respond to its higher aspects you will come in contact with those who, by way of your affections, will benefit you. But should you ever fall into the lower senses you will suffer degradation.

# CHAPTER XXIII.

## SICKNESS.

THE Sixth House of each nativity is concerned with sickness.  It is also the house of work or labour, and of service generally.  It denotes the sicknesses one is liable to if general health is not maintained.

**353.** THE SUN having dominion over the sixth house of your nativity, you should not have many sicknesses during your life; but those you do have may be rather long and difficult to cure.  They will arise chiefly from the state of the constitution, which will have received some shock, or have been impaired by some radical trouble.  You will, however, obtain good attention when ill, and if proper treatment is adopted you should be able to recuperate.  Sun baths will be good for you and plenty of fresh air will do you more good than drugs or physic, the Sun being the best curative medium for all who are sick or indisposed.  You should gain through inferiors.

**354.** THE MOON governing your house of sickness indicates trouble from functional more than any organic complaints.  You should be very careful with regard to diet, as most of your troubles will arise from indigestion, or stomachic complaints.  Never drink too much fluid or indulge in too much bathing, and be most particular to avoid too many starchy foods and indigestible substances.  Sickness may be produced through travelling, or too many changes, but especially through impure magnetisms and unhealthy environments; therefore, see that you have fresh air, and that those with whom you associate are magnetically pure. The Moon governing the sixth house tends to give you tumourous complaints, etc.

**355.** MERCURY having rule over the sixth house of your nativity, most of your ills in life will arise through nervous and also mental troubles.  You should be careful never on any account to worry, if you value your health at all, because a nervous breakdown is threatened you at any time when the mind lets you give way to worry and irritability.

All your sicknesses will generally arise from the condition of your mind and the nervous system. You will have some psychic impressions that will in certain directions affect you, and there is more depending upon the peaceful condition of your mind than you will ever estimate. This influence is a dangerous one when mental troubles press heavily, affecting the mind.

**356.** VENUS having dominion over your sixth house, shows some tendency for the generative system to suffer through excesses, or indiscretion with regard to diet and habits of living. It will, therefore, be well to use temperance in all things, and if you should be led to indulgence in any way, remember that you may trace your indisposition to this fact. The kidneys, throat, and generative system will be liable to attack when health fails.

**357.** MARS governing the sixth house indicates troubles arising from excesses and shows that the muscular system has been weakened in some manner; and to strengthen it the mind must be healthily employed. You cannot be too careful in your habits, and should live purely and quietly, and never exceed temperate limits, for you will be liable to feverish and inflammatory troubles with some danger of operations, accidents, and violent diseases.

**358.** JUPITER governing the sixth house is very favourable for all cases of sickness, as it indicates a speedy recovery through good and proper nursing. Your sicknesses will arise through surfeit, and the condition of the blood, the liver, etc. Keep the blood pure, avoid drugs and live hygienically, and you will then quickly recover from any sicknesses from which you may be suffering. You may escape any liability to sickness by a study of temperance in all things.

**359.** SATURN governing your sixth house shows danger of much sickness at certain periods of your life, sickness that is liable to be lingering, and cured with difficulty. Cold will injuriously affect you, and you will tend to suffer from asthma, also liver and stomach troubles, owing to the condition of the system generally. Study your diet and keep up the circulation by adequate exercise.

**360.** URANUS governing your sixth house indicates a tendency to peculiar complaints likely to become incurable. You should in all cases avoid operations; hypnotic treatment will not always be advisable for you, although in cases that require special attention, electrical, or extraordinary methods of treatment may be useful. Avoid hysteria, for there is some danger of hypochondria shown.   Generally speaking, the position shows liability to peculiar nervous diseases.

**361.**   NEPTUNE being connected with your sicknesses will cause you to suffer from peculiar ailments, and uncommon disorders ; therefore special treatment will be required, should you ever be seriously indisposed, for it is highly probable that you will suffer from what may be termed astral sickness, or disorders that arise mentally, these affecting you astrally.   Great care should be taken when afflicted by any serious ill-health, to see that all your surroundings are harmonious, and not likely to attract unhealthy and injurious conditions.   The mind should be kept balanced, and all tendencies towards hysteria eradicated, and everything done to prevent hypochondria, etc.

# CHAPTER XXIV.

## MARRIAGE.

THE Seventh House, in quite a general way, denotes marriage. On this question a good deal of individual judgment is necessary ; for the aspects to the luminaries, and certain other considerations largely affect marriage. But in a general sense the planet nearest to the cusp of the seventh house, or failing that the planet ruling the sign on its cusp, has most to do with marriage.

Where there is no planet in the seventh, or near its cusp, the position of Venus should be considered, as described in the next chapter. Paragraphs *630 Ga* and *630 Gb* in Chapter XXXII. also have to do with marriage and may be needed in exceptional cases, as there explained.

**362.** THE SUN governs the seventh house of your nativity, the house of marriage. This signifies a fortunate and an ambitious partner, and one whose influence will be beneficial in your life. You will in some way gain through marriage financially, and also socially. Your partner will be very independent, but of great moral integrity, and one who scorns to do anything mean, or not exactly straightforward. It is not the best signification for harmony, but there will be every opportunity for affection to increase, and also happiness produced by success. This influence sometimes delays marriage or makes it very difficult to bring about, either through pride or position.

**363.** THE MOON governs the seventh house of your nativity, the house of marriage. This is rather a favourable testimony for your marriage, and although it may not be considered a social success yet it may be a happy marriage. You will have several opportunities to marry, but you will incline to waver or be undecided about it. Your partner will be sensitive and also inclined to several moods and changes. You should try to guard against outside influences which may seriously affect your marriage prospects. Dark and probably short persons will be attracted to you, or those who are very fascinating and magnetic.

**364.** MERCURY governs the seventh house of your nativity and is therefore the indicator of marriage. This denotes your partner to be very quick and intelligent, fluent in speech and apt to be rather out-spoken at times, but critical and nervous. Some worry and unsettlement is denoted by this influence, and it favours a marriage with a partner younger than yourself. There is likely to be much correspondence in connection with your marriage and it would be well to be cautious with regard to letters as it is probable that trouble may come through papers or writing. Mercury is a very peculiar planet when the significator of marriage partners.

**365.** VENUS governs the seventh house of your nativity, the house of marriage. This is a very favourable significator and promises a partner who is not only happy and well disposed, but one who will bring some fortune into your life destined to benefit you financially and socially. Your marriage should be a happy one and all your relationships after marriage should be most harmonious and peaceful. Venus is the planet governing all love affairs, and tends to improve the life according to the house she governs. It will tend to make your union fruitful and all children should bring with them blessings, greater joy, fortune and happiness.

**366.** MARS governing the seventh house of your nativity, the house of marriage, is not the most favourable planet to rule over the affairs connected with matrimony, Mars being more concerned with passion, etc., than love. You will do wisely to avoid a hasty marriage, or falling in love at sight. It as a rule promises a very early marriage, and sometimes more than one union. You will, in all probability, marry one who is very ardent in feeling and affection, and one who will desire to hold the reins and rule the roost. Still, the martial type is affectionate, although at times given to anger and assertiveness. The person most likely to attract you will be bold and fearless, and full of courage.

**367.** JUPITER governs your seventh house, the house of marriage. This is a favourable testimony for a happy union, for Jupiter is a benefic planet and promises success, and much happiness in all things over which he rules. Your partner will be very noble and also very generous, and fortune should smile upon you after your marriage. It sometimes indicates a partner who is rather proud, though always high-minded. If you marry under the best " directions," much success will come to you after marriage, the union being fruitful and prosperous.

This position sometimes indicates that the partner has either been previously married, or, it may be, is senior by a few years. Still, on the whole it is the best of positions.

**368.** SATURN governs the seventh house, the house of marriage, in your nativity. This planet tends to delay or hinder the marriage prospects. Should marriage take place however, it promises a faithful and steady partner, one who is just though rather grave and serious, very industrious, persevering, careful, thrifty and economical. There is some probability of your partner being older than yourself, with a tendency to court responsibility. It is not a very favourable testimony for prosperity, but it denotes a faithfulness in the marriage state, although care should be taken not to allow coldness to spring up between you at any time, for your partner will not be over demonstrative in affection, and will prefer action to speech and loving deeds in preference to the use of many words of endearment.

**369.** URANUS governs the seventh house in your nativity. This mystical planet will bring some very peculiar experiences into the marriage state, and it is very probable that it may bring you disappointment, or estrangement. It always threatens separation from those who are loved, and this will occur either before or after marriage. Sudden and very unexpected events occur in all regions that Uranus governs, and there are more divorce cases under his dominion than any other planet; therefore see that your partner is original and fond of metaphysical subjects. You will then know the right person described by Uranus, who favours mystics, etc.

**370.** NEPTUNE governs the seventh house of your nativity. This planet is one of the most recently discovered, and therefore we cannot as yet be fully acquainted with its influence. It is supposed to sound a much higher and more spiritual vibration than any of the other planets, and in this respect is said to favour those kinds of marriages that are more the result of soul union, than of the senses. But, it has been found also, that the planet Neptune is also concerned with the lowest conditions, as well as with the highest, and may cause some very strange and uncommon unions, indicating marriage with people who are either crippled, or else afflicted in some way, physically, mentally, or morally.

# CHAPTER XXV.

## MARRIAGE PROSPECTS AS INDICATED BY THE POSITION OF VENUS IN THE SIGNS.

As stated in the previous chapter, there are other influences than the position and aspects of the Lord of the Seventh that affect marriage; of these, one of the chief is the position and aspects of the planet Venus.

**371.** VENUS IN ARIES is a powerful influence, but it threatens you with some dangers in connection with love affairs. You will incline to be somewhat fickle, and have several courtships or love attachments, owing to your desire for change, and will, if you are not careful, become too fond of romance, etc. Eventually you will have sorrow, or sadness, in connection with affairs of the heart, for you are liable to make mistakes in regard to marriage, either through some hasty decision or by the fact of your becoming involved and entangled with another to such a degree that you will be forced into a marriage. You are liable to impulse and there is also a tendency for you to fall in love at first sight.

**372.** VENUS IN TAURUS will give you some trouble in connection with your love affairs, but at the same time you should gain financially and also socially through your marriage. This position of Venus indicates that you have a very strong love nature, with an inclination to let your feelings influence your decision greatly, your emotions being much stronger than your mind. Some happiness will eventually come to you through your marriage, but this appears to be more along the lines of finance than through reciprocal affection. You will, in all probability, have only one love affair throughout the course of your life, for you are more fixed than fickle, and possess a very decided attachment to those whom you love; therefore you should be careful upon whom you bestow your love.

**373.** VENUS IN GEMINI, the dual sign, will bring two love affairs into your life, and through this you will have some trouble, and also sorrow; because it is quite likely that you will have two attachments running at the same time. Relatives will also affect your love affairs, and they will exercise a decided influence over your marriage. This will bring you troubles and difficulties, and it will be extremely difficult for you to avoid being involved in more than one love affair at the same time, this planet in Gemini always giving dualism, and more often than not, two unions with members of the other sex. There is some danger of jealousy, and also trouble arising from correspondence, in connection with your matrimonial affairs.

**374.** VENUS IN CANCER, the house of the Moon, indicates that there is some tendency for you to be rather fickle in your affections and, until you become really attached, you are liable to have many love affairs. You will be attracted to those older than yourself, and also to those who have had love affairs with others. You may meet with your future partner while travelling, or become very much attached to one who is not of the same social standing as yourself. You must avoid all change-ability and inconstancy in matters of the heart, or you will be liable to disappointments and sorrows in connection with your love emotions. You are more receptive to the feelings of others than you suspect, and easily influenced through them.

**375.** VENUS IN LEO promises you a very successful marriage, and a considerable amount of happiness will come into your life through your marriage partner. Through your marriage you will be elevated to a higher position in life than that which you held at birth, and will attain to reputation and social advantages which will considerably minister to your welfare in the world. This influence favours marriage, and quickens the emotional nature to such an extent that your feelings are easily appealed to, producing attachments at the first opportunity. It also lessens your liability to make errors in all matters of the heart; the perceptions being very keen and active in this direction.

**376.** VENUS IN VIRGO shows that you will be in some way averse to marriage, giving greater preference to a life of freedom than legal union with another. Therefore there will be some liability either to a platonic attachment or to clandestine unions. This unique position, however, gives an internal love for celibacy: it is not altogether favour-able for union with the opposite sex. It indicates attachments to inferiors, or to those in a lower station of the social scale than your own, and also the inability to gain the affections of those superior to yourself by birth, that is, so far as social status is concerned.   You will be attracted towards people younger than yourself, also to those persons whose health is weak, weakness in others calling forth the sympathetic side of your love nature.

**377.**   VENUS IN LIBRA, the sign of justice and equipoise, promises you a successful marriage, bringing you prosperity and social enjoyment; but it is quite probable that you will have a rival and this may either cause some enmity, or some opposition to arise, but eventually you will be successful, and should prosper in your love affairs.   You will, in all probability, be attracted to those holding favourable posts in life, and this may bring you elevation or spur you on to greater attainments in the material world.   You will have very strong emotions, but amidst whatever difficulties that may attend the feelings of your heart, you will eventually have success.

**378.**   VENUS IN SCORPIO promises a remarkable intrigue, or strange relations with the opposite sex.   In love matters you cannot be too discreet in your relationships with others, being greatly attracted to and by those persons who have very strong desires, and a tendency to form secret attachments with you.   You will also be very liable to some betrayal, or disappointment, which may cause you sorrow in connection with your emotions.   No matter whom you may marry, you will survive your partner, for you are destined to have some remarkable experiences in connection with love affairs.   Avoid all illicit connections and hasty unions.   You have much self-control, but will not always use it.

**379.**   VENUS IN SAGITTARIUS denotes that you will marry more than once; for this gives a decided tendency for you to survive your marriage partner, and to marry again.   You will have some peculiar episodes in connection with your love affairs, and will, in all probability, meet your marriage partner while travelling, or engaged upon some journey.   You may be involved in a love affair with a relative or with a person not of the same nationality as yourself, and you will have many experiences affecting your heart during the course of your life; but marriage should be good for you, promising success and advancement by your connection with persons socially superior.

**380.**   VENUS IN CAPRICORN denotes hindrances and delays to marriage, and also the probability of some very dangerous and peculiar love affairs, for you are somewhat fickle, and yet, at the same time liable to be involved in very strange attachments, probably with persons older than yourself.   You may be over-ambitious with regard to your affections, and thus bring yourself into critical positions, whereby your honour may be affected. It will require a great deal to touch the depth of your emotions because you either have great control over the feelings or they may be difficult to awaken to their fullest extent. Jealousy may cause you to suffer keenly, for when your affections are awakened you will become remarkably attached.

**381.** VENUS IN AQUARIUS, a Saturnian sign, has some tendency to delay marriage, and will probably bring you some disappointments, etc., in your love affairs, and this will arise through your intuitions being so keen as to guard you from making mistakes in relation to marriage. It also has a tendency to intensify the desires for a celibate life, for you would have your love chaste, and free from all trace of the senses. In some cases, secret connection with the opposite sex arises from Venus in the sign Aquarius, and it seems to favour those attachments, rather than legal unions. It generally produces a very faithful attachment, and sometimes causes long courtships, or friendships of a Platonic nature. You will love one formerly a friend.

**382.** VENUS IN PISCES, a dual sign, and the exaltation of this planet, should bring you success in love affairs, if you do not have more than one attachment going on at the same time. For, this sign being a mutable one, is likely to cause two attachments and this would bring you slander or difficulty in connection with rivals. It is, however, just possible that you may marry more than once, and should you survive your first partner, this will most certainly be the case. This influence favours all attachments having their origin in matters connected with sickness, or, institutions, and it promises a happy marriage if it is undertaken under benefic "Directions." You may meet the one who will affect your life seriously, under rather peculiar circumstances.

# CHAPTER XXVI.

## LEGACIES.

THE Eighth House of each nativity governs legacies, and money coming from others, such as co-workers, partners, etc. It is also concerned with occult affairs, mysterious and secret undertakings; it indicates the sex tendencies.

**383.** THE SUN governing the eighth house of your nativity promises a legacy, most likely from some person holding a position in life superior to your own, or it is probable that you may gain a legacy from a relative. In a general sense the Sun has not much dignity in the eighth house, but it is a favourable position for occultism or matters connected with the deeper things of life. Materially it generally promises gain through marriage or by linking yourself with others, such as partners or co-workers, and denotes that you would do better in sharing undertakings with others than by taking the sole responsibility upon yourself.

**384.** THE MOON governing the eighth house of your nativity, there exists a slight possibility of your gaining by legacy, and very probably from someone who will not be directly related to you, or else you will gain something by public donation, or through affairs in which the general public are interested, and are desirous of rewarding you for some service, or public good that you will have done. It also favours your gaining through partners and co-workers, or by those who may be concerned with you in public undertakings.

**385.** MERCURY ruling the eighth house of your nativity is a slight testimony of gain by will or legacy during some portion of your ife. This position favours your gaining through co-workers or partners, but nothing definite can ever be predicted from a horoscope when Mercury rules the eighth house, with regard to the goods of the dead, owing to the very changeable nature of this planet. Your mind may be exercised concerning any money that may be left you, or you may have to act as administrator, executor, or trustee for someone at some period of your life, and may gain pecuniarily by so doing.

**386.** VENUS having rule over the eighth house of your nativity, promises you certain gain by will or legacy. You will in some way or other benefit through the death of others, also by marriage, partnerships, and co-workers. When this planet is well placed, or aspected by " direction " you will, in all probability, gain money through others. It is a very favourable influence if you are in any way connected with others wherever monetary matters are concerned. You should procure an insurance upon all things in which there is any liability, or risk of any description. This influence promises you a very peaceful end, and preservation from accidents at the close of life, or any sudden termination to your existence, being a benefic influence.

**387.** MARS has chief influence over all matters connected with the eighth house of your nativity, the house concerned with deaths, wills or legacies. You may or may not, gain money by the death of others, but if you should it would be sudden, and in some way unexpected, for Mars is not a good planet to be concerned with money matters. You would find that you had been probably buoyed up by some false hope, and would not gain so much as you had been led to expect. Your own terminus vitæ will be somewhat sudden, although you may live to a good age, but it will be advisable to guard against accidents, and not to run any more risk than is absolutely necessary. You would be drawn to public calamities, etc.

**388.** JUPITER having the chief influence over the eighth house, the house concerned with deaths, wills, legacies, and matters pertaining to the *terminus vitæ*, you will gain by legacy or the goods of the dead, or through marriage, partners, and also through co-workers. This influence brings you good fortune through other persons, and either through insurance, or in some direct or indirect manner you may gain by the loss of others. You will have a very peaceful end to your existence, dying a natural and easy death. There is no better influence than that coming from the planet Jupiter, and all he presides over comes to good in the end.

**389.** SATURN ruling the eighth house of your nativity, the house connected with deaths and with money left by others, is in no way favourable for your interests in these matters. You will be disappointed in your expectations concerned with money coming to you from others; also, with regard to money by marriage, or through partner-ships and co-workers. You may have money left to you, but the indications for this are not strongly marked in your horoscope. Your own *terminus vitæ* will be slow, and you will also have much time to ponder, before the final end comes to relieve you from your physical body. You will live to an advanced age, and should be fully conscious at the end of your life.

**390.** URANUS, the mystical planet, has control over the eighth house of your nativity, the house of deaths, wills and legacies. This influence brings about sudden and unexpected events. You will not obtain all that may be left you, and may gain nothing whatever, or unexpectedly come into money. Nothing is sure where this planet is in any way concerned, and it seems in some way to be concerned with that portion of the fate over which one has no control and which waits for some opportunity to reward or punish. Your terminus vitae will be somewhat of a sudden nature, and I do not think that you will have any long illness at the close of your life. Avoid operations and crowds.

**391.** NEPTUNE presides over the eighth house of your nativity. This is the portion of your horoscope connected with matters con-cerning death or the leaving of the physical body, by all with whom you are related, as well as your own *terminus vitæ*. It is not beneficial for any money or legacy that may be left to you, as you will be very liable to be the victim of fraud, or not get that to which you are entitled. You should take every precaution not to have any drugs administered to you, or any experiments made upon you at any time; for everything that the planet Neptune governs is shrouded in mystery, and peculiar happenings occur in connection with all those matters in which he is concerned. There is some liability of your going into very deep sleeps or becoming entranced. A watery death is not improbable.

# CHAPTER XXVII.

## PHILOSOPHY.

THE Ninth House of every nativity denotes the scientific, philosophic and religious tendencies of the native. It is the house of the "higher mind." It also denotes travel or long journeys from home, journeys which result in a broadening of the mind, expanding the ideas and drawing one away from the petty and *bourgeois*. Such journeys need not necessarily be great as measured in leagues ; it depends upon the general environment. To one, a journey from Slocombe to London will produce a greater change in the mental outlook, than another might experience in going to New York and back.

**392.** THE SUN having rule over the ninth house of your nativity promises you success in all philosophical matters. You have very deep feelings with regard to religion and spiritual affairs ; and your thoughts are lofty and ennobling. You can take very broad views of life generally and are not bound too much by conventionality. This influence will bring you success from all ninth house affairs, such as the law and foreign affairs, also long journeys abroad and those things which concern the higher mind. There is behind you a good spiritual influence, and as your faith increases you will learn to come in touch with the higher part of your real self.

**393.** THE MOON has chief rule over the ninth house in your nativity. You will be drawn toward the higher life and, although you may have peculiar views in regard to religion, at the same time you will be earnest and become enthusiastic in all matters pertaining to the higher thought. It will never be difficult for you to change your mind in regard to any religious view that you may hold and in this way you will escape orthodoxy or limitation to your religious feelings. You could become very philosophical, as you are inclined to take broad views and the mind is more to you than the senses.

**394.** MERCURY having dominion over the ninth house of your nativity is an indication that your higher mind is often more active than the lower.   You have, in a certain direction, the ability to become a philosopher, but not until you have more concentration and continuity. You are very quick in your perceptions and very intuitive, so that you may very much improve your mind during the present life, being in many respects quick to learn and appreciate.   You will take some long voyages, or travel in foreign countries, for this influence is an indication that you are fond of travel, especially long journeys.   You have a metaphysical turn of mind, and love mystical subjects.

**395.** VENUS governing your ninth house, the house of philosophy and the higher mind, will bring you peace either through religion, or through a deeper inner knowledge about the soul and after death states, which will bring happiness and peace eventually.   You are very philosophical in your tendencies, and possess an intuition that will help you in any problems that come before you in life's journey.   You have the right spirit and attitude towards all matters relating to the higher mind, and will make much real and permanent progress this life, in your soul attainments.   You will have good relatives through marriage, and may gain through them in some way, this being a good influence.

**396.** MARS having the government of your ninth house, the house of all matters coming under the head of philosophy, is not very favourable to peace and calm, as would be expected were any other planet in power over this portion of the horoscope.   But it shows you to be enthusiastic in all that you put your mind and heart into ; and you will combat or argue against any system of thought that does not meet with your full approval.   You are very independent in your thoughts and feelings, where religion or philosophy are concerned.   Avoid litigation or disputes, and do not become too expressive, or too outspoken in matters of religion, or you will suffer.

**397.** JUPITER rules over the ninth house of your nativity, the house of science, philosophy, and religion.   This influence inclines you to philosophy and wisdom, in its widest sense.   You will not be so scientific, as philosophical and artistic, for you incline more to accept the broad outlines than the limited and precise details of the higher mind. You would succeed in foreign lands, and probably gain in some way through foreign affairs.   This influence favours all legal affairs, and also religious matters in general.   It gives you some prophetic tendencies and the power to dream correctly and also to bring the dreams through into the physical brain. Take note of them.

**398.** SATURN has rule over the ninth house of your nativity, the house of religion and philosophy. Saturn is the planet of stability and concentration, and this position indicates a grave enthusiasm in all the religious questions that will occupy your mind. You will be philosophical and hold very advanced views concerning all matters connected with the higher mind, and all subjects of a metaphysical nature will prove of deep interest to you. This position of the planet Saturn is, however, unfavourable for legal affairs, or for travel where long journeys and foreign affairs are concerned. Truth is the best means of your awakening the qualities of this ninth house.

**399.** URANUS, the mystical and occult planet, occupied the ninth house of your nativity. This indicates the interest you have in astrology and kindred subjects. You hold very advanced views, and you do not cling to those that are orthodox and conventional. You have a very ingenious and inventive mind, with a great deal of originality in your character. You can explore the region of the unknown, and obtain joy and pleasure from all those thoughts and subjects that are considered in our day " far fetched " and " superstitious," but no matter how much critics may look on you as a crank, your thought is of the advanced and progressive type. You may cultivate the higher criticism to advantage, but be sure that it is the *higher* criticism and impersonal.

**400.** NEPTUNE ruling the ninth house of your nativity, indicates a peculiar and somewhat advanced view of life, with a mental attraction towards psychical affairs, and perhaps to spiritualistic phenomena, and also all kindred subjects. You will have some very true and remarkable dreams. At times you will dream things that have no connection with, or are not in any way related to, affairs of daily life, but at other times you may have warnings in your dreams that will be useful; but to "dream true" successfully, you must live an ideally pure life. The relatives of your partners will have strange histories, and you will do well to avoid litigation, and legal affairs in all forms, to be happy in life.

# CHAPTER XXVIII.

## PROFESSION.

THE Tenth House governs honour, profession and the ambitions generally. Avocation is not, however, judged *solely* from the tenth house; the Sun and Moon must be taken into consideration and also the strongest planet. The second and sixth houses have some share in the matter, too; the second indicating the general financial success ease in making income, etc., and the sixth showing the degree of what may be termed " drudgery." But the tenth house is emphatically that which concerns the *vocation*, that in which one's ideals are to a considerable extent involved, and towards which one's best efforts tend. It is the house of ambition.

If there is no planet in the tenth house, it is best to judge by the quality of the sign on the M.C. (paragraphs 410-412). The remarks in the second paragraph of Chapter XIX. will also apply here, *mutatis mutandis.*

**401.** THE SUN, having influence over matters concerned with your occupation in life, is very favourable, but much will depend upon your opportunities to rise to the height of the Sun and all it indicates. This you may judge from the solar aspects and the sign that the Sun occupied at your birth as described under "Individual Characteristics." Your individual and real character will be concerned in all the pursuits in life with which you are in any way engaged, but in a general sense you are best adapted to be your own master and not in the employment of others, unless it be in Government employ, which in your case would be the best, for you can exercise authority.

**402.** THE MOON is concerned with all your pursuits in life, and her influence favours all employments of a common, or public and universal character. You should follow those professions which have to do with catering for the public at large, and those in which a popular or well-known demand is made. You will have much fluctuation in your pursuits in life ; therefore it will be as well if you adapt yourself to almost any calling or environment necessary to win success out of small or common things. Do not seek any trade or any profession which has fixity and permanency as its base, but where change and fluctuation are the order of the day ; S.P.Q.R. is the motto for this position.

**403.** MERCURY has rule over the tenth house of your nativity. This denotes that all Mercurial professions will be best for you, such as literary work, writing and secretarial pursuits. It is not altogether a favourable influence for permanency with regard to professions, and some changes may be experienced throughout your life. A light employment is better suited for you, and where travel or movement is required you will be in your element. There are many professions coming under the rule of Mercury, such as printing, writing, bookselling, stationery, etc., but all those pursuits where the mind is exercised, such as an agent, interpreter or teacher, etc., will be best suited for you.

**404.** VENUS governing the tenth house of your nativity promises you success in all matters that are concerned with the pleasure of others. Your employment in life should have some connection with the female sex, for Venus favours women and all their requirements. The occupations under the influence of Venus are too numerous to describe, but, generally speaking, they are those which deal with objects and subjects that give pleasure to others. All those professions that are light and refined will be best suited to you so far as gain and enjoyment is concerned. You will meet with success in life through this position, and you will have many good friends to help you.

**405.** MARS presides over the part of your nativity concerned with profession. Mars is the planet governing warfare and all matters of an external nature, also where much energy is required. You should possess some mechanical ability, you would then have success in all matters where mechanical skill and enterprise is necessary. You would also be successful as a chemist, or doctor, and in any pursuit where fire is used for working purposes. There are many occupations under the rule of the planet Mars, and they are so numerous that it is almost impossible to enumerate them all, but you will be able to judge for what you are best fitted, by noting the positions and aspects of the planet Mars.

**406.** JUPITER has chief rule over the tenth house, and therefore indicates that you will follow honourable professions by which you will gain financially and socially.    You will gain through religious affairs and foreign concerns.    This planet denotes success in all matters over which he presides, so that your occupations will be to your taste, and likely to bring you joy and happiness.    There are many pursuits that you may follow to advantage from a judge to a merchant, according to your abilities, but so far as trade is concerned you will do well in businesses that clothe and supply the general public with provisions, etc.

**407.**  SATURN has rule over your profession or occupation, and this denotes power and authority in some way, but brings most fortune and success through industry and perseverance.    You will either hold a leading position or have some kind of responsibility placed upon you.    This Saturnine influence is not good for business matters as there is always some danger threatened, either through the injury of others or the failure to carry to a successful issue whatever projects you have in hand.    Saturn favours gain by labour more than by good fortune.    Matters requiring patience, tact and caution succeed better than any other methods, therefore you should seek the pursuits requiring these qualifications.

**408.**  URANUS having rule over the tenth house of your nativity, signifies that the pursuits for which you are best fitted and adapted will be found amongst all those professions that are original and ingenious in their nature, such as advertising, or those of an inventive nature and those which call forth all the activities of the higher mind. This Uranian influence will, however, upset many of your plans until you get into the right groove.    You will eventually find that you will have to mark out your own career, for after many ups and downs you will come to realise that you have original talent, and either adopt an uncommon profession, or become an inventor and originator of work.

**409.**  NEPTUNE having some concern with professions and employment in your horoscope, indicates that you should follow those pursuits that are rare, unique and uncommon.    In a general sense this planet governs all things of an inspirational and psychic nature, and we find mediums and all uncommon persons in the professional world under this planet.    It bestows upon some a literary genius, and upon others artistic tastes of a peculiar nature.    It is difficult, if not impossible, to hit upon any special or permanent profession to recommend with confidence, especially as so little is actually known about Neptune, most of our ideas about this mysterious planet being at the present time more or less of a speculative nature.

**410.** CARDINAL SIGNS are the indicators of all matters connected with profession and the employments for which you are best adapted, and these denote the power to fill responsible or prominent positions in life. Wherever energy or activity is needed, your ruling influences will find the best opportunities to lead you on to success. You will display some ambition with regard to your pursuits in life, and it will therefore be better for you to fill any post where advancement and responsibility may be acquired. You have all the necessary power to rise in life and occupy lucrative positions. All your undertakings should be upon a large scale, and you should avoid taking part in any business or profession where there is not a sufficient scope for your energies.

**411.** FIXED SIGNS have the greatest and most marked influence in all matters concerning profession or employment, these signs being most prominent in your nativity. This being the case, you would be well advised not to change your profession or employment too frequently. You would have the most success in governmental positions, or in those employments where steady and fixed pursuits engage the energies. The fixed signs favour the medical profession, and those pursuits wherein skill and tact is necessary, also a business of stability, and if not strictly of the conventional order, something that is well established and in no way too original or new. Therefore it will be best for you to engage in old-fashioned and well-established callings, which are recognised as legitimate modes of gaining a livelihood.

**412.** MUTABLE SIGNS governing the profession at the time of birth, show a tendency to follow employments of a more or less ordinary character, but do not give you any great opportunity of fame or success in matters of employment. You would probably have greater success in the employment of others, than on your own account. But if you should ever undertake this responsibility it would be the best for you to engage in those pursuits which receive the patronage of the majority and where the general public are concerned rather than separate individuals. Probably two or more occupations will engage your attention at the same time, dualism being indicated.

# CHAPTER XXIX.

## FRIENDS.

THE Eleventh House governs friendships, hopes and wishes, and the desire for Union. It is closely related to the seventh house and indirectly with the third, and all that it denotes is synthesised in the planet Uranus.

Should there be no planet in the eleventh, then judge by the triplicity to which the sign which occupies it belongs ; (paragraphs 422-425).

**413.** THE SUN has chief rule over the eleventh house of your nativity, the house of friends and acquaintances, hopes and wishes. This is a very favourable position for you in a general sense, so far as friends are concerned, and it will also enable you to realise many of your hopes and wishes during life. You are capable of making some very firm friends in a good position, and they will be willing to help you in several ways. You will make many friends during your life, by whose help, advice, or favour, you will in some way benefit. Associations, and joining with others, is one of the many ways by which success could easily be yours. This position will help you to cultivate hope, and general good will to all.

**414.** THE MOON governs the eleventh house of your nativity, the house of friendship and acquaintance, and this will cause you to have many friends, some among the general public, and many who will be willing to help you. Your chief experiences will come to you through your connection with friends and associates, for you fraternise very easily with those who are congenial to you. Your career will be greatly affected by your friends, who will play a very important part in your life. You will be likely to come in contact with some very peculiar and eccentric people. Your best friends will be found amongst those born between June 21st and July 21st of any year.

**415.** MERCURY governs your house of friends, and much depends upon the aspects to Mercury and the other planets, as to how far this is a favourable position or otherwise. It is probable that you will have many acquaintances, but only a few friends in the true sense of the word. Some of your acquaintances may profess friendship for you, but it will be as well to be on the look-out for any insincerity or deceit; for Mercury unless well aspected ever inclines to be fickle and unreliable. You may have friendship with ingenious persons, and those who are connected with literary work will probably be your best and truest friends, but be cautious in all your dealings with acquaintances until you are quite satisfied that they come under the good side of the dual planet Mercury, when they will make clever friends whose advice will be helpful and useful to you.

**416.** VENUS governs your eleventh house, the house of friends, promising you a merry set of friends and acquaintances, and an association with persons who are fortunate. You will either be advanced or gain socially and financially through your friends, and they will do much to help you, whenever you may require their help. You will do well to trust persons born under the signs belonging to the planet Venus. Those who were born between April 20th and May 20th will be attracted towards you, and those also who were born between September 21st and October 21st will be able to aid you in many ways. It is a very favourable influence for friendships, companionships, etc., and promises you the fulfilment of your hopes and wishes.

**417.** MARS governing the eleventh house of your nativity is not altogether ꞌfavourableꞌ for friendships, for it indicates some disputes and quarrels between yourself and friends, at some period of your life. You will become acquainted with medical, or military men, or persons who are ambitious and enterprising; but avoid serious disputes or wrangling, and be guarded in your choice of acquaintances. This influence denotes a strong desire nature, and implies that you have very potent hopes and wishes, but many of your desires will only be gratified by your own energies, and through much force and earnest endeavour. Do not become surety for anyone, or lend your friends money, etc., or you will lose both friends and money.

**418.** JUPITER governing your house of friends is very good, and a very happy testimony that you will never be in want of a friend throughout your life, and those friends will not only be very willing but also able to help you, whenever you may require their aid. You will have friends or acquaintances amongst religious persons, or those who are very philosophically inclined, very well disposed and anxious to do all the good they can to others. Your friends will be found amongst those born under the planet Jupiter, or generally speaking, from November 21st to December 21st in any year. You will realise many of your hopes and wishes during this life, if you will think clearly.

**419.** SATURN governing the eleventh house of your nativity, will bring some very faithful and reliable friends into your life, but some trouble in connection with your friends and acquaintances is also denoted. You will have friends amongst the aged, in a general sense, or those who are much older than yourself. You will have some bitter disappointments, in connection with either friends and acquaintances, and you will not always realise your hopes and wishes with regard to them. Some of your so-called friends are liable to desert you, when you most require their aid, therefore do not rely too much upon all your friends, this influence giving but few real friends.

**420.** URANUS having rule over the eleventh house of your nativity, promises a rare and exceptional friendship, and indicates that persons who are interested in the side of life connected with the mystical and the occult will help you at some period of life's journey. This influence gives friends and acquaintances of the romantic or bohemian order; some very strange or fascinating and remarkable experiences in connection with friendships, are denoted by this Uranian influence. You have ability to study human nature, and will be drawn to original persons, and those who think more than the average individual. While travelling, you will meet those most likely to become your warmest friends.

**421.** NEPTUNE presiding over the eleventh house in your nativity, the house of friends, will bring you many peculiar and strange acquaintances, and many weird or remarkable experiences will occur through them. It would be well for you to know the persons with whom you associate and mix, as you will find them rather difficult to in any way understand. This position usually brings those coming under its influence into contact with persons who are physically or mentally deformed. It will draw you toward the psychic and spiritualistic side of life, and your friends or acquaintances will influence you in this direction. You should avoid hypnotists, mesmerists, etc. This position indicates a somewhat mystical turn of mind, and shows the fulfilment of your hopes in a manner quite different to your expectations.

**422.** THE FIERY TRIPLICITY has chief rule over the eleventh house in your horoscope, bringing you some very energetic and useful friends, whose enterprising and ambitious nature will considerably benefit you. You will most probably profit through some of your friends and acquaintances at some period of your life, especially when your "Directions" favour help from them. You are intelligent enough to appreciate good friends when they come into your life, and will do much to win their favour and assistance whenever it is required. It is said that there is no better looking-glass than an old friend, therefore encourage those friendships that help the spiritual side of your nature to increase. Theophrastus has said "True friends visit us in prosperity only when invited but in adversity they come without invitation." This is fortunate in your case, for you have that kind of nature which cannot help appreciating true friendship, and whatever influence friends assert over your life will be for good more than for evil.

**423.** THE EARTHY TRIPLICITY has chief rule over the eleventh house in your nativity, bringing you some very practical and solid friendships. Your friends will be found amongst those who possess their full share of common-sense and whose business-like principles will greatly benefit you, for you are apt to be somewhat dependent at times upon the help of others. Mere acquaintances will not be so favourable to you as solid friendships and you should avoid all self-seeking and material persons whose influence upon you will have a chilling effect causing you to feel a want that they are unable to supply. Take Edward Young's advice, "Judge before friendship, then confide till death." Moneyed men and those in position, or persons who have risen in life will become your best and permanent friends.

**424.** THE AIRY TRIPLICITY has chief rule over the eleventh house in your nativity, bringing you intellectual and very refined friendships from which you should gain much profit and benefit, as they will tend to improve your mind and stimulate you into more active thinking and thus awaken a deeper interest in life and its surroundings. You will never rely too much upon your friends, for with Lord Bacon you can say "The best way to represent to life the manifold use of friendship is to cast and see how many things one cannot do for one's self." It is your somewhat independent nature that will win you the admiration of those who are mentally able to appreciate the value of true friendship, and thus although you may have adverse as well as favourable experiences through friends, on the whole your friends and acquaintances will work more good than evil into your life.

**425.** THE WATERY TRIPLICITY has chief rule over the eleventh house in your nativity, therefore you will have many emotional friends, some of whom will have much sorrow and many troubles of their own. You will never be able to place implicit reliance upon your friends and acquaintances, as they will be as unstable as water and liable to much fluctuation in feeling and affection. Some will be dreamy and sensitive, and others will be psychic and mediumistic, while others again will not be firm or in any way self-reliant, so that you will see that you are very liable to be imposed upon by your friends at some period of your life. Never become surety for another or lend money unless you are quite certain that your help will not be abused and lead to evil results. You can be practical where your friends and acquaintances are concerned if you do not become too much influenced by their feelings.

# CHAPTER XXX.

## OCCULTISM.

THE Twelfth House is one of mystery; that is, owing to its cadent and mutable influence it is more connected with the mind than with actual physical manifestation. It has been called "the house of self-undoing," therefore it represents occultism and all that is secret or sacred, and in an occult sense it may be said of this house that, whatever can *be* must be.

Should there be *no* planet in the twelfth house use paragraph 435 unless the sign Leo occupies it, in which case use 426.

**426.** THE SUN ruling the twelfth house of your nativity is a good influence for all matters of an occult nature, and gives you a rather deep interest in all things that are psychic, or beyond the material. But at the same time you are in some manner restricted or limited, and will be unable to express yourself to the full, owing to the conditions surrounding your birth or environment, which are not at all favourable, or conducive to worldly welfare. Therefore let your life be one of devotion to the inner, more than to the outer; for you will then come in contact with those who are willing to assist you in the right direction. The Sun in this house is rising, and therefore you are promised much improvement in worldly affairs as your life advances.

**427.** THE MOON ruling the twelfth house of your nativity, while favouring occult tendencies, is at the same time not very good for your personality, because you may be obscured or kept in the background, and at some period of your life will either suffer confinement within a hospital, or some place where your liberty and freedom is restricted, the twelfth house having to do with all those matters connected with the unseen. Therefore it favours self-undoing, or matters that are concerned with the occult more than mundane things. Also you should never seek to push yourself too much to the front, but must be contented to pass through life more or less unknown and unrecognised.

**428.** MERCURY having rule over your twelfth house will cause your mind to be very much engaged in all matters relating to occult phenomena, and any matters dealing with the other worlds. In fact, you have some sort of ability for investigating spiritualism and occultism generally, for you will be able to put your mind into those subjects. At the same time you should be careful not to let yourself become too much engrossed in the phenomenal side of these things. You should be very careful in your speech as there is a danger of suffering through treachery, in which your liberty might be taken from you, this influence being very much against your material affairs, but better for occultism.

**429.** VENUS is associated with much of the growth or progress you will make in the occult life; it promises you profit, joy, and some pleasure in connection with all psychic and occult matters. In fact, you will, on attaining that stage of growth wherein the influence will operate, obtain your greatest happiness and pleasure from occult and mystical subjects, and will be inclined to interest yourself, if not deeply certainly not superficially, in matters pertaining to other planes, worlds and states of consciousness. It is probable that you will be introduced to the occult side of life by means of the influence of others; but you will be more intuitive than studious in occultism, and it should come easy to you.

**430.** MARS governing the twelfth house of your nativity is not in any way favourable for matters of an occult nature. It warns you to use very great care in dealing with matters that you are not in every way acquainted with, and it would be better for you never to have too many dealings with phenomena or with out-of-sight conditions. This influence threatens you with some confinement at some period of your life, either through accidents, false imprisonment, or some thing that will tend to take away your liberty for a time. Therefore be very discreet in all your actions and thus avoid trouble. Also beware of spiritualism.

**431.** JUPITER is the planet connected with occult matters in your nativity; therefore you will be drawn towards occultism and make great progress during this life in all matters connected with occult thought and study. In some way there is an hereditary connection between yourself and the occult, and no matter how far you may drift from the subjective life, the inner worlds will have some fascination for you. You will in some manner gain by means of your connection with psychic matters, and very little harm will come to you through matters of self-undoing, and you will yet take your life in hand and endeavour to understand much of your inner nature, for you will have a faith in mystical affairs.

**432.** SATURN is so placed as to have principal influence over all matters of an occult nature in your nativity, and probably you will yourself be the cause of your own self-undoing, and may come into the occult life through perseverance, patience, and forethought. But you may also experience sorrow, difficulty and delay, in connection with the occult life ; but whatever you attain to will be permanent, so that your difficulties will only tend to make you build for the future on a very firm and solid basis. You are in many respects much drawn towards the mystical and occult, and should be able to take up the study of astrology and kindred subjects, but use caution in occult matters.

**433.** URANUS is concerned with all matters of an occult nature in your nativity, and all mystic subjects will have a special fascination and interest for you. You possess the ability to enter upon the study of astrology and kindred subjects, and a love of the metaphysical is deeply buried within your nature ; therefore you should seek to awaken this from latency and bring it into activity. You may be brought to a realisation of the higher truths by some remarkable crashes, or through strange and unexpected experiences which may come into your life, but nevertheless, amidst all the strange experiences in your career, you will ever be brought nearer and nearer to the truth, and may, at ength, make very rapid progress.

**434.** NEPTUNE having chief influence over the twelfth house of your nativity, will bring you into contact with peculiar and weird experiences, in connection with what is called occultism. You will either come into touch with mediums, or study spiritualism, and will probably also meet with some very peculiar persons holding strange views on occult lines. It warns you, however, to be careful in your dealings with psychic matters; for you will come in contact with various grades of psychic phenomena, at different periods of your life, but these various influences can only operate, in the highest condition, when a pure life is led, and the tendency is towards higher thought and purity of motive.

**435.** Your twelfth house, the house of occultism and secret affairs, was NOT OCCUPIED by any planet at your birth, therefore its influence over your life was not so strong as would have been the case had a planet stirred this house into activity.   This may have the effect of delaying any special effort on your part to lead the occult life, and whatever tendencies you may have towards occultism will come from other influences in your nativity.   There is one advantage that this gives you, it does not show any very marked sorrow through treachery or the deliberate evil intention of enemies, and all your troubles arising from enmity or jealousy will be more spontaneous, and the result of impulse rather than premeditation.

*§ 6.—Summary of the Horoscope.*

## CHAPTER XXXI.

### SUMMARIES.

EVERY nativity may be summarised, in the first instance, by noting first the position, and next the Triplicity, and finally the Quality of the signs in which the *majority* of the planets were placed at birth. Should there be any doubt as to which Triplicity or Quality has the greatest influence, (owing to there being three planets in each), then those signs in which the Sun and Moon are placed should be allowed a casting vote, the Sun being preferred to the Moon in any case of ambiguity. Sun and Moon both in signs of *same* quality count same as ' majority.' The following brief Summaries are self-explanatory.

### PLANETARY POSITIONS.

**436.** The majority of the planets were RISING AND NEAR THE EASTERN HORIZON at the time of your birth. This denotes that you will rise in life by your own energy, enterprise, and perseverance, and attain to a good position in which you will have power and authority in the sphere in which you may be moving. You will have many opportunities, and the ability to seize them ; thus you will prosper and advance. The majority of the planets rising at birth, denotes ability and self-control, and enables those who are born at this time to have the vibrations of the planets to their hand, so to speak, and thus you will make good use of the operating forces around your ascendant.

**437.** The majority of the planets were SETTING at your birth, denoting less opportunity to govern circumstances, and bring you more under the influence of fate than would be the case had your planets been rising instead of setting. You will find the influence of others affect your life very considerably, and you will not stand alone and create your own destiny : for you are fated to always have some one either

helping you or advising you.  It may seem as though you had less free-will than others, whose planets are rising at birth ; but in reality it has a far more important meaning than this, for it means the merging of the Personality into the Individuality, whenever you are ready to realise the value of this surrender.

**438.**  The majority of the planets in your nativity were ABOVE THE HORIZON at the time of your birth.  This will bring out all the latent possibilities denoted by those planets, allowing you to express their influence easily ; therefore you will meet with some success in life and advance in many ways, beyond the sphere of your birth.  The elevation of the planets also denotes a certain amount of ambition and the ability to stand alone, making you more self-reliant, aspiring, energetic, and persevering.  You will have some very fortunate periods, and success will come to you, whenever you exert yourself, and determine to make the most of the opportunities that will be yours.

**439.**  The majority of the planets at your birth were BELOW THE HORIZON.  This denotes that the latter years of your life will be the more successful.  There is a great deal that is latent in you that you cannot well express, and you will not have very many opportunities in life to improve your position : therefore you should seize every opportunity that comes in your way.  You will succeed better by working with others, and by steady persistence, than by great show and enterprise, and I think you would do much better by allowing others to take responsibility than by asserting yourself ; you work best un-recognised and unknown.  There is more in you than you are aware.

## THE TRIPLICITIES.

**440.**  The majority of the planets were in FIERY SIGNS at your birth which is an indication of a very spirited and idealistic nature. You possess a great amount of force and energy and a full, rich and generous nature, plenty of vitality and enthusiasm and also much hope and activity.  You have deep emotions, can love ardently, and also display much passion, and are never lacking in spirit.  Love of the heroic and intensity of purpose is a very marked feature of your character and disposition.  You will always put a great deal of yourself into all you do and feel, but you should avoid impulse or rashness, and always think carefully before you speak or act.

**441.** The majority of the planets were in AIRY SIGNS at the time of your birth. This will give you an inspirational and also an artistic temperament. You are essentially refined and can live much more in the mind than in the senses. You may love sensuous pleasures, but you will abhor all things sensual. Your soul is alive and you have that very rare quality of feeling things with your mind. You have good intellectual ability and could study with ease, but it is the artistic side of life that appeals to you more than the scientific, unless it be the philosophically intellectual aspect of science. You have splendid ideals, and may subjectively cultivate exquisite tastes.

**442.** The majority of the planets were in WATERY SIGNS at the time of your birth. This denotes a somewhat emotional and also a psychic nature. Your instinctual and sensitive tendencies are very active and thus you are receptive and to a certain extent impressionable. Much will depend upon your conditions, surroundings and environment, as to how you will enjoy and appreciate life, for you have acute and active perceptions and sense things in a peculiar manner through your feelings. You are mediumistic, and very often impressed with feelings and thoughts that come from others either on this or the other side of the grave. Live purely, to be happy.

**443.** The majority of the planets were in EARTHY SIGNS at the time of your birth. This is a sure indication that you will become very practical, thorough and matter-of-fact, and always look to the solid, and concrete side of life. You possess scientific ability, and would have a certain amount of success in any dealings with matters connected with the earth, or any affairs that are tangible and solid. You will be a lover of justice, and will desire that all ideals should be of a practical nature, and easily made manifest. Although you may not be quick, brilliant, or sharp, you will always be painstaking, plodding and persevering, and in this manner you will win much more success than you would by hurry and flurry, being more reliable than showy.

## THE QUADRUPLICITIES OR "QUALITIES."

**444.** The majority of the planets were in CARDINAL SIGNS at your birth. This denotes that you have much ambition, an enterprising and energetic spirit. You are very enthusiastic, and must be at the head of things to be quite happy. In every sense of the word you are a " Pioneer," and will always aspire to take the lead in any concern in which you are at all interested.    You are in many respects self-assertive, independent, and very active.    You will have some fame during your life, and you are, or will be, a noted person in the sphere in which you move.    There is a certain love of change in you, which will make you sometimes capricious and uncertain ; but, nevertheless, changes are good for you.

**445.**   The majority of the planets were in FIXED SIGNS at your birth, and this is a favourable indication of your solidarity, reliability and patience.    At times you will be very firm and rigid, and if this is carried to any excess, you will become dogmatic and even obstinate. But in a very general sense it gives you self-reliance, and a certain amount of independence ; for at the root of your character there is some pride and dignity ; because, although you will not be prepared to admit it, you can be austere and in some ways autocratic.    You will be kind, however, owing to your feelings, of which you have a full share.    You are persistent, sure and reliable.

**446.**   The majority of the planets were in MUTABLE SIGNS at your time of birth.    This denotes that you are versatile, although at the same time rather too indecisive and not sufficiently firm and determined.    But you are sympathetic, and somewhat inclined to be sensitive although if you would make your life more useful, you should cultivate more thoroughness or you will be inconstant, and have a feeling of want and discontent with yourself.    You have a somewhat fickle nature and should try to pull yourself up to the standard of firm self-reliance, which would make your life much more happy and successful.    You are at times very restless and uncertain but are always fond of intellect and intellectual pursuits.

### THE POSITION OF THE SUN AND MOON IN THE SIGNS.

**447.**   THE SUN IN A CARDINAL and THE MOON IN A FIXED sign will cause you to be internally aspiring and ambitious, but externally unable to respond quickly to the inner vibrations.    This may cause some obstinate tendencies to be displayed in your personality. This quality makes you an earnest character, possessing much ability, but although you have the necessary steam, you will not always feel disposed to allow it to move you forward.    In fact you often stand in your own light through the failure to personally answer to the internal and real promptings from the higher part of yourself.  It seems as if you possess internal wit and quick perception, but not the power to understand until opportunities have passed.

**448.** THE SUN IN A CARDINAL and THE MOON IN A MUTABLE sign will give you internal aspirations and ambitions, but the lack of opportunities to carry them into active manifestation, and this may arise through indifference to the internal desires, for the combination of these different qualities is not altogether harmonised, the one showing an active tendency, the other quite the reverse.  But there is this advantage about the above, which is of value: it will cause you to steady the individual characteristic and calm down much of the internal enthusiasm.  This may not be so beneficial from a material standpoint; but from the point of view of the higher life and the Soul, there is wisdom in this arrangement.  Where principle is concerned, be decisive, and never sacrifice the ideal for the sake of detail.

**449.** THE SUN IN A FIXED and THE MOON IN A CARDINAL sign in your nativity will give you more individual firmness than you will be able to express during life, the personal element being changeable and less permanent.  You could be internally satirical, and externally witty, a combination that should quicken your mentality to a great extent, and give you some measure of power over your external conditions.  You are ambitious enough to be able to make your way in life, and will seek to rule, or to be at the head of things generally.  You will be independent, and self-reliant, and possess an internal restraint over yourself which will enable you to pursue with steady purpose any object you desire, your formative will being strong and persistent.  You have strong characteristics.

**450.** THE SUN IN A FIXED and THE MOON IN A MUTABLE sign in your horoscope, shows that you have a blending of the humorous and satirical tendencies, although the one may somewhat counteract the other.  Internally you will be capable of much more than you are able to accomplish externally, probably through the lack of opportunity.  Internally you are firm, steady and fixed, but your external conditions are in a measure restless and indecisive.  This may be the cause of some lack of ambition, and a tendency to let things drift, without enough energy being put forth to alter these existing conditions.  Therefore you will not attain to fame or great things in this life, unless your life is joined with another more ambitious.    Internal decision and external wavering are your dangers, while determination and intellect are your salvation.

**451.** THE SUN IN A MUTABLE and THE MOON IN A CARDINAL sign at the time of your birth will make you personally desirous of fame and recognition, but you will often lack the necessary internal incentive to enable you to carry out your different plans and aspirations.    You should not let yourself be too changeable or individually too uncertain.    Try to remember that during this life you are weaving the web of your future destiny, and that although you may not be able to carry out everything you plan in this life, you will, in the future that lies before you, have the opportunity to reap all that you have hitherto sown.    Your nature seems to be internally peaceful, whilst on the surface you are over active, and somewhat too precipitate.    Nevertheless, you will learn much more through your outward activity than through the inner conditions which are apt to be too uncertain to be relied upon.

**452.** THE SUN IN A MUTABLE and THE MOON IN A FIXED sign in your horoscope will give you internal indecision, and external resolve, so that you may be personally fixed and determined upon any course of action, and yet when driven to the point may be so very undecided as to waver, and thus let many an opportunity pass you by. It will be to your advantage to think very carefully ere you make up your mind definitely, but when once made up, it would be well to carry out your original plan, or you will have to make the thing action when its usefulness has passed by.    It seems as if you would have to learn the lesson of being firm, but not stubborn.    You will not obtain much fame and recognition in this life and will do well to be ever patient.

**453.** THE SUN IN A FIERY and THE MOON IN AN AIRY sign at birth is one of the best influences ; it is in every way harmonious. It will allow you to control your emotions, and to see things from the intellectual standpoint, beside having the motive force behind to raise your ideals to the highest point.    You can be philosophical and very sincere, but may live a little too much in the subjective world.    You will think and also feel in advance of your surroundings, and if you can make your actions harmonise with your ideal, you will indeed make very great progress during this present earth-life.    The quality of your brain is such as to allow you to expand in every way, and you should try to realise that many of your present limitations may be overcome by your own individual effort.

**454.** THE SUN IN A FIERY and THE MOON IN A WATERY sign at your birth indicates the ascendency of the higher emotions over the lower, and this really means that any tendency of yours to encourage the sensational element, is to live in the lower half of your being. You will be very receptive to your surroundings, and will often take on the conditions of other persons and think that their conditions are your own. You are positive to the higher life, and should remember that the true mediumistic spirit is to give allegiance to the higher Self and not allow the habits of mind and body to entirely dominate the soul. You are personally inclined to be impressionable, but when pushed to the centre of yourself can be firm and determined.

**455.** THE SUN IN A FIERY and THE MOON IN AN EARTHY sign at your birth are contrary elements. You will find that you are individually much in advance of your personal conditions and surroundings, and the purpose of this seems to be to teach you to be thorough, and far less on the enthusiastic or emotional plane, and to help you make your splendid ideals practical and real. You will have plenty of opportunity to cultivate patience, and to avoid impulse and over generosity. Internally you are entirely different to your external nature, and this is owing to the fact that you are to acquire the much needed balance between the two states of being. You should try to understand this great difference in yourself, and learn the lessons of both sides; one being expansive, and the other contractive—therefore extremes.

**456.** THE SUN IN AN AIRY and THE MOON IN A FIERY sign at your birth shows that you are far too personally impulsive for your inner or individual conditions. This may cause you to precipitate matters, when it would probably have been better to await fitting opportunities. You will look upon the world from a refined and idealistic standpoint, and will make great progress during the life that still awaits you in the future, and you have little to fear mentally, for you have the ability to carve your own way through the world, but should remember that haste, and also hurry are not the best means to adopt to gain success. You are very intuitive, internally sensing the best in all things, and you are fortunate in possessing a personality that is in harmony with your individual tendencies.

**457.** THE SUN WAS IN AN AIRY and THE MOON IN A WATERY sign at your birth, the former representing what is known as the Individual part of your being, and the latter the Personal conditions. There is some inharmony shown by this. You will in all probability allow the Personal element to almost dominate you entirely and if so you will be very receptive, and also easily affected and impressed by your surroundings, and conditions. The higher part of your nature will be rarely manifested, unless you overcome your moods. Check all tendency towards sensation, and the lower emotional feelings. You will have some periods of inspiration and uplifting, that will be quite out of keeping with the surroundings and environment and give you opportunities to grow spiritually.

**458.** THE SUN WAS IN AN AIRY and THE MOON IN AN EARTHY sign at your birth ; thus you will tend to be internally volatile, and externally practical, so that a somewhat inharmonious condition is denoted by the combination of these two. But it is quite possible that you may make a good use of your life by permitting the practical side of your nature to carry out the dictates of your Higher or Inner Self. You will by accuracy and careful study realise through the objective world, some of the ideals and subjective states of your Soul. Do not allow yourself to be too matter-of-fact, or too critical ; for you have stored up in the inner part of your nature, many gems of artistic beauty. Though your experiences during this life may be on purpose to " solidify," yet you have inspirations within, which you should never forget.

**459.** THE SUN WAS IN A WATERY and THE MOON IN A FIERY sign at your birth, and these are not the most congenial elements to blend. It is a testimony that you will be personally ahead of your individual state, and by the general experiences of this life will tend to raise your emotions and feelings upward to a higher plane. The emotions will often sway you, and your dangers will be through impulses that are unchecked, often carrying you far beyond the place of safety, where feeling is concerned. You are internally mediumistic and externally positive, and the reverse of what you would wish to be, and this will often cause you to reflect upon conduct that is contrary to your innermost desires, and thus give rise to discontent.

**460.** THE SUN WAS IN A WATERY and THE MOON IN AN AIRY sign at your birth. This denotes that internally and individually, you are more emotional than you are personally, but you have the ability and also the opportunity during this life to reason upon your sensations, and gain sufficient control over them and thus evolve more rapidly than if you had a less refined personality. You would be able to express your soul through painting or any professional work wherein the feelings or emotions could guide the mind. Your conditions for progress are helped by your surroundings and environment, but deep within you there is a receptivity, which brings you in touch with unseen forces and this is the motive power of all your actions. You are inspirational and may become psychic, especially if you live purely.

**461.** THE SUN WAS IN A WATERY and THE MOON IN AN EARTHY sign at your nativity, and therefore harmony between your Individual and Personal conditions will be obtained from this unity of the elements. Personally you will be objective, practical, persevering and fond of science, but internally you will be inclined to dream or be restless, and not so practical; therefore the opportunity will be given you this life to make many of the internal conditions more solid. You will always be receptive, and never too positive; but you may tend more towards the external than will be altogether good for your progress. You will learn much by studying the laws of hygiene and also by study of scientific matters. There is a certain amount of complexity in you, and this makes you a difficult subject to know.

**462.** THE SUN WAS IN AN EARTHY and THE MOON IN A FIERY sign at your nativity. This in an indication that a practical, solid, determined, internal nature governs the personal characteristics. But with the fiery personality, you will often go beyond your individual desires, and thus find a difficult path opening up before you, the ideal which you pursue being much ahead of your own true growth. This will tend to bring you many opportunities to break up crystallised ideas of the past, so that you may progress in the future. You will often act upon impulse and regret the action after its consummation. The two extremes in your nature will be a great problem to you, until you realise that you are sowing in the present for future reaping. A tendency to be internally slow, and externally quick, sums up much of the life in a few words.

**463.** THE SUN WAS IN AN EARTHY and THE MOON IN AN AIRY sign at your nativity. Your inner nature will be much more practical than the external, the latter being more volatile, causing you to be much more refined externally than you are internally. You will, owing to this, find yourself amidst surroundings which will not altogether harmonise with your individual requirements. The whole tendency of your life will be to refine the inner nature and eliminate any crystallised conditions of the past. The virtues of Truth and Justice will become very attractive as you realise more concerning the complexity of your nature, for you are complex inasmuch as you are negative internally, and positive externally, giving rise to extremes.

**464.** THE SUN WAS IN AN EARTHY and THE MOON IN A WATERY sign at your nativity. This will give you a receptive temperament causing you to obtain impressions from without, and inclining you to the side of life which is easily influenced by mixing the surroundings, and their conditions, with yourself, so that you identify yourself with your feelings and emotions. Never allow yourself to be hypnotised by others or you will absorb the whole of their conditions and lose much of your will power. You will tend to become internally practical, but externally restless. It will be well for you to draw yourself out of sensations, or you may become a slave to a habit or custom to your soul's detriment and progress onward. You should cultivate firmness, and endeavour to strike the balance between fluidity and rigidity.

# CHAPTER XXXII.

## SUPPLEMENTARY PARAGRAPHS.

"SUPPLEMENTARY" paragraphs are to be used judiciously where the horoscope shews the necessity of adding them, for the purpose of strengthening it or filling in gaps, after carefully considering the effect the additions will have upon the whole reading. They should be sparingly used, and not given indiscriminately.

The " rising planet " will of course be that which is on the eastern side of the map and nearest the cusp of the ascendant; for the nearer the ascendant, the more does the power of the rising planet tend to be thrown into the field of consciousness and brought under the control of the will. It is not advisable to give this page unless there is a planet either in the first or twelfth houses, or else in the former half of the second or latter half of the eleventh. The rising planet's influence will be much modified by the sign in which it rises, its distance from the ascendant and the aspects it receives from planets in other houses, etc.

The paragraphs described as " personal colouring " are suitable for persons having a special interest in psychic matters and anxious for any information concerning the aura, wishful to know what are suitable and harmonious colours to wear, etc., etc., in fact for any who have a special interest in colour. In the majority of cases, the " personal colouring " paragraph need not be included; but where there are no lunar aspects to tabulate, this paragraph serves usefully to supplement what the reader might otherwise feel to be a somewhat scanty treatment of the Personality.

Beginners are advised to omit the paragraphs in this chapter altogether.

## THE RISING PLANET.

**465.** THE SUN rising at the time of your birth is a very fortunate position, bringing dignity and honour into the life and upholding you under any stress and strain that you may be called upon to pass through.

You will command respect and good feeling from those around you, so that you are able to hold responsible positions, and to exercise some authority over others.  This is not only a fortunate position for worldly affairs but also very favourable for your moral growth.  You will scorn all mean or sordid actions, but will ever strive to do right only for the sake of right, and therefore you must in time merit the esteem of others.

**466.**  THE MOON rising at the time of your birth will give you a mutable disposition: you will be a lover of change and novelty. This position will make you very receptive, not only to the thought-spheres of others, but to your own surroundings also: feeling will play a prominent part in your life.  It is important for you to exercise great care with regard to your companions and acquaintances, for there is some liability for you to become easily psychologised and quickly influenced by them.  You will love travel and may be a little restless sometimes: much will depend upon your environment and home life however.  You are very sensitive and somewhat impressionable.

**467.**  MERCURY rising at the time of your birth is good for your mentality: you will be very sharp and acute, also active and quick both in your thoughts and actions.  This position will render you in many ways a unique character, for not only will you have splendid imitative powers, but you can be "all things to all men."  You will be shrewd and diplomatic and very well able to argue for or against anything according to your inclinations: you also possess literary ability, so the mind will never fail to find out some device to keep you busy.  Like quicksilver, which Mercury represents, you will rise or fall just like a barometer, according to that environment in which you may be placed.

**468.**  VENUS rising at the time of your birth is very favourable, giving you a very pleasant, agreeable and cheerful disposition. It will bring good fortune into your life, and you will be loved and respected by all you come in contact with.  You have ability for music, or singing, and you love art, and everything beautiful or refined.  You would have success in such matters as give pleasure to others ; and you should always seek for very refined employments, and take up with those pursuits that minister to the happiness of others : not only to reach success in life, but also because your sunny influence will be beneficial to them.  The planet Venus rising gives one of the best dispositions.

**469.**  MARS rising at the time of your birth will give you plenty of *vim* and confidence in yourself, and you will never be short of what the world calls "pluck." You will be courageous, energetic, and, at times, somewhat consequential and inclined to assert yourself needlessly: so that you must avoid giving way to impulses and doing things rashly, also jumping to conclusions. You will rise in life by your own efforts, and can push yourself forward well enough when occasion demands; still you should try to conserve some of your energies, so as to reserve your force for the period when it may be more to your advantage to use it. In other words, always *think* before acting.

**470.** JUPITER rising at the time of your birth is very favourable for your success in life, promising you good fortune and bringing you what is termed "good luck." This will however, chiefly arise from a noble and generous disposition, and from the fact that you possess both benevolence and sympathy. Your buoyant, hopeful and inspiring nature will readily win the confidence of others, who will constantly wish you well. You will be a success socially and you need never fear any social undertaking provided hope does not fail you; the more hopeful you become, the more will you come under this benefic influence. You may create for yourself a splendid future.

**471.** SATURN rising at the time of your birth is not fortunate, so far as your worldly prosperity is concerned, as it indicates that the environment into which you were born was not the most favourable for progress or prosperity: you will have many obstacles to contend with, and your success depends more upon your own efforts than upon any help from outside. You are industrious and plodding, and you can be very persevering, and economical, also prudent and reserved. Your goal eventually will be Chastity and Justice: the more you cultivate moral virtues the nearer will you approach the true saturnine qualities, Meditation, Contemplation, Truth.

**472.** URANUS rising at the time of your birth (especially if in the first house) marks your nativity as one quite out of the common, for Uranus is the planet of originality, invention, and oft-times of genius also. It will however, at times, cause you to be considered peculiar, strange, and eccentric, inclining you to be abrupt and very unconventional. This position has much to do with your love of the mystical, and it also gives you the ability to study astrology and metaphysical subjects. You love everything that is wonderful and profound. Some romance will come into your life, or some very sudden and unlooked-for change, with either reversals of fortune, or unexpected gain or benefit.

**473.** NEPTUNE rising at the time of your birth, will affect your life in an uncommon mannner. You will be romantic and mediumistic, or psychically inclined. Some very strange experiences and also some remarkable episodes will occur in your life. It is only the very few who can in any way respond to the subtle, spiritual vibrations of the planet Neptune, and they are the souls that live the purest lives. You must be on your guard against hypnotic suggestion, and should be very choice in your associates and acquaintances. You will in all probability have some very remarkable dreams, which you should endeavour to remember. You will not escape being very mediumistic and hypersensitive at times.

## PERSONAL COLOURING.

**474.** The Moon occupying the sign ARIES at birth, your personal Aura will be tinged with a bright red, or scarlet and pink colouring. This will cause you to look upon the world through rosy spectacles, making your personal bias more telescopic than microscopic. Therefore you will have to make a few of your ideals more practical and stable than is your usual wont, for it will cause you to be venturesome, speculative, and at times a little too enthusiastic and over imaginative. It will tend to make you enterprising, high spirited and well able to organise, plan and scheme, so that you will never be at a loss through lacking to seize all the opportunities that will come in your way during your present life. For you will colour all things more or less RED, and this will give you hope and the energy required to carry out all your projects.

**475.** The Moon occupying the sign TAURUS at your birth will tinge your personal aura a pale blue which will make you look upon the world through blue coloured spectacles, and this will tend to accentuate the affectional part of your nature and give you that stability and affection which will cause you to look upon the world from a more hopeful and higher standpoint than would have been the case had you not this blue colouring in your aura. It will make you sociable, pleasant and fond of giving pleasure to others, stimulating your affections and thus making you more demonstrative, kinder-hearted and more tender and sympathetic than is the case with those who have not as much of the blue colour in their aura. Of course all the other influences in your nativity will tend to modify this considerably, and the aspects of Venus will accentuate it; therefore endeavour to discover the quality of Venus in your nativity and how it acts upon you from this standpoint.

**476.** The Moon occupying the sign GEMINI at your birth will bring a certain amount of the pale yellow ray into your aura, but as this is a dual sign, the colouring will depend very considerably upon the strength of your intellect, or the direction in which you are turning it, for while this yellow ray gives the elements of wisdom, at the same time the mind may be used for more or less selfish ends, and whenever there is a tendency to be undecided and not sufficiently concentrated, then there is a danger of there being orange patches, as it were, in the aura, instead of the clear and bright yellow which Gemini should give.  Now, much will depend upon Mercury and its aspects in your nativity as to how far this yellow ray will affect you, and I would strongly advise you to practice continuity and try to extricate your mind from the sensations which will come to you from the animal side of your nature, for the more you purify this yellow, the keener will be your intellect, especially for all matters of a refined nature.

**477.** The Moon occupying the sign CANCER at your birth, will tinge your personal aura with a pale violet ray, and as this will colour the whole of your life, you will look over the world through this violet ray of the spectrum, which will heighten your sensitiveness, and make you much more keenly alive to your surroundings and environment, affecting you very considerably when thrown in contact with other people, inasmuch as the violet ray tends to absorb the colours from the other planets and generally is affected considerably by the various planets in the nativity.  It will make you highly sensitive, very keen to feel all the impressions around you and the psychological conditions into which you will be thrown, especially if you study occult subjects, and give your mind to matters connected with the psychic world; you should live as purely as you can, if you would have this colour purified, for much depends upon your habits of life as to how far this influence will permeate the whole of your aura.

**478.** The Moon occupying the sign LEO at your birth will tinge your personal aura with the orange ray. This will give you much vitality and will greatly strengthen your health aura, for it will enable you to throw off disease quickly, and will in many ways give you that brightness, hope and joyousness which will enable you to look upon life from a far more cheerful standpoint than the majority are able to do. But you should remember that this will be chiefly owing to the fact that your vitality is strengthened considerably by this orange ray, therefore do not abuse its strength by giving way to pleasure which Leo has ever a tendency to lead one into. It will give you the ability to study art and music, and at times gives poetic tendenc es whenever the orange ray is sufficiently purified to enable it to blend with the other colours in the aura, as would be seen by the planetary positions in the nativity.

**479.** The Moon occupying the sign VIRGO at your birth will tinge your aura with a pale orange ray and cause you to become wiser the more that you absorb its colouring, for you will view the world chiefly from the standpoint of knowledge, and this will cause you to be somewhat critical and analytical, but the yellow ray will ever be stimulating you to discriminate, and the more you can use this faculty of discrimination, which the yellow ray gives you, the more you will be able to overcome the more or less animal tendencies into which we are all born. This is a purely human colouring and tends to make one more refined, with a desire to live more to the mental side of the nature than the animal, for the ray coming through Virgo, the sign of the Virgin, is that of purity, and those who are ready to wear the yellow robe are always those who have dis- criminated sufficiently so as to be able to view all things with equanimity without using the lower criticism.

**480.** The Moon occupying the sign LIBRA at your birth will tinge your personal aura with light sky-blue, making you compassionate, affectionate, sympathetic and generally kind hearted. At the same time you must be careful not to let other people's minds and conditions affect you too much, for those who have this colour in their aura have a tendency to be swayed by environment and psychic emanations. It will make you very refined and religiously inclined, tending to bring out all the finer qualities which belong to the planet Venus which this colour is directly under, therefore all artistic pursuits will tend to accentuate this portion of your aura and you will view the world generally from a more balanced standpoint than the majority. This ray will strengthen your powers of comparison, and the more balanced you become, the more will you lean towards the side of justice and tend to harmonise yourself under the Venus principle. Therefore try to discover as much as possible the strength and influence of the planet Venus in your nativity.

**481.** The Moon occupying the sign SCORPIO at your birth tinges your personal aura with a deep red, and this causes you to have a very strong personal aura which may be easily moved to passion, pride, or jealousy, and knowing that these weaknesses are coming to you through this red ray, you should try to change its colour from the deep heavy red to the finer and more rosy qualities which eventually lead to the spiritual red or crimson. Now, to do this, you should study your own nature thoroughly and use all the self-control which Scorpio usually gives. You will ever have a belief in the mystic side of things, but will also incline to be careful of yonr own interests, and if the other colours of your aura do not change the deep red into a brighter shade, there will be a danger of your becoming far too personal, for this accentuates everything connected with the personality.

**482.** The Moon occupying the sign SAGITTARIUS at birth, will colour your personal aura with the Indigo ray, and much will depend upon the influences coming from the other planets as to how far this indigo will be affected, for it is of a deeper and stronger colour than any other sign in which the Moon may be placed, therefore much will depend upon Jupiter's position as to how this influence will affect you, but if you overcome any tendency to rebel against the law and order of your being, the more you will be able to purify this colour and realise its spiritual influence. It will cause you to feel more or less all religious vibrations, and will put you in sympathy with everything to do with the religious side of life, and if this is not the case, you may know you have not brought yourself under the true Indigo ray which is chiefly governed by Jupiter. Your past lives have had much to do with your present conditions, therefore try never to rebel against circumstances, endeavouring to harmonise them.

**483.** The Moon occupying the sign CAPRICORN at your birth, will colour your aura with light green and tend to considerably accentuate the other colours in your aura. And through this you will clearly perceive the conditions that are around you, for this colour absorbs to some extent the red given off by the planet Mars, thus tending to purify you and cause you to lean more towards the ascetic life, and if you can refine this green, until it becomes like the fresh green of young trees, you will be able to cultivate all those enduring and refining qualities which are signified by the green colour. It will tend to make you fond of knowledge, to rise higher than the sphere in which you were born, for it generally makes one diplomatic, careful and prudent.

**484.** The Moon occupying the sign AQUARIUS at your birth, will tinge your personal aura with many colour; in fact, this is the only sign of the zodiac that may be said to represent the tartan, or the " coat of many colours." This is owing to the fact that it is merging out of the green into variegated colours in which all seem to be blended, and those who can respond to this very wonderful combination, may make their lives remarkably useful and beneficial. It gives that keen judgment of human nature which enables one to see the world from many standpoints, and if you can cultivate tolerance, and endeavour to live up to the sixth race principle, which is that of harmony and union, you will indeed have done much during the present life with the aura which surrounds you. But very few can respond to this remarkable colouring, and only those who are living to the human side of their nature can really respond to this vibration.

**485.** The Moon occupying the sign PISCES at your birth, will tinge your personality with a silvery grey colour which has more to do with the psychic world than the physical. It will make you very receptive therefore, and incline you to become either mediumistic, or so impressionable as to receive thoughts and feelings from the astral plane, which will considerably affect the whole of your life. Now, the purer you can live, the more refined will this colour become, and as it has some relation to the planet Neptune, much will depend upon the associations that you form, and the companions with whom you associate. Endeavour to live as much as possible in the higher side of your nature, as you have some very hopeful and kindly feelings, and your nature is generally sympathetic and very easily influenced by good surroundings. It will make you especially tender to all dumb animals, or those who are in pain or suffering, as this ray awakens the sympathetic side of the nature.

### GENERAL ASPECTS.

Under this same heading of Supplementary Paragraphs may be considered a matter that else might easily be overlooked, and that is, the consideration of planetary aspects other than those to the "ruler." A moment's reflection will show that if the system explained in this book were followed quite blindly, some very important influences might easily be omitted altogether.

Suppose, for instance, a nativity in which Mercury is the ruling planet. Filling in the Chart as described elsewhere we can see that such an aspect as Mars square Saturn would have no paragraph allotted to it, since neither Mars nor Saturn is ruler and no provision is made for other aspects.

It is quite true that in such a nativity, Mercury being ruler, the influence of ♂ □ ♄ would be very much obscured ; its influence would be almost negligible in comparison with what it would be in a nativity where either Mars or Saturn was ruler. Still, it would make itself felt to a certain extent.

It is at this portion of the Chart, then, that such an aspect should come in for consideration. Any *powerful* aspect, a square, opposition or conjunction, etc., between really significant planets should be entered under this head ; not more than two however, or three at the outside, as the reader is likely to be confused by a number of aspects. The " boldest " should be selected, and any other tending to confirm it or (should it so happen) neutralise it, added.*

These aspects need not necessarily be kept to this particular part of the delineation, in fact any of these Supplementary Paragraphs may be inserted wherever it appears desirable, — which will depend on circumstances, of course.

## PLANETS IN SIGNS.

In the same way any planet strongly placed, either as regards house or sign, may be taken as *S. P.*

Thus suppose in any nativity Mars is in Aries, and therefore essentially dignified. Then, even though Mars be not the ruler, and though it receive no aspect, still " The Influence of Mars " should find a place in the delineation ; for Mars in Aries is an influence that does not hide its light under a bushel. The same will hold good of any planet in its exaltation, *e.g.*, ♂ ♑, ♃ ♋, ♀ ♓. And likewise also of a planet angular; *e.g.*, ♂ in ♓ or ♋ in the 10th or 4th house will show out powerfully in the life.

Still, here, as elsewhere, no hard and fast rule will always avail. The student must ever rely upon the development of his own judgment.

---

* It would be absurd to take ♅ △ ♆, for instance, in most cases, since this aspect remains in force so long as to be found in the horoscopes of nearly all people born during a certain year. Not unless either planet is angular, or in some special way thrown into prominence, should such an aspect as this be included in the delineation. Similar remarks apply to aspects between ♄ and ♅, or ♃ and ♄.

# CHAPTER XXXIII.

## THE "POLARITIES."

IT has been remarked elsewhere that the "Polarities," as they are often termed, or in other words the combination or blending of the Solar and Lunar sign-positions, have been already given in an earlier volume of this series to which the reader was referred. But after the former part of this book was actually in type it was decided to include them, in a somewhat condensed form, in the present work; and that for two reasons. First, because it was thought desirable that this book should be quite self-contained, and secondly, because the "polarities" given in the earlier book are put in the third person instead of, as here, the second—which might cause inconvenience to those who wish to give a written delineation to friends.

The choice of this word may perhaps seem strange at first, but it is designed to convey the idea of the two 'poles' of man's nature represented by the terms Individuality and Personality; and it is the particular *mode* in which the man is thus 'polarised' that such a phrase as "the polarity of Sun in Aries and Moon in Taurus" is intended to express.

The proper place for the Polarity in a horoscope delineation is just after the Lunar Aspects in §3. The Solar positions and aspects indicate the individual powers and limitations, as do the Lunar positions and aspects the personal; the Polarity, then, in quite a general fashion describes the blending of the individual and the personal—that combination of character and disposition which may in a practical sense be termed the every-day man himself. It is a very important part of the horoscope, and may be looked upon as the 'minor focus' of the whole, just as the Summary is the 'major focus.' It should of course be remembered that the remarks here given are brief and cannot pretend to more than hint at the true powers of each combination or "polarity." The student should always strive to develop *his own* powers of blending two or more different influences; there is no other way to become an astrologer

## POLARITIES OF THE SUN IN ARIES.

**486.** Blending the influence of the Sun and Moon in the sign ARIES, it may be judged that you are a very independent and self-reliant character. You are endowed with much wit and brilliancy of thought, but you are inclined to view life from intellectual and idealistic standpoints, rather than from the practical, or emotional side. You are in danger of becoming self-centred and will thus run some risk of becoming intolerant and limited. You need not fear the expansion of your feelings, for you are apt to live rather too much in your head; and you thus induce such complaints as insomnia, neuralgia and headache. You should not worry or become over-anxious, or your mind will suffer. You can be clever, but are liable to over-reach yourself by being too independent and impulsive. Grief or worry would bring you danger of brain troubles or nervous exhaustion. When your blood is out of order it will show itself by eruptions upon the head or face.

**487.** Blending the individual and personal characteristics by synthesising the influence of ARIES-TAURUS in your nativity, it may be judged that you have excellent discriminative power and ability to judge the quality and conditions of things generally. You have the ability to study hygiene and should be successful in the search for the cause of disease in yourself and others. You have much determination of character when you wish to exercise it, but you have also a tendency to receptivity, or mediumship. You are fond of all practical sciences, for the ideal and the practical are fairly well blended. But of all things you love harmony best; and I judge that you are very sensitive to the least discord in the condition of your surroundings. As life advances you will become more concentrated, steady and determined.

**488.** Blending the individual and personal influence of ARIES-GEMINI in your nativity, it may be judged that you have a very intense and active temperament. You are both desirous and able to express your thoughts clearly and well, but there is a tendency for you to overdo things with your intense nature. Therefore it may be judged that you will be somewhat restless and exacting at times, this probably arising from your tendency to take upon yourself too many things at once. You have ability for art and some mechanical genius, but you should never strain or overtax the brain, or you will induce nervous and brain trouble which will arise more or less from nervous exhaustion. Learn to concentrate and finish one thing before starting another, and do not scatter your forces too much. You cannot be too practical and should cultivate the "every day" virtues, for this is a very idealistic combination.

**489.** Blending the individual and personal characteristics it will be seen that the active centres of your horoscope are ARIES-CANCER, from which it may be judged that you are very sensitive to inharmonious conditions, and especially those arising from other persons. Although you have a very clear reasoning mind you are apt to worry and become over anxious, particularly if financial conditions are not as satisfactory as you wish. You love science and all that pertains to the mind. You would command success in life as a writer, for you have splendid image-making faculty, retentive memory and logical ability. You will never be quite happy unless you are at the head of all that you undertake, and you desire to excel in everything you do. You will suffer in life through the magnetic conditions of others, therefore be very choice in your acquaintanceships.

**490.** Blending the individual and personal characteristics, the main centres of your horoscope are ARIES-LEO. This will give you a very keen and intuitive mind; both reason and intuition will seek to unite in you, and at times your thought will reach ahead of the race in which you are living. The combination of your individual and personal characteristics shows that you possess a very warm and sympathetic love nature, but you are rather sensitive to the feelings of others and cannot bear disapproval. If you could but live up to all that your nativity indicates, you would have a marvellous image-making faculty; so much so, that you could by practice visualise clearly and carry a mental picture of all that you had once seen. You have deep spiritual inclinations and can be very original in your ideas, but probably have not yet realised to the full all that your nature is capable of. Live always to your highest, and allow the intellect to draw you from the thraldom of the senses.

**491.** Blending the individual and personal characteristics, the chief centres of your horoscope are ARIES-VIRGO, from which it may be judged that you have a very discriminative and critical mind. You are capable of engaging in scientific thought and could study to advantage the exact sciences. You love order, system and method; this in reality springing from your clear, logical and reasoning brain. You can, however, be very sceptical and would require evidence in all things before you gave your willing belief; and this especially where religious matters are in any way concerned. You have the ability to teach others; also for literary pursuits, but should not engage in physical labour as you are best adapted for mental work, in which you could make great attainments, for you are persistent in all that you undertake in any direction.

**492.** Blending the individual and personal characteristics, the main feature of your horoscope is the ARIES-LIBRA combination, from which it may be judged that you are just and honourable. You desire to be equitable in all your undertakings, and should be able to help and counsel others; not so much from an intellectual standpoint as from your intuitional and reasoning power. You are not always quick to comprehend when ideas are first presented to you, but they come out very clearly and take their proper shape on reflection. You possess some originality of thought but are apt to be conventional where action is concerned. You are fond of home, and can be very conjugal and attached to domestic ties. It is essential that you should avoid all stimulants in order to preserve your intuitions, and allow your reason and comparison to act.

**493.** Blending the individual and personal characteristics, the main centres of your horoscope are ARIES-SCORPIO, in which the positive and the negative elements are well balanced and of the martial type, making you at times very high tempered, combative and determined. It will be to your interest not to allow yourself to be carried away by your feelings, or you will exhibit strong passions, and at times be in danger of fits of jealousy. Therefore you should never allow yourself to act upon impulse, but always think carefully beforehand. You can safely cultivate all your sympathies and allow kindness to take the place of irritation and resentment- Extremes in your case are dangerous and likely in the end to lead to disaster. Cultivate temperance and avoid all things that excite and stimulate the aggressive side of your nature.

**494.** Blending the individual and personal characteristics, the principal centres of your horoscope are ARIES-SAGITTARIUS, a combination that endows you with much activity of mind and body, thus making you liable to extremes, over-anxious and restless, which will eventually impair your health unless some restraint is exercised. You will be inclined to be hasty in action and also in speech, and should always endeavour to think before speaking or acting. Avoid hurry and excitement. You have some taste for music, and also for public speaking, but there will ever be that danger of going to extremes in all that you do; therefore seek to be more peaceful, calm and thoughtful, so that the innate rebellious and independent spirit may be guided instead of guiding you so much.

**495.** Blending the individual and personal characteristics, the main influence of your horoscope is ARIES-CAPRICORN, which makes you positive, active and determined. You have the ability to economise and make the most of your surroundings, and could if necessary live by your wits, for you have a prolific imagination full of ideas and schemes for success. You love to be appreciated and recognised, and will strive to attain fame, or at all events, good standing in society. You have keen political interests when aroused, and admire persons of intellectual ability and education. Avoid all extremes and do not become too exacting, or your nature will get warped. You have some ability for, or love of, music, but may lack the necessary patience to become skilful or very proficient. There is some liability to brain troubles if you strain your brain, or over-exert yourself mentally.

**496.** Blending the individual and personal characteristics, the major influence of your horoscope is ARIES-AQUARIUS, a combination that should make you a good judge of human nature and allow you to become quickly interested in strangers. You would make a splendid entertainer, for you have not much difficulty in pleasing others. You can not only adapt yourself to others, but can easily go out to them, understanding them in a way that few can. You will make many friends and acquaintances during life, and it may be judged that you would do well in connection with associations and public bodies. You will be interested in any work that is directly concerned with the helping and amelioration of the condition of the people, and could in some way originate and invent methods that would generally conduce to the welfare of others. There is a true mental intuition in you which will act potently if you avoid impulse.

**497.** Blending the individual and personal characteristics, there is a mixture of fire and water in the ARIES-PISCES combination, which will give you an inclination to study and gain knowledge of mysterious things. You will be interested in spiritualism, or psychical matters, but there is an innate restlessness in you which may prevent your getting at the truth of things during this life. You love details, and mechanical things ; are philanthropic and can be kind and sympathetic, but you are inclined to be dissatisfied with your life, for it may be judged that you will meet with many an obstacle and be inclined to worry more than is wise. You are likely to be too much affected by the conditions of others, and should therefore try to be more self-reliant; for while you love harmony it is necessary to remember that we can each, more or less, make it for ourselves.

## POLARITIES OF THE SUN IN TAURUS.

**498.** Blending the influence of the Sun in TAURUS and the Moon in ARIES representing your individual and personal character, it may be judged that you have the ability to begin and accomplish great undertakings, with some adaptation to mechanics, mathematics and things of a constructive nature generally. You must try not to be too exacting, not to demand too much of others, and if you make laws of life try to see that they are just. You are liable to go to extremes and are a little headstrong. You have also a certain amount of dignity, and a respect for education and knowledge of a practical kind. Your chief danger will be an inclination to be too stiff-necked and too much disposed to lay down the law. You are exceedingly conscientious, however, and very positive, and, what is more useful, open to reason and reflection. Your personal nature will often be restrained from within.

**499.** Blending the influence of the Sun in TAURUS and the Moon also in TAURUS, representing the individual and personal character, it appears from this combination that you are an exceedingly independent character, very hopeful and buoyant, with animation of thought, brilliancy and vivacity. You have excellent self-control in everything, but like to be within your own sphere and are not inclined to travel, or to take up with new enterprises. You have a fairly determined nature and a very strong character in most ways; and, other things being equal, are capable of making great attainments in life in the financial world, as also in other directions, and becoming a very useful member of society. You are not so much affected by the influences of others, but are desirous of living your own life in your own way, independently.

**500.** Blending the influence of the Sun in TAURUS and the Moon in GEMINI, representing your individual and personal characteristics, it may be judged that you are endowed with some artistic ability with a tendency towards, and an inclination for, scientific knowledge. You have also some mechanical ability. You love order and beauty, but have a somewhat restless nature, liking to rule and be at the head of things. You have great physical endurance and can accomplish more than many people around you; but you must avoid obstinacy, self-will and any inclination to dominate others. You have ability to take up almost any profession or department of business. You have also capacity for public speaking and, other things in your nativity agreeing, would succeed as an orator, having great linguistic ability.

**501.** Blending the influence of the Sun in TAURUS and the Moon in CANCER, representing the individual and personal character, it can be seen from this combination that you are exceedingly sensitive, economical, very persistent and active in your undertakings, whether of a business nature or otherwise, but somewhat anxious about monetary affairs. Your thoughts centre around your home and are generally engrossed in that sphere. You should ever seek to act from reason rather than from sensation or emotion, because you are endowed with a clear mind and ability to reason, provided you do not allow the sensational side of the nature to over-ride your mind. You have a very active imagination and should be careful of what mental energies you set up and the kind of romances you read and dramatic entertainments you attend. You are much attached to family and home life.

**502.** Blending the influence of the Sun in TAURUS and the Moon in LEO, representing your individual and personal character, it would appear that you will be subject to great extremes in your nature, and that you are liable to be very easily influenced by your associates. You may be frequently deceived and misled by placing confidence in undeserving persons, as you are somewhat over-confiding where feeling is concerned. You will require to subordinate your sensations and emotions to the reins of reason and self-control, or your life is in danger of being made very unhappy. You should try and realise that love lies in action more than expression, and that really the strongest and deepest love is apart from sensation and emotion altogether.

You have a powerful imagination and will at times have strange and vivid dreams.

**503.** Blending the influence of the Sun in TAURUS and the Moon in VIRGO, representing the individual and personal character, it can be seen from this combination that you have fine intuitions and discriminative power. You will be fond of learning and an admirer of literature, but have a good business mind notwithstanding. You will have somewhat acute judgment and will be accurate and precise in everything. If you cannot get exactness, you are apt to be impatient when it cannot be obtained in each and every direction. You are exceedingly

critical and are apt to criticise those whose capacities do not come up to
your own.   As a rule you will succeed in most things you undertake, but
you must try to be just and not be too intolerant of others.   It is as
natural for you to be critical and see defects and imperfections in others
as it is for some to see the good.

**504.**   Blending the influence of the Sun in TAURUS and the Moon in
LIBRA, representing the individual and personal character, it may
be judged that you have a very sincere, positive and decided character,
quick in decision and extremely determined when that decision is reached.
You will work not only by law but also by intuition.   This combination
is sometimes apt to give a little conceit and some severity of nature, with
a certain amount of separateness ; although you have much kindness and
love for those whom you regard, which will eventually lead to unity.
You sometimes make peculiar decisions which you expect others to abide
by.   You are somewhat jealous and have the capacity for either love or
hatred strongly marked, and do not readily forget an injury ; but you are
very conscientious and a law unto yourself.   You will be able to modify
many of the defects in your character by the combination of the positive
and negative Venus elements.

**505.**   Blending the influence of the Sun in TAURUS and the Moon in
SCORPIO, representing your individual and personal character,
you will see from this combination that you have a very strong passional
nature, one that needs restraint in several directions.   You are very
positive and determined, and at times somewhat lacking in forbearance.
You think a great deal of educational attainments in others, and have an
innate love of the mystical and psychic, and a desire to understand
something of the hidden mysteries of life.   You must try to avoid pride,
conventionality and selfishness, for these are the three special weaknesses
of this combination.   You can be exceedingly firm and have a strong
will, and if you choose to exercise it you can, so to speak, eradicate weeds
from the garden of your own personal character.   The Venusian and the
Martial influences are blended in your nativity, representing the higher
and lower natures.

**506.**   Blending the influence of the Sun in TAURUS and the Moon
in SAGITTARIUS, representing your individual and personal
character, you may learn from this combination that you are liable to go
to great extremes in anything you undertake, and will be very positive
and decided in all you do.   You are inclined to be hasty in speech and

too ready to act on impulse, or from the first thought that comes into your mind. You are altogether too quick in your impulses and if you gave way to anger would become very intolerant. Yours is a combination that needs a great amount of self-control. You should cultivate dignity and self-restraint. You have good executive ability and in many ways are very practical, but are somewhat too liable to be swept away by feeling, emotion and impulse.

**507.** Blending the influence of the Sun in TAURUS and the Moon in CAPRICORN, representing your individual and personal characteristics, it may be judged that you have a very positive, determined and independent nature, with ability to turn the mind to either general principles, business interests, music, or art. You will have a great love of wealth and grandeur, and will desire to obtain position and honour in public life; you have also a disposition to reason and plan well, and to be cautious before taking action. At the same time you are very independent, and yet curiously conventional. You have excellent ability for organising, a strong will, power of self-control, and ability to control others. You could remain quite unmoved even under exciting circumstances. This combination therefore fits you more for public than private life.

**508.** Blending the influence of the Sun in TAURUS and the Moon in AQUARIUS, representing the individual and personal character, it may be argued from this combination that you have a disposition and aptitude for pleasing people. You can easily form acquaintance with strangers, for you have a good deal of tact and confidence, and this will give you personally a great deal of pleasure. Other things being equal, —that is, your power to respond to the vibrations,—you are well adapted for a literary calling and have a strong inclination in that direction. You like to come into touch with the public and would prefer public work to that of a private kind, and will have unusually good ideas as to what would please or displease the public. You will make many friends and acquaintances, and be desirous of forming associations. The motive power behind you is deep feeling, and the power to express this will depend upon your own determination as affected by your feelings.

**509.** Blending the influence of the Sun in TAURUS and Moon in PISCES, representing your individual and personal character, it may be judged that you have a very practical, mechanical and ingenious mind, and a disposition to be constantly doing something. Your internal nature is restful, but your external nature is often more active, making you at times dissatisfied ; therefore, unless controlled, you will become combative and somewhat irritable.   You have an inclination to study and to reason, also the ability to make money and save it.   There is some latent desire to investigate phenomena not connected with this plane of matter, and having a receptive nature you like to be orderly and have a rule of life, as it were ; but you will sometimes feel there are many obstacles in your way and that everything is against you.   Try to be hopeful, and never give way to despondency or despair.

## POLARITIES OF THE SUN IN GEMINI.

**510.**   Blending the influence of the Sun in GEMINI and the Moon in ARIES, representing the individual and personal character, it is clear from this combination that you have a strong will and aspiring mind, a love of knowledge and a good understanding.   You are fond of books and can express thoughts contained therein.   You are somewhat ambitious and worldly, yet capable of making very high attainments. There is one danger to be avoided, and that is going to extremes.   You must not allow yourself to become too independent, and it would be as well for you to realise the necessity of sometimes bending to circumstances. You are somewhat disinclined for conventionality and do not like set rules and customs.   You have, however, the power to carry out most things you desire and the capacity for self-control if you wish to exercise it.

**511.**   Blending the influence of the Sun in GEMINI and the Moon in TAURUS, representing your individual and personal character, it may be judged that you are intelligent, far-seeing and sensible, with a determined and persistent character.   You are somewhat liable to be led by feeling and emotion, and therefore you should try to overcome the sensational side of your nature, which would tend to lead you away from reason.   You have an energetic, active nature, and desire to be at the head of things.   You have also a very strong love of Nature and a desire to study her workings.   You should have, through this combination, a full share of vitality and vigour.   You have ability for studying medicine and in some ways are a natural doctor, for hygienic methods and the study of the laws of health appeal to you strongly.   The more you can reason upon your sensations the more will you realise your inner and true nature.

**512.** Blending the influence of the Sun in GEMINI and the Moon also in GEMINI, representing your individual and personal character, it will be understood from this combination that you have an independent character, great clearness of thought, and that you are fairly well balanced. You must avoid any tendency to self-conceit or lack of sympathy with others, as you have a determination to carry out the inclination of your own mind, at times, regardless of the effect it may have on others. You are not easily turned from your own decisions but there is in you a certain duality, springing from the combination of Gemini with Gemini, which will sometimes make you want to do two things at a time. All things in connection with the literary world will attract you. You have a very clear mind capable of becoming illuminated, and possess quick perception and keen observation. Strive to learn to hold the balance between the objective and subjective, the material and the spiritual, the transitory and the eternal.

**513.** Blending the influence of the Sun in GEMINI and the Moon in CANCER, representing your individual and personal character, it may be judged that you are active, intelligent, economical, and anxious generally about business, family matters or home affairs. You are somewhat restless and inclined to seek sympathy from others, with a curious longing for an unknown something ; and the sympathies of others do not seem to meet or satisfy that longing. You have a great degree of sensitiveness to other people's conditions, thus making you liable to sense their feelings. You would succeed if you turned your mind to business matters, or matters to do with the home and domestic sphere. You will ever be receptive to the psychological conditions of others, but should endeavour to control your feelings and emotions, or you will find yourself becoming liable to too many moods and changes of opinion.

**514.** Blending the influence of the Sun in GEMINI and Moon in LEO, representing your individual and personal character, it would appear from this combination that you are somewhat lacking in energy and determination, especially in business directions. Thus you will not be so successful as you could be, probably owing to despondency and a feeling of inefficiency ; to counteract this, become as practical as you possibly can. You will have a tendency towards poetry and music, with a love of philosophical pursuits and a desire to study religious questions. You will also have the elements of a growing faith, with a belief in the supernatural, and will feel at times that some peculiar destiny or unseen force is hindering you in life. You will have a desire to reach out for love from the opposite sex and will be in danger in this direction unless very careful. You are sympathetic, kind-hearted, and have at times spiritual inclinations and aspirations, and some very high ideals.

**515.** Blending the influence of the Sun in GEMINI and Moon in VIRGO, representing your individual and personal character, it may be judged that you have a very studious and mathematical mind, being critical and analytical, and this will, in all probability, give you a desire to study Nature, anatomy, physiology and hygiene, or even chemistry and medicine. You have a keen love of beauty in form and nature : also a love of honour. You are very orderly and tidy, and neatness in your surroundings is essential to your comfort ; you are also very particular about keeping things in order when you once get them so. You have a very strong will and are somewhat difficult to please, being so extremely critical ; but you must try not to be too critical and irritable. You have a desire to investigate phenomena of a psychic nature.

**516.** Blending the influence of the Sun in GEMINI and Moon in Libra, representing your individual and personal character, this is a combination which shows that you have a peculiar spiritual tendency with a love of the occult and the unseen, also a very intuitive and far-seeing mind. You have great accuracy and quickness of decision and will appreciate the study of nature and philosophy. You have good imitative powers and these will enable you to hold your own in all departments of life, but you are more especially fitted for literary pursuits. You often come to your decisions quickly through intuition rather than reason, and have a wonderful appreciation of beauty, art, and everything of an ennobling character. You are liable to be affected by others, and it is essential that you associate with pure persons, if not, you will absorb much of their influence and perhaps be led to think that it is your own. Learn to distinquish between your own views and opinions and those of others.

**517.** Blending the influence of the Sun in GEMINI and Moon in SCORPIO, representing the individual and personal character, it may be judged that you are positive, determined and imitative, but are however able to conceal your disposition and keep it out of sight so that if you wished you could appear very different from what you really are. You are not very sensitive and if annoyed could be somewhat harsh. You could, however, rule in some public position. You are very determined and can use tact and subtlety if necessary to gain your desires.

You are somewhat inclined to argue, and have a very strong passional nature, yet you can use self control in this direction if you choose to do so. You are capable of very keen criticism and can sense the weakness of others.

**518.** Blending the influence of the Sun in GEMINI and the Moon in SAGITTARIUS, representing the individual and personal character, it would appear from this combination that you are far too active, both mentally and physically, also over-expressive, overdoing all things; indeed, if rest, calm and quiet are not at times enforced there will be serious danger to the life. You are inclined to be mentally although not physically combative, and there is some danger to the brain and a threatening of nerve trouble in this combination. You have some prophetic ability, and will at times " dream true " or have intuitions of some coming event. You are somewhat inclined to religious thought, with innate aspiration and some devotion. It would be well to impress upon yourself the necessity of always taking plenty of rest and repose.

**519.** Blending the influence of the Sun in GEMINI and the Moon in CAPRICORN, representing your individual and personal character, it is clear from this combination that you have a careful, practical and active mind, with considerable business ability. You are somewhat suspicious and distrustful, and will be subject to some disappointment unless you assiduously cultivate your intuitions. You love beauty, grandeur and eloquence, also elegance, and would be inclined to work very hard for a position of eminence and honour. You are qualified for a business life, much more so than for a domestic sphere. Honour is exceedingly dear to you, and in some ways you are very conventional. You are industrious, plodding and hard-working.

**520.** Blending the influence of the Sun in GEMINI and the Moon in AQUARIUS, representing the individual and personal character, it would appear from this combination that you will succeed well in any public sphere, having natural qualifications for dealing with the public. Your life will only be satisfied in its expression in some position where there is a great deal of activity, excitement and change. You are well fitted to take the head of things, or have others under you, and in partnerships or associations with others you would gain success. Other things being equal, you would do well in politics, oratory and medicine. You get on well with strangers and easily make friends.

**521.** Blending the influence of the Sun in GEMINI and the Moon in PISCES, representing the individual and personal character, it would seem that you have a very studious mind, but are somewhat too restless and anxious, which will tend to result in dissatisfaction. There is sometimes an inclination to feel that you are being opposed in your undertakings, and this causes an unsatisfied state of mind. It is necessary for you to have harmonious surroundings, and when you have subordinated your lower nature to the control of the will, the tendency will be towards study and research, enabling you to make great attainments. You will be somewhat drawn to mediumship, spiritualism and psychic phenomena. You should try to understand the difference between your Personality and Individuality.

## POLARITIES OF THE SUN IN CANCER.

**522.** Blending the influence of the Sun in CANCER and the Moon in ARIES, representing the individual and personal character, it may be judged that you have a very determined will and indomitable persistence in whatever you undertake, with a natural desire for supremacy, and capacity to lead and control in the mental world. There is a danger sometimes of going to extremes, with a difficulty to change, even under the dictates of reason. You will have an innate hatred of being controlled or even influenced by the mind or will of another, which will make you liable to many mistakes and losses through life. You will prefer to deal with general principles rather than with the minutiæ of daily life. The danger of this combination is that it gives a silent, stubborn persistency. Be careful to avoid extremes in work.

**523.** Blending the influence of the Sun in CANCER and the Moon in TAURUS, representing your individual and personal character, it would seem from this combination that you will be somewhat inclined to allow the sensational part of your nature to influence you too much. You have a great love of the sublime and grand in nature, but this combination renders you too liable to be psychologised by the mental and physical conditions of others, which does you grave injury. You must always cultivate in yourself positive self-control, and resist the power of other people's influence, realising that by will you can face the most unpleasant conditions with a determination to rise superior to them. As you are so liable to take on the conditions of others you should try to study yourself and become a graduate in the school of self-knowledge.

**524.** Blending the influence of the Sun in CANCER and the Moon in GEMINI, representing your individual and personal character, it may be judged that you have a great thirst for knowledge in all directions, allied to great activity and energy. You will either desire to enter into the sphere of art or to take up educational pursuits, and will have some inclination towards public life, either in speaking or writing. There is too much of duality, however, in this combination, giving a disposition to worry about small things ; the mind, nevertheless, is able to receive illumination indirectly as well as through education. Still, you should try also to realise the feeling and emotional side of your nature, as well as the intellectual, for a true understanding of yourself will be of great value to you. You have perhaps too keen a desire for knowledge of an intellectual kind.

**525.** Blending the influence of the Sun in CANCER and the Moon also in CANCER, representing the individual and personal character, it may be concluded from this combination that you have a clear, keen intellect, and that your intentions are also very reliable. You will prefer general principles to details. This combination needs all the educational help it can get, as with it you can enter upon almost any sphere of life you may desire. You are opposed to being subjected to the laws and rules of others, and can be very independent and self-sufficient. Yet you are very sensitive to the conditions and feelings of others, and at times inclined to be a little despondent. You will need to understand the laws of life, and should try to educate the sensational side of your nature.

**526.** Blending the influence of the Sun in CANCER and the Moon in LEO, representing the individual and personal character, it may be judged that you are far too receptive and sensitive to the condition of other minds and feelings ; so much so, that they affect your own considerably. You have strong feelings, and if you are considered unreliable it is because you are so sensitive to other people that they affect your will. In this combination you have really more desire for friendship, love, sociability, affection, ease and pleasure, than for hard mental work. You have a great deal of quiet power, and an intuitive understanding that does not come to you through the brain centres. You have a large heart and are capable of great devotion to those you love, and when you have turned your sensitiveness *inward* you will make great progress individually.

**527.** Blending the influence of the Sun in CANCER and the Moon in VIRGO, representing the individual and personal character, it may be judged that you have a keen, critical, discriminating nature in all matters to do with the emotions. You are somewhat changeable and curiously psychic. You have an inclination towards the study of anatomy and physiology, and you could take up literary work and become an author. You have a strong passional nature, and should be very careful to lead an absolutely pure life, otherwise you are liable to spoil your career. You should realise the law of use and abuse, and that the greatest good lies in the balance between the two extremes ; for though you have a good intellect, desire for pleasure is keen. You have a very keen critical sense, but do not allow it to cause you to become unsympathetic or separative.

**528.** Blending the influence of the Sun in CANCER and the Moon in LIBRA, representing the individual and personal character, this combination shows that you have a very fine intuition, and keen perception. You are domestic and social. If you live a pure life you will possess a fine well-balanced mind, with clear intuitions and prophetic insight, capable of perceiving not only present conditions but events yet to come. You could become a very fine idealistic writer, with keen perception in all matters relating either to the domestic or social life, but you will have to subjugate your passional nature so that the force, otherwise wasted, could be called into action for the use of the mind. You should seek to discipline your will and practise self-control.

**529.** Blending the influence of the Sun in CANCER and the Moon in SCORPIO, representing the individual and personal character, it may be judged that you are somewhat inclined to be conventional, but have great aptitude for public work and the power of making money. In many cases you may be very severe towards your opponents, and you do not readily forget an injury. You will have much self-control over your passional nature, a very determined will, much persuasive tact, and the ability to get your own way. You must avoid being too severe or vindictive, also try to overcome pride and jealousy. You are more especially fitted for an external and public life, although you will be interested in psychic and peculiar subjects, liking to see the interior of things generally.

**530.** Blending the influence of the Sun in CANCER and the Moon in SAGITTARIUS, representing the individual and personal character, it would appear from this combination that you have an over-energetic and active personal nature, good mechanical ability, great industry and energy, but too much activity for your individual stamina. You should be content to do only half of what you desire to do, otherwise you might induce trouble with your physical form, including disease of the digestive organs and stomachic affections generally. You have good intuitive ability, can often foresee coming events, and will occasionally have strange and peculiar dreams. You will be drawn to science and religion, and these two factors will find some expression in your life ; but unless you check your activity and seek repose you will greatly shorten your life. The personal conditions are such as to awaken the individual characteristics for the purpose of inner realisation.

**531.** Blending the influence of the Sun in CANCER and the Moon in CAPRICORN, representing your individual and personal characteristics, it may be judged that you have an idealistic nature, together with practical business tendencies. There will be some opposition between your inner nature and its outer workings, resulting in a peculiar feeling of uncertainty. You will try to produce the ideal conditions that you feel inwardly, in manifestation around you, and so are placed as it were between the external and the internal. You may be considered eccentric in some ways, as you are sometimes uncertain of what you are going to do yourself ; but if you cannot always express your thoughts to your own satisfaction, you would be very successful in any business enterprise you might engage in. This combination gives some musical ability, the sense of hearing being keen in you or easy to develop.

**532.** Blending the influence of the Sun in CANCER and the Moon in AQUARIUS, representing your individual and personal character, this combination indicates that you are very truthful, and dislike prevarication, but you also dislike being blamed and disapproved of. You are adapted for public work, particularly partnerships, societies and co-operation. You are cautious and do not readily give a decisive Yes or No, but usually take time to consider. You would not readily give a promise unless you intended to carry it out. You are likely to make many friends in life and would succeed very well in any business or work that brought you in touch with large bodies of people. You are disposed to self-justification, and ever desire to give satisfaction in any position in which you may be placed. You are determined, though cautious and careful in speech and action.

**533.** Blending the influence of the Sun in CANCER and the Moon in PISCES, representing the individual and personal character, it would appear from this combination that you have a bright, active mind, a keen sense of the inner meaning of words, and that you can readily understand the mind and thoughts of others. You have a keen sense of the fitness of things. You should always keep your mind active and never go day-dreaming or let yourself become mediumistic, hysterical or imaginative. You will be industrious and studious, having an immense hungering for knowledge. With mental activity you should always combine suitable enjoyment and diversion, so as to keep the system in good health. You will desire to embody your ideals practically, and will be very careful about details. You can easily sense and feel the mental conditions of others, but should not let this sympathetic and receptive side of your nature go to extremes.

## POLARITIES OF THE SUN IN LEO.

**534.** Blending the influence of the Sun in LEO and the Moon in ARIES, representing your individual and personal character, it may be judged that you will be apt to go to too great extremes in all things. If you believe a thing is right or wrong, you will be as immovable as it is possible to be : kind and non-combative, but persistent ; and if you engage in study, philosophy or business, you will carry it to the utmost extreme. If religious, your zeal will be unbounded ; therefore you must be careful to always maintain an equal balance between brain and heart, or brain trouble might ensue. It is well for you to listen to reason and subject your will to it, as you are over-tenacious and your extreme tenacity often forces you into positions and conditions you would rather not take up, but having determined to do so you will carry them through to the end.

**535.** Blending the influence of the Sun in LEO and the Moon in TAURUS, representing your individual and personal character, it is clear from this combination that you have good business intuitions, but you will greatly prefer the realm of the mind, and therefore mental philosophy will probably engage your attention. You will love to study nature in all its departments : especially human nature, mental and physical. You would, other things being equal, succeed well in the medical profession ; in any case you will love the study of hygiene and think very much about the laws of health. You have a strong love nature and are exceedingly determined.  You will be rather anxious to succeed in life, and if you are wise in regard to the restraint of sensation and emotion you should be successful.  This combination gives good health.

**536.**  Blending the influence of the Sun in LEO and the Moon in GEMINI, representing the individual and personal character, it will be apparent that you are very active and almost inclined to overdo your powers, either physically, mentally or emotionally.  All matters dealing with education will appeal to you and you have ability to take up almost any branch of it ; you are also fond of art, and have some constructive ability.  You like to have a law by which to work and this law to be absolute and undeviating.  You should be careful to restrain and guide your nature, ever having in view the usefulness of all that you do ; and remember that by taking care not to overstrain any part of your system you will be using your powers wisely and to the best advantage.

**537.**  Blending the influence of the Sun in LEO and Moon in CANCER, representing your individual and personal character, it may be judged that you have great sympathy and are very sensitive to the thoughts of those you love ; but there is a liability to go to extremes.  You are sometimes changeable in moods ; at one time buoyant and happy, and at others sad and depressed.  You are almost too sensitive, as you are liable to be wounded by a thoughtless word or look.  You have much business energy, and a clear, logical and scientific tendency of mind, with some qualifications for a literary life : but you will always have a great love and thoughtfulness for home and family, having a strong love-nature.

**538.**  Blending the influence of the Sun in LEO and the Moon also in LEO, representing the individual and personal character, it will be seen from this combination that you have a very independent, clear-minded and intuitive nature, which is not readily affected by the likes and dislikes of others.  You are capable of standing alone, going your own way and prosecuting your own aims and wishes, thereby making great attainments in life.  You are always able, so to speak, to understand your own feelings and mind apart from others.  There is only one danger, and that is that you may become rather too selfish and self-centred, shut up as it were within yourself.  You will be very intuitive and have a strong desire nature, and it would be as well for you to train that nature to seek the noblest things in life.  You will realise all that this combination means the more you allow yourself to EXPAND.

**539.** Blending the influence of the Sun in LEO and the Moon in VIRGO, representing your individual and personal character, this combination shows that you have a very strong desire for purity of condition and harmony of surroundings that is not always easy of attainment ; so that it will sometimes give you a restless, anxious, dissatisfied feeling, and critical tendencies. You are sometimes impetuous, but are well-disposed, although you are peculiarly sensitive in some small matters, having your own little idiosyncrasies. Your internal nature makes you critical on the plane of *thought*, but with the combination of Virgo it will give criticism in relation to words,—external things as well as internal. It will be difficult for you to realise that you should restrain your natural inclinations and use reason.

**540.** Blending the influence of the Sun in LEO and the Moon in LIBRA, representing your individual and personal character, it would appear from this combination that you could easily adapt yourself to literary and educational pursuits. You have great power of interior intuition, and if you lead a perfectly chaste life would be a natural prophet. Your perception and feeling about things almost amount to what would be called second-sight, but great purity of life would be necessary to allow your spiritual perception the right channel through which to act. You often come to decisions rapidly, yet at the same time are generally correct. You have strong feelings and a deep love nature, and are peculiarly receptive to the conditions of others. Be careful in the choice of friends and acquaintances, and especially also in marriage.

**541.** Blending the influence of the Sun in LEO and the Moon in SCORPIO, representing your individual and personal character, it may be judged that you have a very positive character, and though you have sympathetic tendencies through your Leo nature, yet your personal self will be rather proud, somewhat egotistical, and you will have a great love of external appearances : you will desire to appear well in the world's eyes. In this combination the internal nature of Leo cannot be very well expressed. A great deal depends upon your own attitude towards the world in general, and your own environment in particular as shown by the other planetary conditions. You will have much tact, and will be somewhat critical and sceptical.

**542.** Blending the influence of the Sun in LEO and the Moon in SAGITTARIUS, representing your individual and personal character, it would appear from this combination that you have a very restless, active and positive mind, with an undercurrent of dissatisfaction. You will desire an unknown something, you cannot yourself tell what. You have a love of, and inclination for, the study of science and religion, but this combination will only intensify all the activity of your Leo nature and make you an extremist. You will have a desire for law, order and rule, and an intolerance of any deviation from what you consider the right in your own mind. Try to have a time for work, a time for rest, and a time for recreation, or you will cause serious physical exhaustion from doing too much.

**543.** Blending the influence of the Sun in LEO and the Moon in CAPRICORN, representing your individual and personal character, this combination shows you to be well adapted for business or trading, and that you could take on a somewhat large concern, other things being equal. You will have considerable power to make money, and were it not for the Leo nature behind, would be rather selfish. You are inclined to judge others by yourself, and can sometimes be a little hard or exacting. You are a great lover of music and harmony, and a discordant note will cause you pain, You must try not to be too fastidious in a physical world that is not an ideal world. You will have much ambition and a great desire to be at the head of things, and could become an excellent manager on a large scale.

**544.** Blending the influence of the Sun in LEO and the Moon in AQUARIUS, representing your individual and personal character, it will be seen from this combination that you have a strong desire to mix with the public, can please people readily, form acquaintances easily, and have some inclination for travel. If the other conditions of your horoscope and the planetary influences agree, you are adapted for a public life, or some career which will enable you to travel. You must be in large cities where the multitude is. You would also be successful in forming associations, societies, institutions and organisations generally. Your sympathies are strong and will run out to the many. You have a strong liking for society, and would be unable to live comfortably in a quiet country-town or village.

**545.** Blending the influence of the Sun in LEO and the Moon in PISCES, representing your individual and personal character, it may be judged that you will have an inclination for study and research ; but the outcome depends very largely upon your own attitude, and unless other planetary conditions harmonise, this polarity will make you very restless, always giving you a desire to be moving, walking, or travelling. You are liable to some dissatisfaction in your family relations and are prone to worry over details and small matters, which is nevertheless quite foreign to your internal nature, for that is harmonious, idealistic and expansive. You have a keen desire, however, for knowledge, and if you took up any mechancial work you would be diligent, accurate and practical in it. You love detail, and if you can overcome the spirit of unrest which sometimes dwells in you, you may make great attainments in mental spheres.

## POLARITIES OF THE SUN IN VIRGO.

**546.** Blending the influence of the Sun in VIRGO and the Moon in ARIES, representing the individual and personal character, this combination indicates that you have a great deal of mental strength, firmness and stability, with a keen sense of order and harmony, which would be much disturbed by disorderly surroundings. There is, however, a tendency to be rather too intense and sometimes too obstinate ; and through your desire to be at the head of whatever you engage in, you will be inclined to overdo yourself, to live too much in your brain, and in that case would suffer much through your eyes, which would grow weak by over-use. You have great intellectual ability but are somewhat too stubborn for your own good. You have a keen sense of the ridiculous and can be very mirthful.

**547.** Blending the influence of the Sun in VIRGO and the Moon in TAURUS, representing the individual and personal character, this is a combination denoting that you have a fine intuitive mind and ability to take care both of body and brain. You act more or less from the higher intuitional faculties within you, which guide you in the affairs of life. You are keenly sensitive to the unspoken thoughts and intentions of others, have keen insight in relation to the future of business transactions, and will be rarely surprised at the result. You are rather too active for your own good, your energy somewhat exceeding your strength, but your keen perception of the laws of hygiene tends greatly to counteract this. You have good business ability and would be successful therein, this being a very practical and commonsense-giving combination.

**548.** Blending the influence of the Sun in VIRGO and the Moon in GEMINI, representing the individual and personal character, this combination shows that you have a very active mind and a great readiness of speech, yet there is a liability of your being too rapid in speech which might cause you to find utterance difficult. You are very artistic, with great love of the beautiful, much aptness for education and a desire for a public life. You have good constructive and mechanical ability. The difficulty of this combination is that you are too active and it inclines you to nervous difficulties in consequence. You have some duality in your composition although you have a very strong will. This is a somewhat peculiar combination, and inclines to over much attention to detail; endeavour to reach out to the principles underlying methods.

**549.** Blending the influence of the Sun in VIRGO and the Moon in CANCER, representing the individual and personal character, it may be judged that you have a great love of beauty, harmony and peaceful surroundings; indeed, these things are absolutely essential to your well-being. You are so exceedingly sensitive to inharmonious conditions that discordant surroundings would affect your health. You have an ideal in your imagination of a world that is very different from this, and often find it hard to endure your present environment. You are disposed to be economical and industrious, anxious concerning those dependent on you, and about laying by for the future. You are very kind to your own immediate circle,—indeed, somewhat exclusive; yet your love of family could be extended to a larger field.

**550.** Blending the influence of the Sun in VIRGO and the Moon in LEO, representing the individual and personal character, it would appear in this combination that you have a strong and deep love nature, which is apt to control all your thoughts and actions. Your love, though, can be turned from one object to another; for the fact is that you have imaged an ideal passion, which creates the desire for some unattainable condition. With this polarity you should try and realise that your emotional nature is somewhat unbalanced, and if you are not careful you may often jump from the frying pan into the fire where the heart is concerned. It would be well for you to make the most of life and develop conjugality as far as your nature will allow you, so that you may not be over balanced through your strong feelings.

**551.** Blending the influence of the Sun in VIRGO and the Moon also in VIRGO, representing your individual and personal character, this is a combination denoting that you have a great love of nature and harmony; and are innately pure and faithful. You are capable of being very devoted to another, and yet are a very independent and self-reliant character. You have an insight somewhat amounting to the gift of foreknowledge, and thoughts are apt to come to you in audible words, reporting a knowledge of what is to come. Your organic quality is very fine, and you must have surroundings of beauty, harmony and love in which to grow, as refinement is the very breath of life to you ; for you have an innate dread of anything coarse or common, or that which is not refined and pure. Tolerance and compassion for others should be your watchwords, or you may become too reclusive and unsympathetic.

**552.** Blending the influence of the Sun in VIRGO and the Moon in LIBRA, representing your individual and personal character, this combination indicates that you are remarkably perceptive, yet inclined to philosophical reasoning, independent in your thought, and that when the other planetary indications coincide you will be able to write on philosophical and scientific or occult subjects. You must beware of too great mental strain or activity or you may suffer with your eyes. You are very fond of reading, and quick and intuitive in learning. You have the ability to ' catch on ' to general ideas in regard to philosophy and science and to formulate and utilise them as your own. Everything will depend in your case upon the control you exercise over your emotions and sensations. This combination shows extremes between the inner and the outer nature.

**553.** Blending the influence of the Sun in VIRGO and the Moon in SCORPIO, representing your individual and personal character, it may be judged that you are somewhat inclined to be conventional, imitative, etc., but you will be persistent in your own chosen course of life. You must guard against selfishness and an inclination to be some-what careless of the feelings of those around you. You incline to social life, but really prefer the society of your own sex. You are somewhat quick-tempered, and do not readily forgive. This combination, however, gives you that positive nature likely to bring you success in the outer world. It is of the utmost importance to you to have a thorough education and the mind well trained and disciplined. As you are so imitative it would be well for you to be careful in your choice of companions. There is a very strong psychic element in your combination which can only be advantageously developed by cultivating the mind.

**554.** Blending the influence of the Sun in VIRGO and the Moon in SAGITTARIUS, representing the individual and personal character, it is apparent from this combination that you have an exceedingly active organisation both physically and mentally ; in fact you are somewhat too intense. You concentrate all the powers of your body and mind upon whatever you desire to do, and often push it to an extreme far beyond reason. You have a great love for work and are extremely executive ; inaction would be death to you. You would make a good teacher, especially if you restrained your impulses and did not jump to conclusions. You have a desire for religious and scientific thought, and a leaning towards the study of hygiene and mental and moral philosophy. You must be careful not to speak too hastily or sharply, for when you give way to impulse you are apt to go to extremes.

**555.** Blending the influence of the Sun in VIRGO and the Moon in CAPRICORN, representing the individual and personal character, this combination shows that you have considerable business ability, with decided musical inclinations. You have a practical mind, are fond of activity, business, society, music, and public entertainments generally. You are somewhat independent and rather opposed to restraint or control. You are more inclined for public than for private life, yet would take a pride in the possession of a stately home. Public recognition and honour in the world's eyes mean much to you. You like to be proficient in what you do, yet are perhaps more inclined to generalise than to go into details. You will like to be at the head of things generally.

**556.** Blending the influence of the Sun in VIRGO and the Moon in AQUARIUS, representing the individual and personal character, this is a combination denoting that you will have a great love of society, order, mental and physical harmony, etc. You have superior tact and the ability to adapt yourself to others, and therefore you will not have much difficulty in pleasing people. In a business of a constructive character, or in some musical or artistic pursuit, you would be very efficient and almost sure to succeed. You are very active physically and mentally, your intellect is clear and bright, and you have the ability to control the persons with whom you associate. You have a fair love of home, a wide range of business ability, and are more suited for city than for country life.

**557.** Blending the influence of the Sun in VIRGO and the Moon in PISCES, representing the individual and personal character, this combination indicates that you have a practical business mind, good constructive ability, a great deal of industry and adaptation to literary pursuits. You have a desire to obtain and utilise knowledge in many ways. You are somewhat restless, however, and have a love of variety, therefore it may be judged that there is some desire for travel. You will love power and personal respect and will be remarkably sensitive to blame. You have a very high ideal of the love life, and should be very careful in the choice of a partner. You are somewhat drawn to  ychic and peculiar phenomena, and desire to investigate the occult.

## POLARITIES OF THE SUN IN LIBRA.

**558.** Blending the influence of the Sun in LIBRA and the Moon in ARIES, representing the individual and personal character, it may be judged that you have a strong will and great powers of self-control under all circumstances, with ability to conceal thoughts feelings and emotions. You have also power to control others, and can put great intensity into your speech. You would be firm and reliable in all conditions and positions. This combination increases the mental powers and somewhat illuminates them. You have great perception, together with reason, and can reflect as well as observe. As you can so greatly influence and even psychologise others, you will need to cultivate the moral nature, kindness and sympathy.

**559.** Blending the influence of the Sun in LIBRA and the Moon in TAURUS, representing your individual and personal character, this combination denotes that you will be quiet and harmonious, yet persistent in business, with good continuity, carefulness, patience and perseverance. You are very tenacious in your undertakings generally, particularly in whatever you judge to be right. You are very sensitive and susceptible to the influence of others, also very intuitive internally ; yet with this combination you will show great ability for philosophy and science. You must be careful to realise yourself apart from others and control over-sensitiveness. You have a great love of hygiene and interest in hygienic conditions, which will be a useful field of study for you. You have a fairly strong will, and some ability for medical work.

**560.** Blending the influence of the Sun in LIBRA and the Moon in GEMINI, representing the individual and personal character, it is manifest that you have an active, restless mind, well adapted to shine in all intellectual and educational spheres. You have high aspirations, with some taste for the fine arts, also constructive power and mathematical ability. In some ways you are an encyclopædia of knowledge, but must guard against extremes, as you are restless and inclined to take too much out of yourself. You have high ideals and aspirations; ability to come before the public as a teacher, and could succeed as a writer, other planetary indications agreeing. You have some duality or indecision in your nature which you should try to overcome.

**561.** Blending the influence of the Sun in LIBRA and the Moon in CANCER, representing your individual and personal character, it may be judged that you have an ambitious and a very sensitive nature, and incline to worry yourself unnecessarily at times. You have much continuity and will not be anxious to change your pursuits frequently. You will have an inclination to embark in business pursuits and would meet with fair success therein. You will always be anxious for the welfare of those you love, and your intuitions and perceptions will be very good when turned to domestic uses. You will be eager to come before the public, and there is some prospect of success in this direction, but avoid worry and sensitiveness about small matters. You must live a pure life or you may suffer physically, especially from the lungs.

**562.** Blending the influence of the Sun in LIBRA and the Moon in LEO, representing the individual and personal character, it would appear from this combination that you have very strong feelings and a very active love nature. You have a great love of spiritual things, and at times have a vivid presentment of truth almost amounting to inward vision. You are guided by the influence of the unseen and by your intuition. It is hard for you to understand this somewhat prosaic world, for your interior nature opens out into an ideal world where Love is lord. But you must also keep the intellectual faculties active, thus making yourself more useful and of greater service to others; because it needs the intellect to explain and expound these inner realities to others. Discipline your emotions; you will not feel the less because you control them.

**563.** Blending the influence of the Sun in LIBRA and the Moon in VIRGO, representing the individual and personal character, this is a combination which gives you a very active and critical mind, quick in perception, and loving music and art generally. You have strong feelings and sensations, and need to bring this side of your nature under the control of the reason. You are intuitive, but need the balance of reason. You will have very good success in business pursuits, especially where buying and selling could be effected quickly. You will need to live a very pure life in order to gain the greatest success, as by dominating sensation and the lower nature you will have splendid intuition and inner guidance.

**564.** Blending the influence of the Sun in LIBRA and the Moon in LIBRA, representing the individual and personal character, this combination indicates that you are remarkably perceptive and have great balance and harmony in your nature, so that there is little likelihood of your being influenced and controlled by others. You will have a clear, bright intellect and practical business qualities. You are not, however, inclined to seek society, for you can grow within a circle of your own selfhood, being somewhat self-centred. You are very sensitive to existing conditions and considerably gifted mentally, especially where the higher type of mental activity is concerned. You should be successful in most things you undertake, being very courteous, affable, polite and agreeable.

**565.** Blending the influence of the Sun in LIBRA and the Moon in SCORPIO, representing your individual and personal character, it may be judged that you will be somewhat ambitious yet desirous of pleasing others, though rather perhaps from a love of approbation than otherwise. You will incline to the materialistic sciences and will be rather combative, somewhat selfish, high tempered, yet tolerably quick in overcoming anger. You love mystical and occult subjects, and have intense mental curiosity, which can seldom find its full and perfect satisfaction. There is some amount of discord between your inner and outer nature, and at times a sense of dissatisfaction with yourself and the conditions around you. You are particularly sensitive to atmospheric and psychic surroundings. You dislike to be subjected to the will of others.

**566.** Blending the influence of the Sun in LIBRA and the Moon in SAGITTARIUS, representing your individual and personal character, it would seem that you have a somewhat peculiar nature, being very active and excitable, and too much excitement is disastrous to this polarity. Ethics, as well as education, will be necessary to overcome the faults of this influence, and your eventual success in life will depend very largely upon whether you allow the calm, balanced Libra nature to dominate the impetuosity and excitability of Sagittarius. It will be absolutely necessary for you to have a little quiet time each day in which you can concentrate and draw in your outgoing activities, so that you may be of real use both to yourself and others.

**567.** Blending the influence of the Sun in LIBRA and the Moon in CAPRICORN, representing your individual and personal character, it may be presumed from this combination that you have good, clear general ideas in most directions, are largely governed by intuition, and have the ability to be successful in almost any pursuit. You have strong feelings of sympathy and kindness, and could develop great musical talent. The whole tendency of your nature will be towards mental rather than physical pleasures, and while you are well adapted for a commercial career there is no special business or profession for which you have any marked propensity. You have a great love of purity and chastity, and a great sense of the fitness of things ; the ideality of Libra being well balanced by the practicalness of Capricorn. You will have good insight into business ; perception and reflection being well balanced.

**568.** Blending the influence of the Sun in LIBRA and the Moon in AQUARIUS, representing the individual and personal character, it may be judged that you have great power to read character at sight, and if other planetary conditions permit, you will make remarkable developments in this direction. You can if you wish determine the thoughts of others and sometimes even the words they are about to utter. You have fine constructive power, but at the same time you are very approbative. All intellectual pursuits will be good in your case ; and with a good education you would make a good teacher and make high attainments. You will try to please and serve the public in every way possible, and could if you desired readily make friends with strangers. You are well adapted to come into contact with the many, this combination giving you the necessary mental ability to feel the minds of others.

**569.** Blending the influence of the Sun in LIBRA and the Moon in PISCES, representing your individual and personal character, this combination shows that you have a great aptitude for the acquisition of knowledge and are very industrious in all directions, though at times rather restless in character. You must beware of giving way to despondency, which however will only come about when your forces are exhausted ; and you should try to remember that this physical life is meant to be appreciated,—even the good things of the world. Try to realise that the world is always full of opportunities for sunshine and happiness and that every dark cloud has its silver lining. Cultivate hopefulness, and realise that knowledge has to be used and given forth to the world and that this is the only use of its acquisition. Cultivate a due amount of mental positiveness.

## POLARITIES OF THE SUN IN SCORPIO.

**570.** Blending the influence of the Sun in SCORPIO and the Moon in ARIES, representing your individual and personal characte, this is a combination denoting that you are inclined to be rather too hard a d positive, with a tendency to go to great extremes in anger, having too much physical and mental combativeness. You are somewhat jealous, and you need when in any employment to be where you can control others by your will. However, provided you can keep your will under the control of reason, you would be capable of holding responsible positions. You will be disposed to gratify your feelings sometimes, utterly regardless of the consequences. Your feelings and passions are very strong, and you need to cultivate to the full all your reason in order to govern your personality. For this combination, the golden rule of doing as one would be done by should be strictly adhered to.

**571.** Blending the influence of the Sun in SCORPIO and the Moon in TAURUS, representing the individual and personal character, there is no doubt that you are very fond of the study of nature, and love order, rhythm, dancing, music, and all that makes for harmony. Other things being equal this position gives the ability and the intuition fitting you for the study of medicine. You have a studious and somewhat intellectual mind. This polarity tends to bring the Scorpio nature into submission to law and custom. You dislike to be blamed and greatly desire those you love to approve of you. You have a large amount of conjugality and the capacity to love very strongly and deeply. You are very fixed and determined when your mind is made up. You will be anxious to provide for the welfare of those to whom you are attached, and will be careful and thoughtful about the feelings of others.

**572.** Blending the influence of the Sun in SCORPIO and the Moon in GEMINI, representing your individual and personal character, it may be said that you have a great love of art and science and are an admirer of mental ability and oratorical power in others. You love to teach, and aspire towards high attainments in education. You would be unlikely to follow any system of thought which was unpopular, and would be very circumspect in your external life and habits. You are somewhat proud and dignified, and would dislike hard physical labour or any condition of life in which ease and a good social position were not concomitants. You love elegance and grandeur, and desire to rise in life; for which purpose you will probably put forth both energy and industry to bring about better conditions.

**573.** Blending the influence of the Sun in SCORPIO and the Moon in CANCER, representing your individual and personal character, this combination shows that you have a clear, logical mind and a great desire for harmony, especially in domestic life. You have a great desire for sympathy and love from the opposite sex, but it will be necessary for you to control sensationalism and let reason have full sway over passion and emotion. You must beware of jealousy and of being too easily misled by others. You are extremely sensitive, and where feeling and sensation are concerned do not use enough discrimination. You have, to some extent, a feeling of dependence upon others,—especially with regard to sympathy, and need to study the characters of those whom you meet, lest you suffer through mis-placed confidence.

**574.** Blending the influence of the Sun in SCORPIO and the Moon in LEO, representing your individual and personal character, it may be judged that you have a very ardent and intense nature, and are liable to be almost wholly governed by and act from the feelings and emotions, which are very intense. It is absolutely necessary for anyone having this polarity to understand thoroughly the law of their being, and you should try and always live as pure a life as possible, so that your future health and happiness may not be jeopardised. You have the ability to heal others and could study medicine, but to be successful it is necessary for you to be careful in diet, to abstain from all stimulants and narcotics, and to avoid all passion and excitement, or the heart's action may be impaired. This combination gives that intense inner feeling which always makes for strong character.

**575.** Blending the influence of the Sun in SCORPIO and the Moon in VIRGO, representing your individual and personal character, it may be said that you are endowed with much activity, positiveness and criticism. You have a great love of reading, and a tendency towards literary pursuits. You will never like to be in a subordinate position, but always desire to be where you can exercise control. You must beware of fault-finding, and a disposition at times to be rather unfeeling and hard. You have some passion when roused and should be careful to restrain anger, for if you habitually give way to it you may render yourself liable to asthmatic affections. You are fairly self-possessed, have a practical and clear mind, and may make excellent use of the critical faculty if you will train yourself to recognise the good as well as the imperfect in things and people.

**576.** Blending the influence of the Sun in SCORPIO and the Moon in LIBRA, representing the individual and personal character, this combination indicates that you have an inner penetration, with an inclination to doubt, scan and interrogate the future, which will develop your intuition and sometimes, when the other planetary influences are favourable, favour clairvoyant vision. You have a tendency to blend reason with intuition, which promotes dignity of character, with some nobility of feeling and disposition. You have business perception and a predisposition to succeed therein. You have also some literary ability and love of science, and fairly good judgment. Your perceptive power is very keen, and you have the ability to take on both physical and metaphysical forms of thought, predisposing to success in life. Therefore this is on the whole a good combination.

**577.** Blending the influence of the Sun in SCORPIO and the Moon in SCORPIO, representing your individual and personal character, it is manifest that you will be very firm, disposed to independence and self-reliance, standing alone in the world and seeking few intimate friends. You are somewhat materialistic in thought and feeling, and seldom get beyond the realm of the five senses, but you are very clear and logical in practical things. Subjects of business, government, and those concerning education interest you. You are somewhat conventional, inclined to venerate and support established institutions, and have little inclination to take advice from others or be led by them. You have a certain amount of pride and dignity, and some self-sufficiency, great powers of criticism and analysis together with a strong will. Cultivate sympathy.

**578.** Blending the influence of the Sun in SCORPIO and the Moon in SAGITTARIUS, representing your individual and personal character, it may be judged that you love law and order, but are inclined at times to be sarcastic and cutting in language, being liable to speak out what first comes into your mind, without regard of consequences. You will like public life, but you must beware of being too hasty and reckless. Much self-control and culture are necessary to bring your very intense nature into subjection. One of the greatest troubles arising from this combination will be jealousy, and you may suffer greatly if you allow jealous thoughts to dominate you. Never suffer yourself to become reckless, but try to think first and act after, or you may under a momentary impulse, do something which you will regret all your life.

**579.** Blending the influence of the Sun in SCORPIO and the Moon in CAPRICORN, representing your individual and personal character, it is manifest that you have a nature well suited to govern and organise, plan and arrange. You have a great love of grandeur, display, etc., and like to have the richest and best of everything, and would prefer to patronise only the most expensive and aristocratic places whenever opportunity and circumstances allow. You are inclined to be rather conventional and desire to follow out rigidly set rules and customs. You are very ambitious and desire to gain honour and fame in the world, and you prefer a public to a domestic sphere and would be inclined to study hard to become proficient in whatever you undertake, and thus are likely to be successful in business plans or enterprises.

**580.** Blending the influence of the Sun in SCORPIO and the Moon in AQUARIUS, representing the individual and personal character, one would judge that you are very conservative, and will be attracted by public gatherings and theatres, especially those patronised by the wealthy and aristocratic classes. You are a good judge of human nature and are adapted to serve the public in some form or other. You have great regard for public opinion, indeed, you value external appearances almost too much. You are active in mind and practical generally. You are faithful in service and can adapt yourself to business life, but will be in danger of overdoing things by reason of your desire to excel everyone else in display. You have ability to read character, and a curious knowledge of human nature is innate with you.

**581.** Blending the influence of the Sun in SCORPIO and the Moon in PISCES, representing your individual and personal character, it may be judged that you have a studious nature, yet you are somewhat restless, and take too much anxiety and thought about your success in life. You will in all probability have great veneration for people of high educational and literary attainments, as you have the desire and ability for acquiring such attainments. You will be much drawn towards mediumistic and psychic phenomena, and have great desire to know something about the unseen side of life. You have some duality in you, and should beware of despondency, depression, worry and anxiety, and try to cultivate a hopeful and cheerful state of mind. The personal tendency is towards indecision and depression, whilst the individual is towards pride and dignity, which will pull up the lower ; the whole blend, however, is psychic.

## POLARITIES OF THE SUN IN SAGITTARIUS.

**582.** Blending the influence of the Sun in SAGITTARIUS and the Moon in ARIES, representing your individual and personal character, it appears from this combination that you have great will power and mental energy, and are very determined. You should never be in too much hurry, but take time to do things. Try to be more thoughtful and rather less active. You will have to learn to overcome your activity and excitability. Work is good for you in moderation, but there is a limit to bodily endurance, and this combination is one that requires you to take care of your personal self ; if you do not, you will suffer greatly from nervous difficulties and headaches. You have good mentality, and if you abstain from over-exertion will be successful in life.

**583.** Blending the influence of the Sun in SAGITTARIUS and the Moon in TAURUS, representing the individual and personal character, it may be judged that you are very thoughtful, kind and sympathetic, and have a great desire to help those who are suffering. You have a natural inclination towards hygienic habits, and will be inclined to study and practise the laws of health, either as nurse or doctor. You are almost inclined to go to extremes when your sympathies are powerfully excited. You will be very sensitive ; peculiarly so, and would rather not meet strangers or many people. You do not care for the public or public places, therefore you will not be anxious to form new acquaintances. You love Nature and have a taste for natural science in all its departments. You are in many ways prophetic, and have a generous nature.

**584.** Blending the influence of the Sun in SAGITTARIUS and the Moon in GEMINI, representing the individual and personal character, this is a combination denoting that you have a great love of order and beauty, also much educational and artistic ability. You have musical gifts and may, if you make any effort, succeed in becoming proficient in this direction. There is one point concerning which a warning should be given, and that is your intense and excessive activity ; for this will, if not kept in check, cause nervous exhaustion. You are more adapted for mental rather than physical pursuits, and any business of an intellectual nature you could do well at, or any work connected with literature. You have much duality in your nature and will always feel yourself wanting to do two things at a time. Seek rest and recuperation, or you will suffer from nervous and neuralgic troubles.

**585.** Blending the influence of the Sun in SAGITTARIUS and the Moon in CANCER, representing your individual and personal character, it will appear from this combination that you have a very economical and industrious nature, with a great love of family, so that you will always be anxious about your dear ones, and will like to feel that you have a little money laid by " for a rainy day." Be careful in your circle of acquaintances, and in dealing with the opposite sex, as their influence is likely to prove a strong one in your life, and if you were to form an unhappy or unworthy alliance your whole nature would be blighted. Study the *character* of people, and do not fall in love with the *form*. You are likely to cling tenaciously to the object of your love, somewhat careless of consequences.

**586.** Blending the influence of the Sun in SAGITTARIUS and the Moon in LEO, representing your individual and personal character, it may be judged that you have a strongly active emotional nature, and are capable of very deep and ardent feeling. You have some psychic gifts, and could become very mediumistic. You will have at times curious and remarkable dreams and visions, and in these you have much faith and belief. You have the power to sense coming changes of a public nature, as you feel the condition of the public mind, as well as the minds of your friends and acquaintances. You are disposed always to act from your feelings, and your activities are mainly of the inner or heart nature. You are very kind and noble-hearted, and sympathetic, but rather too sensitive at times ; a cross word or look affects your heart greatly. You will act and speak from the heart, being moved by your impulses rather than by thought.

**587.** Blending the influence of the Sun in SAGITTARIUS and the Moon in VIRGO, representing your individual and personal character, this combination shows that you are fond of harmony and take great interest in and are devoted to music, and you could become successful in the musical profession. You are very discriminative and are capable of studying mathematics, mechanics, and also the fine arts. You have refined tastes, some prophetic power, and can often foretell coming events. You should never combat or argue, as it injures the higher side of the nature and prevents that peace and harmony which is the soul's atmosphere for growth.  Do not be too critical.  Always seek to be hopeful and cheerful and never allow yourself to worry.

**588.** Blending the influence of the Sun in SAGITTARIUS and the Moon in LIBRA, representing your individual and personal character, the indications are that you have fine intuition and perception, and ability to quickly weigh everything in the balance of reason.  You can be cool, quiet, yet prompt and active both mentally and physically.  You have a fine business mind, and adaptability for thought, education and science You are mentally very independent.  Your perceptions are accurate and your judgment generally correct, especially where perception is one of the faculties in making your decision.  This is a good combination, giving intuition and reason, and ability to decide with accuracy.  You have the capacity to attain wisdom.

**589.** Blending the influence of the Sun in SAGITTARIUS and the Moon in SCORPIO, representing your individual and personal character, one would judge that you have a positive, determined character, much pride, and a tendency towards conventionality.  You must be careful in your speech, and avoid using hard and sarcastic language.  You will succeed well at any physical employment, for you have much personal ability, but you rather lack judgment and reliability.  You have a somewhat sharp temper at times and like to argue, are strong and impetuous, but as with many others your "bark is worse than your bite."  You will need to exercise care in your choice of associates as they are liable to lead you astray.  It will be well for you to carefully consider this point.

**590.** Blending the influence of the Sun in SAGITTARIUS and also the Moon in SAGITTARIUS, representing your individual and personal character, it may be judged that you have a well-balanced nature, both mentally and physically, and are free and independent.  You will incline to be very liberal, rather careless, yet withal prompt and industrious. You have a generous nature, taking it all through, a clear and decisive mind, and are but little affected by surroundings or associates.  You have a faithful nature, patient and persevering.  You have an excellent business mind, and are thorough ; though more adapted for general principles than the minutiae of things.  You will at some period of your life be drawn towards science and religion.

**591.** Blending the influence of the Sun in SAGITTARIUS and the Moon in CAPRICORN, representing your individual and personal character, this is a combination showing an excellent business mind, fertile and executive and abounding with plans and schemes. You are practical and thorough, but more inclined for business than social or domestic life, as the business element is very strong in you: you will make all things bend to that. You have a quick ear for, and probably a great love of, music, which if developed would amount to almost a passion. You will love the beautiful and grand, and things must be on a large scale for you.

If you turn your attention to art you will do fairly well, but I think that business will be more likely to absorb your mind.

**592.** Blending the influence of the Sun in SAGITTARIUS and the Moon in AQUARIUS, representing the individual and personal character, this combination denotes that you have keen, active, and alert perceptions and are well adapted to enter into any business pursuit, for you can readily and quickly form pleasant and profitable acquaintances. You would have much success financially by selling commodities, and can on the whole be fairly fortunate at money making. You must, however, endeavour to live a very pure life, or you are liable to spoil your intuitions and consequently come to grief through misplaced confidence. You will not feel satisfied with domestic life, but will yearn for a sphere of public activity. All business work attracts you greatly, and you have the capacity to form large associations and great undertakings.

**593.** Blending the influence of the Sun in SAGITTARIUS and the Moon in PISCES, representing your individual and personal character, it may be judged that you will be very anxious and careful in whatever direction your mind may turn. You are studious and love books, and have also some constructive and mechanical skill. You are very faithful and industrious, but inclined at times to be fretful and worry, are hard-working and persevering, and not inclined for many changes. You will love the quiet of the country, and will not desire a public life or be eager to come before the masses. What you do, you will do well and thoroughly, and you can attend to details. You are not particularly self-confident, and are rather inclined to under-estimate your abilities. You would do well to cultivate concentration and continuity.

POLARITIES OF THE SUN IN CAPRICORN.

**594.** Blending the influence of the Sun in CAPRICORN and the Moon in ARIES, representing your individual and personal character, one would judge you to have a very active brain, full of ideas and plans.

and a practical and very persistent mind which will enable you to carry these ideas into daily practice. You have a great deal of pride in your composition, with very high ideals and aspirations. You generally feel your own ideas are right, and are at times inclined to force them into operation. You have large ideas of intellectual attainments and some egotism. You have not so much capacity for detail, but have an unbending will, which will carry you into any position you desire to occupy eventually.

**595.** Blending the influence of the Sun in CAPRICORN and the Moon in TAURUS, representing your individual and personal character, it is manifest that you have a very powerful and persistent mind and are somewhat combative, with a strong idea of and adherence to social customs generally. You have strong and ardent feelings : also a desire and adaptation for the study of hygiene and the laws of health. You are very sensitive, and the mental conditions of others affect you. You have innately some spiritual feelings, and if you cultivate your mental nature will be earnest and zealous in all educational pursuits, with plans for the elevation of humanity. You desire to be at the head of things and are well adapted to lead and manage.

**596.** Blending the influence of the Sun in CAPRICORN and the Moon in GEMINI, representing your individual and personal character, it will be seen from this combination that you have a very studious and intensely active mind, with a love of science, literature, oratory and the fine arts. You are a good organiser and excel in laying out plans. You have ideals at times far beyond your power and ability to execute, and will thus be fond of building castles in the air. You will be a good speaker if you cultivate the faculty. You will in many ways prefer a public life to a domestic one. You could be successful in a literary profession, or a position where the intellect could be used, and are not so well adapted for physical labour. You have a keen sense of the value of words.

**597.** Blending the influence of the Sun in CAPRICORN and the Moon in CANCER, representing your individual and personal character, this combination shows you to have a great love for and aspiration towards beauty, elegance, ideality and grandeur. You love accomplishments and people who are clever. You are exceedingly careful and cautious ; at times too much so. You are very prudent and careful where money is concerned. You must not carry economy too far however, and should avoid becoming too anxious about monetary affairs. You are very sensitive and feel all that goes on around you. You will always desire power and to be at the head of things. You have ability to attend to details of things and can always do so without effort. You will as time goes on tend to balance the feelings and the intellect.

**598.** Blending the influence of the Sun in CAPRICORN and the Moon in LEO, representing the individual and personal character, it would appear that you have a strong love nature and must be guarded where the feelings, appetites and passions are concerned. You are very spontaneous in action and ardent and zealous in all you do. You will not care about control or self-restraint as you have an exceedingly strong will, but if you submit your will to your reason and intuition you will become a bright, kind and philanthropic person, zealous in good works and plans for the protection of the poor and needy. You are apt to be too liberal with your money for your own good. You have some adaptability for the religious element, and would desire to understand spiritual things. Love and honour will be the principal pivots upon which your fate will turn, and between love and duty your most vivid experiences will be realised.

**599.** Blending the influence of the Sun in CAPRICORN and the Moon in VIRGO, representing your individual and personal character, it may be said that this is a splendid blend of the earthy triplicity, and will cause you to develop a very thoughtful and discriminative mind, and will give you the ability to follow either literary or scientific pursuits easily. Your mind will be orderly, logical and both analytical and critical, and there are few branches of study that your mind could not enter. It would enable you to hold responsible positions with tact and diplomacy, and also gives you that business type of brain which can fully understand value, and estimate objects at their true worth. All other things being favourable in your nativity this is an excellent polarity for expression, as it will tend to make you thorough and painstaking, although at times you may be lacking in initiative. You could study the laws of hygiene to advantage, and providing you do not become too retiring and reserved you would be able to realise the true meaning of service.

**600.** Blending the influence of the Sun in CAPRICORN and the Moon in LIBRA, representing your individual and personal character, it may be said that you are keen and intuitive, with ability for literary pursuits. You would be thorough in business, for your plans and arrangements are carefully thought out so as to make them successful. You have a good deal of foresight, and a desire for metaphysical and spiritual things, and if you cultivate thought control and live purely you could often discern events beforehand.    You have some power for public speaking, and usually turn your energies and faculties into the interior; so that in speech you would sometimes say much that you were not aware you knew until the moment of utterance.    Your perception is very good and you have reason and coolness as well.    This is a blending of Saturn and Venus, indicating chastity, refinement and sincerity.

**601.**    Blending the influence of the Sun in CAPRICORN and the Moon in SCORPIO, representing your individual and personal character, it may safely be said that you are very reserved, positive and dignified, and have far more inclination to write your thoughts than to speak them. You are rather inclined to be conventional and apt to develop a commanding positiveness, and sometimes may be a little too exacting where others are concerned.    You will somewhat dislike manual labour but have great ability to manage, arrange, plan and organise.    You must beware of anger, for when you are once offended with people you will not desire to have anything more to do with them; yet you will not let them see it, as you can conceal your feelings.    The Saturnine and Martial influences in your horoscope are very pronounced, making you an exceptionally strong character.

**602.**    Blending the influence of the Sun in CAPRICORN and the Moon in SAGITTARIUS, representing your individual and personal character, one would judge that you will have great mental activity and be inclined to act on the first thought or impulse without maturing it, or making it practical; consequently you will be liable to business failure and mistakes.    You will have through your individuality a great love of grandeur and elegance, and are therefore liable to be somewhat too extravagant and to lack due appreciation of money.    You are over lavish where finance is concerned, and will have to be careful in this respect or you may become poor.    Industry and economy should be cultivated, or you are not likely to be successful as you might otherwise be.    You love oratory, and expression through speech.    You will also be fond of nature generally.    Both contraction and expansion are denoted by this combination.

**603.**    Blending the influence of the Sun in CAPRICORN and the Moon also in CAPRICORN, representing the individual and personal character, you are shown to have a clear active brain, much concentration of purpose, and ability to carry forward all you begin. You are not adapted for physical labour, but to general business and planning, management, etc. You love order, harmony and elegance, and desire to maintain such surroundings if possible. You are very independent and not disposed to be confidential or take on intimate friendships. For the most part you turn all your attention to business and educational subjects. You have excellent powers of self-control. You are not over partial to family life, still you will make it very harmonious. Do not allow yourself to become too distant or frigid towards strangers or inferiors.

**604.** Blending the influence of the Sun in CAPRICORN and the Moon in AQUARIUS, representing your individual and personal character, it may be judged that you have a very active, restless nature, with some pride. You could not be satisfied with a lonely or quiet country life, you must come before the multitude if possible. You have ability for all mercantile pursuits, and some taste for political economy. You will like home and family : yet the world almost better. It would be well for you not to engage in any form of partnership unless you could join with those who are in a good position, for a public or more external life would be much more congenial to you than a quiet one. You have ability to form accurate judgments of human nature, and could make some very high attainments if you gave yourself up to a study of your own inner nature.

**605.** Blending the influence of the Sun in CAPRICORN and the Moon in PISCES, representing your individual and personal character, you are shown to have a persevering and industrious nature, which makes you studious and economical, loving science and general knowledge ; but you may be at times almost over-anxious and too inclined to worry. You are not much given to generalisations, but are good in all matters of detail, and you will always be wanting to know the use of the thing. You have mechanical ability, and would make a good superintendent or overseer in any kind of business. You are very independent in character and action, yet sympathetic and kindly, and you will seek to be thorough in what you undertake.

## POLARITIES OF THE SUN IN AQUARIUS.

**606.** Blending the influence of the Sun in AQUARIUS and the Moon in ARIES, representing the individual and personal character, it may be judged that you have a very decided character, disposed to push any issue to great extremes. You have a quick nature but are sometimes inclined to be a little stubborn and obstinate. You do not always disclose your plans and decisions to others, and like to hold full control in any sphere in which you may be engaged. You have great self-control in almost any department of life, and like to have your own sphere of business occupation. You will always be disposed to lead, and will have to guard against being too extreme in your views. You are very keen, quick-witted and shrewd, and have a very strong will; disliking to be led or controlled in any way by others. It would do you no harm if you endeavoured to become a little more plastic.

**607.** Blending the influence of the Sun in AQUARIUS and the Moon in TAURUS, representing the individual and personal character, this combination denotes that you will be very sensitive to physical and mental surroundings and that you have the ability to judge both human and animal nature. You will be very active and practical in business matters, and exceedingly industrious in all the minutiae of life. You can be very loving and harmonious as a companion and would make a very good partner. You are inclined to be over-anxious about those under your care, having all their needs at heart. You will have a curious love of farming, and similar pursuits, having a passion for Nature in all her moods, so that you are quite happy when alone. This combination gives a great deal of determination and brings faithful friends who will befriend you financially if necessary.

**608.** Blending the influence of the Sun in AQUARIUS and the Moon in GEMINI, representing your individual and personal character, it may be seen that you have a love of intellectual pursuits and an inclination for public speaking. You will be very interested in all educational matters, will have great constructive power, and will desire to excel in whatever you undertake. If you study you will be quick to understand and comprehend, but you are not likely to adopt too confining a profession. You are orderly, and greatly love refinement. You are somewhat inclined to be nervous, and should be careful not to overdo yourself either physically or mentally. There is some duality in your personal nature and also some restlessness, but you are capable of much mental advancement.

**609.** Blending the influence of the Sun in AQUARIUS and the Moon in CANCER, representing your individual and personal character, one would judge that you will be very industrious and economical, carrying your economy into very small things and that you will love knowledge and desire to acquire it.   You will be very susceptible to the diseases and conditions of others all through life.   You have some self-control, yet none too much.   You should therefore be careful in your choice of associates or friends, as you are liable to be led very much by what they do, although you have a fair amount of firmness in other respects ; you will have to remember that you are very susceptible to the psychological influence of others.   Learn to discriminate between your conditions and those of others.

**610.**   Blending the influence of the Sun in AQUARIUS and the Moon in LEO, representing your individual and personal character, I find from this combination that you have great kindness and sympathy and a very devotional nature.   You can love very deeply, almost worshipping the one to whom you have given your affections.   You are so tender-hearted that you are not so well adapted for the rush and bustle of town and city life as for the quieter and more natural life of the country.   You will be easily led by associates, and so susceptible to psychological control and so liable to extremes that you will be wise to try to realise the character of others ere you give your heart to them, and so save yourself much suffering.   You are liable at times to go to extremes in your views, and to be deceived and misled in love affairs.   Be guarded where your affections are concerned.

**611.**   Blending the influence of the Sun in AQUARIUS and the Moon in VIRGO, representing your individual and personal character, one would judge you to have a clear logical mind, very sensitive in regard to the opinions of others.   You have some pride, yet have personal ability, and will be very capable of rendering service to another.   You have some constructive ability and a natural adaptation to trade.   This combination will give you a tendency towards the study of anatomy, physiology and hygiene, and makes for carefulness in diet and habits. You like and are disposed to have critical reasoning and clear points in your arguments.   You are economical and saving, yet have large ideality. You will be inclined to the practical things of life and like to turn all things to use, and are, in the main, a utilitarian.

**612.**   Blending the influence of the Sun in AQUARIUS and the Moon in LIBRA, representing your individual and personal character, it may be said that you will be very keen, quick, active and discriminative, weighing up and balancing the qualities and conditions of things. Your perceptive ability is very good, though you are almost wholly governed by intuition, and thus will exhibit superior mental qualities. You will have ability and foresight in any pursuit in which you are engaged. You have some occult ability or spiritualistic power and often get visions of things to come. You are a good judge of character and can read the disposition of others at a glance, and form quick and accurate judgments. This combination should give you some musical ability.

**613.** Blending the influence of the Sun in AQUARIUS and the Moon in SCORPIO, representing your individual and personal character, I find from this combination that you will be very keen, quick, and adapted for trade and the driving of bargains. You have some selfishness and a strong, quick temper when aroused, and will be inclined to remember any injury received. This is a combination in which one needs to discipline the lower nature, as the personality is very strong, inclining you at times to be too hard and unaccommodating. You will be fairly successful in literary, educational or public life if other planetary conditions are favourable. You are somewhat conservative, and yet have a desire for the uncommon, the wonderful and the extraordinary. You will desire to know what lies at the back of things, and will be disposed to try and ferret out Nature's secrets.

**614.** Blending the influence of the Sun in AQUARIUS and the Moon in SAGITTARIUS, representing the individual and personal character, this combination shows that you will be very active in physical and mental pursuits, and that you must be careful always to speak and act with due thought and preparation, as it may be judged that you are somewhat too hasty and premature for your own good, and a little liable to go to extremes in all you undertake. You have fine constructive power and some artistic ability, also a keen conventional sense of right and wrong. You will be industrious in whatever you may engage in, very neat and orderly, with a strong love for home, family, and friends, etc.

**615.** Blending the influence of the Sun in AQUARIUS and the Moon in CAPRICORN, representing the individual and personal character, it may be judged from this combination that you are very active, nervous and excitable, both in brain and body. You have some inclination and adaptability for public life, also for mercantile pursuits, but you prefer a business on a large scale and large transactions generally. You would never be happy unless in some sphere affording opportunity and great activity for brain and body. You have a strong idea of honour and some class prejudice. You must try to control your excitability or your health will suffer. You will love music, and if it were not that this combination rarely makes a student, you could become clever and proficient therein.

**616.** Blending the influence of the Sun in AQUARIUS and the Moon also in AQUARIUS, representing the individual and personal character, this combination denotes that you have an active, prompt and positive mind, with clear perception as to a definite business or public career. You will be independent, frank and expressive, and display great discretion and wisdom. This is a good combination as it harmonises and intensifies the Aquarius nature, making you a good representative of this sign of the zodiac. You will be apt to tie yourself to one pursuit in life, and will desire some kind of work that brings you into touch with the public, and this you will be well fitted for. You have a capacity for business, and you will be a good judge of human nature, in short a good character reader. You will readily take to strangers, who will soon become friendly to you. This is one of the most refined of the 144 polarities and shews much ideality and artistic ability.

**617.** Blending the influence of the Sun in AQUARIUS and the Moon in PISCES, representing the individual and personal character, it may be seen from this combination that you are endowed with great perseverance, activity, and carefulness, but are adapted for mental rather than physical labour. You will love books and incline very much to all literary pursuits. You have a very high sense of honour and integrity of character, yet you will be over anxious concerning your career and success in life. You will be successful in the minutiæ and details of life, for you have formed a habit of economy. Be careful not to overdo yourself or you may suffer from nervous debility. Try and be as hopeful as you can and do not let despondency or worry overtake you, for there is some tendency in this direction.

## POLARITIES OF THE SUN IN PISCES.

**618.** In blending the influence of the Sun in PISCES and the Moon in ARIES, representing your individual and personal character, one would judge that you have an active and restless but very determined nature, and that you can be very self-willed, headstrong, positive and difficult to govern. You have one of those natures that cannot be forced, but is more easily led than driven. You have a very great love of knowledge and much strength, self-reliance and self-control, yet there is a danger of your doing too much and weakening your nervous system. You should try to train yourself to habits of moderation, remembering that you are in a physical vehicle and that you must use this vehicle well or you will find it fail you at the time you most need its services.

**619.** Blending the influence of the Sun in PISCES and the Moon in TAURUS, representing your individual and personal character, this combination shows that you are very quiet and easy-going externally, although very active internally. You have strong desires and feelings and an intense love of Nature, with an interest in medicine and the natural sciences. This combination intensifies the honour and integrity of the Pisces nature, making you considerate of the welfare of others as well as your own. You are subject to melancholy, but are persistent in all you take up. Always try to become as hopeful and joyous as possible. You are very sensitive to the conditions of others and often isolate yourself from them, preferring a quiet occupation where you can remain alone.

**620.** Blending the influence of the Sun in PISCES and the Moon in GEMINI, representing your individual and personal character, it may be judged that you have a great love of knowledge and a disposition to usefulness. This combination intensifies the activities of the Pisces nature, and sometimes increases the anxious worrying nature Pisces gives. You should ever strive to look on the bright side of things and encourage the cultivation of a joyous, happy spirit, remembering that it is weak and unworthy to indulge in forebodings and morbid imaginings, and thus you may counteract the somewhat unfavourabte tendency of this polarity. Always keep the bright side of life before you if you would avoid brain troubles and nervous restlessness. It would be well for you to get as many educational advantages as possible, for you are able to profit by these.

**621.** Blending the influence of the Sun in PISCES and the Moon in CANCER, representing the individual and personal character, it is manifest that you will have a very sensitive nature and a disposition to excessive industry that may lead you at times to overtax your strength. You have a great love of knowledge and wish to see educational institutions prosper ; you will also be greatly interested in the education of the family and improvement of home interests. You are more inclined to generalise than to enter into details. You have a strong and persistent will, and are disinclined to work under others, preferring an occupation of your own. You will be very sensitive to the influence of others, and should be careful in your choice of friends and acquaintances.

**622.** Blending the influence of the Sun in PISCES and the Moon in LEO, representing your individual and personal character, this combination indicates that you have a high ideal of unity, love and harmony and a strong disposition towards union with another. If this union is realised it will give you a disposition to work for the elevation of humanity and the common good in all ways. You are very industrious and studious, loving the occult and all metaphysic subjects. You have a strong desire nature and a wish to understand the mysteries of nature, but your mind will not work well except your heart be satisfied. You must be careful in the bestowal of friendship, being liable to mistakes. You are kind-hearted and confiding, and would suffer very keenly where your heart is concerned, so that any disappointment or misplaced confidence would have a most ruinous effect upon your life generally.

**623.** Blending the influence of the Sun in PISCES and the Moon in VIRGO, representing the individual and personal character, one would judge that you have a clear, logical mind, inclined to the study of the natural sciences, and (other planetary conditions being favourable) you would be well adapted for the study of medicine. You have a love of mathematical problems and all abstruse subjects. At times you will be rather positive and exacting and somewhat difficult to please ; so that you should always be careful to guard against becoming in any way selfish. You should try to make your surroundings as happy and harmonious as possible. You have some intuition and at times inspirational power. You also have artistic and musical ability.

**624.** Blending the influence of the Sun in PISCES and the Moon in LIBRA, representing the individual and personal character, you may be said to have a very deep, quiet, earnest, thoughtful nature, with carefulness and foresight for everything, being somewhat indisposed to take counsel from any. You have a large interior life, and an inclination for poetical subjects and literary pursuits. You will love all new ideas and experiments, and are a somewhat close student, being persistent in thought, reason and investigation. You are much inclined to philosophy bordering on spirituality, and are better adapted for business than domestic life. You must avoid nervous excitement, overdoing, and the worrying of the mind, or reaction would bring you melancholic or desponding endencies.  Cultivate all the hope and compassion you can, and strive for " balance " in all things

**625.** Blending the influence of the Sun in PISCES and the Moon in SCORPIO, representing the individual and personal character, it may be judged that you are very quiet, thoughtful, and often inclined to be a little reserved.  You are at times, according to circumstances, conventional, with some pride in personal more than individual ability. You love great attainments and education, but this combination is not altogether a harmonious one, and you must be careful not to become too hard or positive, for the dregs of the lower self are strong, and it will be somewhat difficult for you to overcome the lower nature as the personality is very powerful and strong.  You will be inclined towards a public life and are a supporter of established systems and public institutions.  It is everything to you to live a pure and chaste life, as you are very receptive to the magnetic sphere of others ; being receptive to evil as well as good when the personality is uppermost.

**626.** Blending the influence of the Sun in PISCES and the Moon in SAGITTARIUS, representing the individual and personal character, it would appear that you have a very active, restless nature, tending to extremes in many directions.  You are internally excitable and irritable with no great power of self-control.  You have some constructive ability, a tendency towards art and an inclination to investigate religious thought. You are excessively industrious and are perhaps too active and thus liable to impair your health.  You should try to be thoughtful and careful in speech and action and avoid extremes in all things.  When prompted to rebel against irksome restrictions remember that it is necessary to respect the rights and feelings of others.  Be careful of your health. Try to keep your own secrets.

**627.** Blending the influence of the Sun in PISCES and the Moon in CAPRICORN, representing the individual and personal character, it may be judged from this combination that you have decided business talent and ability, with an inclination to speculate and enter into more business schemes than you can bring to maturity.  You are disposed to deal with general principles rather than details and minutiae, and may sometimes fall short in many of your undertakings on account of this disposition.  Other planetary conditions conducing, you will have great love for music and the fine arts.  Superintendence and management are your forte.  You will be disinclined to work with your hands, and are better fitted for mental pursuits. Your love of knowledge lies in a business direction.

**628.** Blending the influence of the Sun in PISCES and the Moon in AQUARIUS, representing your individual and personal character, this combination indicates that you have a cheerful, happy mind, and can form acquaintances and make friends quickly. You would soon turn strangers into friends. You are adapted for all kinds of mercantile pursuits, and indeed for any work that brings you before the public. You are fond of travel and change, and will not care about the confinement of a home. You are not so much inclined to study as to mix with, and be of service to humanity at large. You will never be happy away from public life, and you are well adapted for it. Your hopes, desires and wishes are very strong, and you often see them gratified.

**629.** Blending the influence of the Sun in PISCES and the Moon also in PISCES, representing your individual and personal character, it may be judged that you are very active and persevering in all your undertakings, but lack confidence in your powers and abilities. You will be shut up, as it were, within your own sphere of thought, and may at times become morbid and anxious. You have a love of intellectual pursuits and some inclination towards public speaking. You can ,attend to details and all you undertake will be done thoroughly. Guard against melancholy and never let yourself despond or your health will suffer. If you follow this advice it will add much to the comfort of life, for this polarity generally gives old age.

# CHAPTER XXXIV.

## A Few Explanatory Paragraphs.

With this chapter the student who procures this book chiefly for his own instruction need have little to do, but it will be of use to those beginners who have friends for whom they are anxious to "do a horoscope" and who will be glad of a few hints founded on a wide experience. The paragraphs in this chapter are what may be termed "extras," and form no part of the actual horoscope itself; yet they may be of considerable service where a written delineation is being sent to a distant friend, as they will help to put the reader in a receptive frame of mind and may also perhaps anticipate and answer certain criticisms which might possibly arise in his or her mind, and which even if unuttered would militate against the general effect of the delineation.

For convenience of reference these paragraphs are all given the general number *630*, with an added letter for purposes of distinction.

They will explain themselves almost, but it may be said that *Aa, Ab* are alternative "Introductions," either of which may be used at pleasure, while *Ac* may wisely be added if the particular person for whom the delineation is intended is of a particularly Mercurial or critical temperament; *B* need only be used if the birth-time, and hence the ascendant, is uncertain. Paragraph *C* sometimes comes in usefully to clear up the frequently met with confusion as to what "under a sign" means, and if used should precede *D*, which latter it is almost essential to include in most cases, as only the vaguest ideas on this subject prevail amongst the general public. Paragraph *E* will very rarely be necessary, as it is far wiser to omit all reference to any minor aspects as a rule; but sometimes a semi-square or sesquiquadrate is the only aspect to, say, the Sun and in such case this paragraph is useful, since the general delineation of an "adverse" aspect is worded rather too strongly to be applicable without some qualification.

Paragraphs *Fa* and *Fb* are frequently useful and in some cases can hardly be dispensed with. Suppose for instance we have a horoscope with $☽ \ast ♂$, $☍ ♄$.  How is the consecutive reading of paragraphs *233* and *240* likely to strike the reader ; will he not say that what is given with one hand is taken away with the other ?  In such cases paragraph *Fa* meets the difficulty, and in a similar way *Fb* can be used where such a position occurs as, say, Aries rising and Moon in Capricorn,—where everything said about the rising sign appears to be contradicted by the description of the Moon's influence.  In this way the reader is led to analyse his own nature ; and it is by no means certain that a judgment in which the astrologer attempted to combine the two influences and gave a joint description would prove half so useful in the end as drawing attention to the two warring influences and describing each separately.

Paragraph *Ga* is for use in the comparatively rare cases when the significant luminary is " void of course " (*v.c.*) ; that is, passes out of the sign it is in before making any aspect to another planet.  The Sun is the marriage significator in a woman's horoscope, and the Moon in a man's ; but any judgment on this matter must not omit consideration of the seventh house, for if there is a planet therein it is better as a rule to take that as the significator, as described in Chapter XXIV.  If the Sun or Moon or other marriage significator is in one of the " double-bodied " signs (*d.b.*), paragraph *Gb* may be used, but a little tact is necessary in deciding this, as it is not always wise to hint at the possibility of a second marriage.

With regard to paragraph *H*, similar remarks will apply to what has just been said about *E*, and the student should exercise his own discretion as to when it is advisable to employ it.  Mercury retrograde is very much less eager and alert, far less keenly mental, than when moving swiftly ; similarly too in the case of Venus and Mars ; the slower planets are perhaps somewhat less severely handicapped by retrogradation.

The next paragraph, *I*, is sometimes useful to introduce before the Summary, especially in delineations intended for readers unfamiliar with the distinction between the two words generally recognised in Theosophical literature, and in these books.

Paragraphs *J* and *K* are General Summaries, respectively *adverse* and *benefic*, and may precede the pars. from Ch. XXXI.

Paragraphs *L*, *M* and *N*, are introductory of the FUTURE PROSPECTS, dealt with in the next chapter, and explain themselves.  The same may be said of *O*, *P* and *Q*, which are general summaries of the Future Prospects, respectively *adverse* (*a*) *benefic* (*b*) and *mixed* (*m*), the latter being for use in those cases where the aspects are various and of a contradictory nature, so that as a whole they can neither be termed fortunate nor unfortunate.

Paragraph *R* explains itself. It adds finish to a delineation, and is worth the trouble of copying out.

The last paragraph in this chapter, *S*, may be found useful in certain cases, either as supplementary or alternative to *Ac*. It may come either at the beginning or end of a delineation, and is distinctly useful in the case of the sceptical friend who is apt to parry every home truth with " Oh yes, but you knew that about me all along, so that's no proof of Astrology." It relieves the writer from any personal responsibility for the opinions quoted on the one hand and on the other will perhaps gain a more respectful hearing for the delineation, from a certain type of person, than if it were supposed to be the work of 'only an amateur.' Though to be sure we are all but "amateurs" at present, and will be for many years to come, where Astrology is concerned.

---

## INTRODUCTION.—(*a*).

**630.** Students of Astrology are convinced that it is a perfect system **A a** of study whereby an understanding of the Delphic oracle *Man, know Thyself* may be obtained. But the stars only *incline*, they do not compel, and it is the attitude of the soul that decides the result, for :—

> One ship drives east and another drives west
> With the self-same winds that blow.
> 'Tis the set of the sails
> And not the gales
> Which tells the way to go.

> Like the winds of the sea are the ways of fate
> As we voyage along through life :
> 'Tis the set of the soul
> That decides its goal
> And not the calm or the strife.

That is, by knowledge, and will, we may rule our stars through our own inherent character. It has been said that CHARACTER IS DESTINY, and it is in this belief that the following delineation is written ; it is in this spirit also that it should be studied.

INTRODUCTION.—(b).

**630.** The True Purpose of Astrology is to serve as a guide through
**A b**　　physical life, but the soul must have awakened before the real
value of a horoscope can be fully appreciated. The writer believes that
CHARACTER IS DESTINY and that we, in our past lives, have woven the
web of destiny by our own thinking, and thus to-day are weaving the
web of our future horoscope. All sin is a result of ignorance or non-
knowledge, therefore to KNOW ourselves is to become wise and thus to
master fate. All fate, good or evil, is made originally by our own
thoughts and actions and has its roots in our *character*. The horoscope
is the indicator of the Divine Law in action and thus helps us to discover
much of our destiny.

[*The following paragraph may usefully be added to the "Introduction" in certain cases.*]

**630.** A word or two will make plain the principle adopted in this
**A c**　　Delineation. Each planetary position or aspect is separately
noted and its general effect described, entirely apart from that of any
other aspect, though where any two tend to conflict a note to that
effect is added. In this way is gained an analytical presentment of the
character and fortunes which could not otherwise be arrived at, and
the analytical horoscope thus obtained can of course be "synthesised" at
any time. An interesting account of this system, and the reasons which
led to its adoption, will be found in *Modern Astrology* for December,
1903, under the title of "The History of the Test Horoscope." The
article alluded to was written in reply to a critic who had objected that
no such system of delineation could give accurate results, since two
people having the same aspect would receive exactly the same delineation
as regards that particular aspect. But the point is, not whether two
people may be told the same thing regarding some details of the horoscope
but whether the delineation as a whole *is true*.

PREFACE.

(*Where birth-time is uncertain.*)

**630.** The following delineation of your nativity is the best judgment
**B**　　that can be given you, from the scanty data supplied. Astrology
depends upon fixed laws, but you will easily see that it is no easy task to

delineate all that concerns your particular horoscope when there is any uncertainty as to the actual star under which you were born. However, everything has been done to make the reading as reliable as possible, for the pages have been so arranged that the faulty portion will be in what immediately follows, so that the latter half of the judgment will be found to be the more correct, especially that which refers to the Planetary Positions, and the Summary.

## "What Sign am I Born Under?"

**630.** The following quotation from *Everybody's Astrology* will serve
**C** to clear up an element of doubt that often arises in connection with this question.

"Astrologers use the expression 'under' any sign, or 'under the influence of' any sign in three quite different ways, as follows:

(1) When under the Sun's influence through that sign, *i.e.*, the Sun is in that sign at birth.

(2) When the Moon is in that sign at birth.

(3) When born under a certain sign of the Zodiac, *i.e.*, that sign is on the horizon at birth. ("Rising Sign.")

. . . . . . Thus, in the case of any given man or woman for (1) it would merely be necessary to know the month of birth, for (2) it would also be needful to know the very day, and for (3) the actual time and place of birth. This fact gives us a hint as to the relative importance of the three senses in which the phrase is used."

In the popular articles on Astrology which appear from time to time in the weekly papers the term "born under" such and such a sign usually refers to the sign occupied by the Sun, and *not* to the Rising Sign, a practice which is to be regretted as it often causes confusion.

## What is Meant by the Term "Rising Sign."

**630.** Each point of the zodiac rises, culminates, and sets once in every
**D** 24 hours; this is caused by the turning of the earth on its axis. The zodiac, consisting of 360 degrees, is divided into 12 "signs," or portions of 30 degrees each, and the sign which is on the Eastern horizon at birth is known as the Rising Sign or Ascendant. (See *Everybody's Astrology*, pp. 93, 94.)

The "Rising Sign" describes your form and temperament, your

disposition and general tastes and likings.   It denotes the form fitted for the environment, and it is the most important point in your nativity to consider.   Next comes the planet which governs your sign, your " Ruling Planet," together with any planets that may be rising upon the Eastern Horizon at birth ; and after that the Sun and Moon.

## A Minor Aspect.

**630.**
**E** The foregoing aspect is one of those minor positions between the two planets mentioned from which it is never safe to expect any strongly marked influence, for it almost entirely depends for its effect upon powerful " directions " or the progression of planets to a place in your nativity where the aspect can be stimulated into action.   It is only noted for the purpose of giving you some idea of its expression when moved into action either by " transits " or by the period spoken of being reached, when you can either set it more actively in motion or seek to control its influence by an exercise of the Will.   However, the influence is there as described, but in what may be termed a more or less latent condition.

## Contradictory Paragraphs.

### (Conflicting Aspects.)

**630.**
**F a** The remarks in the two previous pages are slightly contradictory there being two opposing aspects to the same planet.   You will notice that one aspect is benefic in its nature and the other adverse, and much will depend upon yourself as to which is to dominate your life. In your past life you  probably set two causes in motion, one having good results, the other harmful, and so you now come to reap the result of your past sowing.   The future action of these aspects will eventually depend upon your own mental attitude towards them.   The tendency of the evil aspect may be accentuated by encouraging that attitude of mind, while the good aspect may overpower the evil if you will allow its influence to guide you in the right direction.

### (Contrary Influences.)

**630.**
**F b** The remarks in the foregoing paragraph should be taken in con-junction with what has previously been said on this head.   If you will carefully weigh the two statements, conflicting though they may appear at

first sight, you will easily be able to see how far each is true in its own particular sphere. Now it lies with you yourself to adjust the balance between these warring influences, by strengthening the weaker points of your character and by ridding yourself of undue predilections in any one direction, so that harmony may be restored. It is in the close study of conflicting influences of this character that the very greatest value and use of astrology lies, and you would be well advised to pay very special attention to this part of your horoscope, for it is not unlikely that upon this point the most momentous events of your life will turn.

## MARRIAGE.—(*v.c.*).

**630.** The Sun (Moon) in your nativity applies to none of the planets
**G a** ere it leaves the sign that it is in. This is somewhat against marriage, and signifies delay and hindrance, and the possibility of either a disinclination on your part to marry, or lack of a suitable opportunity. This solar (lunar) position is distinctly unfavourable for marriage, therefore I judge it will be in many respects best for you to live a single life. Probably you will not or cannot mate with the man (woman) likely to make you happy, but should you become acquainted with a person in whose horoscope the Moon (Sun) was in the same degree as your Sun (Moon), marriage might be advised. In any case you would do wisely to give any contemplated marriage very careful consideration.

## MARRIAGE.—(*d.b.*).

**630.** The planets concerned with marriage in your nativity are placed
**G b** in what are termed "double" signs, indicating that you will in all probability marry more than once, or seriously entertain two prospective alliances before coming to a definite decision ; this influence being more favourable to union with others than the desire to live single and free from domestic ties. You have the right kind of nature to enable you to love and appreciate home life, and I judge that you will be more happy married than single. When marriage planets occupy "double" signs, a dual experience seems to be quite necessary for the soul's progress, so that in some way married life will probably be known to you in two distinct phases.

## A Retrograde Planet.

**630** This planet is "retrograde," that is, moving backward in the
**H** Zodiac, which is found by astrologers to very greatly debilitate
its influence.   Retrogradation, as is well known, is only *an appearance*
due to the Earth moving forward at a greater rate than the retrograde
planet, when the latter is in a certain position in relation to the Earth and
to the Sun; but it is found to have a very hampering and restricting
effect upon planetary influence, and this effect must be taken into account
in its bearing upon the remarks given on the foregoing page.   It is
noteworthy that *all* the planets can under certain circumstances become
retrograde, but the Sun and Moon never do.

## Individuality and Personality.

**630.** Before summarising your horoscope it should first be explained
**I** that the nativity is divided into two parts : one half dealing with
the internal or higher subjective or " Individual " part of the nature ; and
the other concerned with the lower, external or objective manifestation,
generally termed the " Personal."   To go fully into the matter, however,
demands a more detailed treatment than is possible in this class of
horoscope, so that we will pass on to a study of the elements predominating at your birth and their general influence.   Should you desire fuller
information, in such books as *How to Judge a Nativity* and *The Art of
Synthesis*, the subject is gone into more fully.

## General Summary. (A.)

**630.** Yours is not altogether a fortunate nativity, for there are many
**J** cross aspects, bringing obstacles in life.   But the strongest souls
often have the most to fight against, for it is they who realise life's
purpose, and by taking up their cross and working off their past accumu-
lated debts win freedom in the near future.   So that looked at from the
occult standpoint the most adverse nativities are the most progressive,
since an unfavourable environment gives opportunities for the soul to
grow stronger and more self-reliant.   In the foregoing delineation an
effort has been made to condense and explain your natal influences as
succinctly and lucidly as possible, and you should weigh carefully all that
has been said.   [The following summary should be well pondered.]

## GENERAL SUMMARY. (*B*.)

**630.** You have a favourable nativity, and will have opportunities to
**K** develop your character, and use your mental faculties wisely.
You will gain by studying your horoscope, for you have the ability to
profit by the good influences operating at your birth, the planetary
positions giving you some power in the world, no less potent because it
may not be open and public. The judgment has been given as succinctly
and lucidly as possible, and you should ponder well what has been said,
so as to catch any inner meaning that may attach to any paragraph,
remembering that the whole delineation is given with the main view of
helping you to progress. [The following is a brief judgment of the
whole combinations denoted by the nativity.]

## YOUR FUTURE PROSPECTS. (*a*)

**630.** In the previous pages there has been given a reading of your
**L** past and present conditions, the whole of which has been judged
from the nativity. *Every horoscope is progressive*, however, and several
paragraphs now follow giving a brief outline of the most important influences in operation during the ensuing years. The respective influences are
strongest during the year mentioned, but overlap to a certain extent into
the previous and succeeding years. Should you require details for any
year, " directions " need to be calculated, as explained elsewhere. It
should be mentioned that the most important aspects are those formed to
the Sun; next those formed between the planets; and lastly those formed
by the Moon.

## YOUR FUTURE PROSPECTS. (*b*)

### *Directions.*

**630.** In certain horoscopes the word " Directions " may be mentioned,
**M** and as those unfamiliar with astrological terms may not understand what is meant, it may be well to give a brief explanation. The
word " Directions " is used in reference to a judgment given upon the
planetary positions since the time of birth, it being necessary to erect a
fresh horoscope for every year after birth, so that by a study of the progressed positions we may discover the possibilities and influences operating

or any given year of life. It is wise in certain cases to have the Directions calculated, for often detailed advice can be given for each month in any year.

The " Future Prospects " which follow give a rough outline of your Directions for the ensuing   .  .  .   year(s).

## YOUR FUTURE PROSPECTS.  (c)

**630.** Although any attempts to give accurate predictions with regard
**N**   to the future are based upon astrological laws, at the same time it must be remembered that astrologers are very far from being infallible.  These words of the wise Ptolemy to his pupils should be well pondered :  " Judgment must be regulated by thyself, as well as by the Science.  For it is not possible that particular forms of events should be declared by any person, however scientific, since the understanding conceives only a certain general idea of some sensible event, and not its particular form.  It is, therefore, necessary for him who practises herein to adopt inference.  They only who are inspired by the Deity can predict particulars."

## FUTURE PROSPECTS.—SUMMARY.  (A.)

**630.** You are now under a train of rather evil influences, though it should
**O**   be remembered that these are of a secondary or minor nature as compared with the radical influences to be found in your horoscope at birth.  It will be well for you to act as discreetly and as carefully as you can during this period, avoiding all new undertakings, also doing nothing that is likely to incur displeasure from others, or give your mind anxiety. For you are now by your mental attitude shaping *your future*, and much depends upon the nature of your present thoughts and your attitude towards circumstances, for this will determine the fate that you will reap from the present sowing.  The lunar aspects now in operation are holding in solution fate that at length may crystallize into action in the future.

## FUTURE PROSPECTS.—SUMMARY.  (B.)

**630.** You are now under a train of benefic influences, and all seems to
**P**   go well with you.  [There is no special aspect that calls for more

comment than another, for all the lunar and solar applications are now good] ; though to know the precise nature of the good lunar aspects it would be necessary to make a further study of the matter. This should be done at any time that your mind is desirous of taking advantage of any special date, for while these good influences are in operation will be the most favourable opportunity for you to commence any new undertakings that you have been in any way contemplating. This is the time to sow good seed for future profitable reaping. Therefore make the most of it, for good " directions" unaided by *effort* accomplish little.

## FUTURE PROSPECTS.—SUMMARY. (*M.*)

**630.** In the foregoing paragraphs the Solar, Planetary and Lunar
☿  influences have been briefly outlined. The Moon's passage through each sign and house will indicate the tendencies of your fate during that period ; within the scope of these influences, you possess a certain amount of freewill, enabling you to act in the way that will be wisest under existing circumstances. "*The stars incline, they do not compel.*" You see the aspects and nature of their influences : therefore it lies chiefly with you to guide affairs and act accordingly. So the general tendency of the directions having been pointed out it will be fitting to conclude with the ancient dictum—*tempus omnia revelat.*

## CONCLUSION.

**630.** As time goes on you will have opportunities to awaken that
R  which is latent in your nativity, and in accordance with your earnestness and adaptability you will be enabled to live up to all that your planets indicate. You may not recognise the whole of the foregoing characteristics perhaps, yet if your birth-time has been correctly taken every word should appeal to you. Astrologers believe that " Character is Destiny," and that during this life we must work to develop our characters. In the far future we are destined to take an active part in the management of the world's evolution, and to this end we should fit ourselves; for eventually we must become perfect.

## Explanation.

**630.** By adopting the system explained in *The Key to Your Own*
**S**    *Nativity*, a system which was devised by the astrologer ALAN
LEO after much careful experiment, I have been enabled to give
you a purely scientific reading of your nativity without introducing
any personal bias or separate opinions of my own.   So far as the general
knowledge of Modern Astrology has brought us up to the present day, you
have in the foregoing pages the cream of a well-known astrologer's experience, representing many years of thoughtful investigation and
painstaking effort.   The judgment given is based solely upon the laws of
Astrology and none of my own knowledge of your character can have
entered into it in any way, even unconsciously.

## CHAPTER XXXV.

### THE FUTURE PROSPECTS.

THE Future Prospects, or periods of good and bad fortune operating in every nativity, may easily be obtained by noting the progression of the planets from their radical positions and observing the aspects the progressed planets form to the radical positions.

The progressed horoscope is obtained by counting each day after birth, in the ephemeris, as a year of life. This method is fully explained in Volume V. of this series, *The Progressed Horoscope ;* and a detailed delineation is there given for all the progressed planetary positions that can occur in a lifetime.

The method of using the present abbreviated system of delineations is as follows :—

(1) The planetary positions as given in the Ephemeris for the day succeeding the day of birth, show the progressed positions for the first year of life; those for the second day after birth, the second year of life; and so on, counting forward a day for a year.*

(2) Note the age of the person for whom the delineation is being made, count forward to the day corresponding to that age, and see whether any planet on that date is in aspect to any planet in the horoscope of birth, and if so, whether it is a conjunction, a benefic or a malefic aspect. Then refer to the paragraph giving the delineation of that aspect.

(3) Similarly for the next day (year), and the next; and so on.

It is quite unnecessary as a rule to calculate the exact date to which the aspect measures when complete, for every solar or planetary aspect lasts roughly speaking for about three years ; one year before that in which

---

* For this the ordinary Ephemeris must be used, as the condensed Ephemeris given in *Astrology for All, Part II.*, is not suitable.

it becomes complete, during which time it is slowly forming and growing in strength; the year in which it becomes complete and therefore attains its maximum strength; and the year following, during which the influence gradually wanes. *Strictly speaking*, the positions should be calculated for exactly 24 hours, 48 hours, 72 hours, etc., after the moment of birth; hence the positions given in the Ephemeris, which are calculated for Greenwich Noon, will be somewhat too much or too little as the case may be. But for the purpose of the present Chapter such precision is not necessary, as the aim is merely to outline the general indications, and not to go into detail.

By way of example King George's progressed planetary positions for 1910, the year of his accession, may be given. Counting a day for a year, this measures to July 18th, 1865, on which date the Ephemeris shows us the positions as below :—

| ☉ | ☽ | ☿ | ♀ | ♂ | ♃ | ♄ | ♅ | ♆ |
|------|------|------|------|------|------|------|------|------|
| ♋25.48 | ♊2.25 | ♌13.7 | ♊10.10 | ♍2.59 | ♐20.25℞ | ♎23.56 | ♋1.22 | ♈10.35 |

A glance shows us that Venus has reached the sextile aspect of the place of Neptune at birth. We therefore write down, "*Venus in benefic aspect to Neptune, 1909-10-11.*"

For the Lunar Aspects a little more trouble must be taken. Since the actual moment of birth is obviously the starting-point of the progressed horoscope, the Greenwich Time at birth—(1.18 a.m. in the case of our example, King George)—will clearly measure to the birthday of the year in question, that is, June 3rd, 1910, in the present instance. Therefore noon of the same day will measure to a later date in the same year, as can be seen by a rule-of-three sum: As 24 hours is to 12 months, so is 10hrs. 42min. to 5 months 10½ days; 10h. 42m. being the time between 1.18 a.m. and noon. Then 5 months 10½ days added on to June 3rd brings us to November 13th, which is consequently the date to which the noon-positions given in the Ephemeris will measure; it may conveniently be termed the "limiting date."

Having obtained this date the rest is easy, for as the Moon moves on an average about 12° per day (year), each degree corresponds to a month. We have, therefore, only to see how many degrees the Moon is behind or in front of the exact aspect, and add or subtract as many months from this date—and the thing is done. Thus on Nov. 13th, 1910, King George's progressed Moon, we see, was ♊2°25.

It therefore wants 10° of the Sun's place at birth, equivalent to ten months later, and so we write down "*Moon conjunction Sun, September, 1911.*"

---

The paragraphs which follow explain themselves.

The student will be well advised to give these paragraphs on Future Prospeets very sparingly when furnishing the delineation of a horoscope. He should pick out two or three of the leading aspects in the years just ahead, and content himself with them. Where there are no aspects to radical planets, the same paragraphs may be used with but trifling modification for aspects of the progressed planets among themselves. Thus, in our example Mercury is in ♌13.7 and Venus in ♊10.10, and they are therefore just separating from the sextile, a benefic aspect, which was complete on July 15th, 1865, measuring to the year 1907. The aspects of the progressed planets among themselves, however, are found to be less effective in most cases than those of progressed planets to radical.

They are numbered with Roman Numerals, to prevent any possible confusion with the paragraphs in the other part of the book relating to aspects in the horoscope of birth. To find a given aspect quickly, turn up the paragraph number in the Chart at the beginning of book.

## SOLAR ASPECTS.

i.
The CONJUNCTION of the Sun and Moon is at all times an important conjunction, the Sun being "the greater light that rules by day"; the Moon the lesser ruler by night. From any point of view, the luminaries in conjunction is important enough, but from the esoteric and internal standpoint it wakens the lower part of the nature and brings more power into the life. To those who have not a strong, healthy constitution it impairs the health, bringing too much vitality into the system, and when it is going to affect the health injuriously the eyes usually begin to suffer, a sure sign that important changes are at work in the system, warning sufficient to be noticed by the wise. It often marks an important epoch in the life when changes are about to take place either in the environment or the general conditions.

ii.
The Sun having progressed to a BENEFIC aspect with the Moon, you have now come under favourable and prosperous influences.

This aspect will in a great measure improve your horoscope for the time of its operation. You will meet with persons who will be favourably disposed toward you, also ready as well as willing to assist you in all directions. This solar influence is good for spiritual and material welfare, but much will depend upon your power to respond to all that it implies, for it often brings an awakening of the consciousness to higher states of being, and gives all who are ready, opportunities to advance in all directions either socially, financially, or psychically, etc. Pleasure and domestic felicity, also speculation, and investments prosper under its benign favours. Therefore endeavour to find the best outlet for your efforts whilst it is in operation.

iii.    You have now reached a stage in your evolution in which the solar ray in your nativity comes into ADVERSE aspect with the Moon. This influence indicates troubles and difficulties, delays and hindrances, losses and some trials of various descriptions, the personality for a time being under a cloud, and you will have to garner some experiences that will cause you to remember this period, which is not by any means good for worldly affairs. It will be well to safeguard your health, as your vitality will not be so good. Take care of your eyesight and do not overstrain it. Seek no fresh undertaking, nor act in any way likely to bring upon yourself future trouble.

iv.    The CONJUNCTION of the Sun and the Mercurial planet will bring much activity into your life, all matters connected with the mind being more to the fore than at any other period of your life. You will either travel under this potent position, or be engaged in mental flights, the imagination carrying you into the creation of many plans, the working out of which will in a great measure depend upon the ability to carry into practice your ideals, and give expression to the formative will. To some the conjunction brings changeable and unsettled fancies, causing the mind to waver and become too indecisive; but to the progressive person the mind is re-vitalised by the sun-ray and thus energised ready for greater power of thought, and consequent freedom of action, by the mental foresight that precedes the mental activity. Make the most of this time mentally.

v.    The Sun and Mercury being now in BENEFIC aspect, will bring much mental activity and incline you towards study. You will become very desirous of change, therefore seek to improve your condition generally, but mostly in connection with learning and study. You will be strongly inclined towards all things concerned with correspondence and literature. This should be rather a successful period as the mind will be more acute and active, and some illumination will come into your brain by this aspect. You should strive to make the most of it, as it always denotes an expansion of the mind and consciousness, and brings you the opportunity for much activity although much depends upon the position of Mercury and his aspects at your birth.

vi.     The Sun has progressed to an ADVERSE aspect with the planet Mercury, and this will produce some anxieties and worries, or cause your affairs to proceed less smoothly than usual. It is not a serious affliction that is operating, for the Sun and Mercury are always so closely connected that it is difficult for their adverse aspects to produce more than minor troubles, in which the mind is generally unsettled, and given to brooding or fretting over matters that are not in reality as serious as they look at first sight. It will be well to avoid controversy or any actions that would involve you in legal disputes, whilst this affliction is operating. The period now under consideration will, however, be very much what you yourself make it by your thoughts and actions.

vii.     The CONJUNCTION of the Sun with the beautiful planet Venus will now bring you pleasurable unions of all kinds, you will form unions with others, or make lasting attachments which will bind you to those you love and desire to be united with, both in mind and body. This conjunction can only be fully appreciated by those who are refined and value art and beauty for its own sake; music and the fine arts engaging the attention of those who have sufficient of the Venus nature in them to come under this excellent conjunction. You will now have opportunities to enjoy life from its pleasurable side more than has hitherto been your wont. Now is the time to make your life as happy as your environment will allow for fortune will bring you many opportunities to enjoy to the full, all you are able to take.

viii.     The Sun has progressed to a BENEFIC aspect with the planet Venus, a very favourable and indeed often one of the most fortunate of aspects. It brings pleasure and success, new friends and attachments, and tends generally to unions or the making of new and lasting ties. All things go well under an aspect of this nature and new undertakings prove satisfactory and in all ways beneficial. The Sun giving life and new energy to all that it affects by its rays, causes the beneficent influence of Venus to be translated in the most favourable manner possible, and thus all latent benefits, and opportunities will now have the medium through which good of some kind will be brought about, and if your "directions" are now favourable it will be a splendid period of your life.

**ix.** The Sun has now progressed to an ADVERSE aspect with the planet Venus, and although this planet is benefic, the adverse aspect of the Sun will keep back many good influences, and instead of blessings being showered upon you, it will rather be the negation of these things that is indicated by this aspect. If you are careful in your actions, avoid extremes and live within your income, the aspect will not be so serious as it might if you committed acts that would allow the aspect to act adversely. You cannot be too temperate, or cautious in avoiding extremes and extravagance, and taking care not to give offence to others. A death is likely to occur in your circle.

**x.** The CONJUNCTION of the Sun with the fiery and impulsive planet Mars will now quicken all your life force, bringing an abundance of fire and life into your constitution; therefore much will in every way depend upon your mode of living and the power of restraint which you possess, for it is necessary to restrain and check the forceful and impulsive tendency of Mars when in conjunction with the Sun. To the untrained there is danger of accidents through impulse; to the reckless and careless danger of fever and feverish tendencies. For those who are easily excited there is danger of quarrels and to all alike it will in a measure awaken that which is latent within, and stimulate into activity the whole forces of the animal side of the nature. It will give renewed health to those who are temperate, inflammatory tendencies to those who give way to impulse, and those lacking thought are easily unbalanced.

**xi.** The progression of the planets in your nativity since birth has now produced a BENEFIC aspect between the Sun and the planet Mars. This influence will strengthen your physical constitution, increase your vitality, and awaken all your latent energies. You are now coming into a very active period: you will make the acquaintance of martial men, or those who are positive and assertive. Your affairs will tend to go well, and you will have more vitality and hopefulness than usual. You will be more dauntless, intrepid, and inclined to entertain adventures and new enterprises. You will now begin to assert your personality to your own advantage, will and desire going hand in hand to further and promote your material welfare.

**xii.** The Sun and the planet Mars having progressed to an ADVERSE aspect will produce troubles of a martial nature. The nature of its influence will depend to a great extent upon your own attitude and state of progress. However, it warns you generally to take care of your health, and to guard against accidents and all inflammatory complaints. It tends in some manner to injure the body; therefore it is necessary that you should avoid excitement and rash action. Mentally, it tends towards impulse, rashness in speech, and a rather turbulent state of mind, but its nature may be judged by the lunar influences operating at this period. The inner meaning of the aspect is conflict between the will and the desires.

**xiii.** The CONJUNCTION of the Sun with the benefic planet Jupiter, marks an epoch in your life which it will be well for you to fully understand, and appreciate. You have now reached a stage wherein you may take a choice of great spiritual and moral development, or, material and worldly advancement. Your vital forces will be renewed, and your mind will become calm and peaceful, so that you will be able to take advantage of the opportunities and preferment that will now come in your way. This influence is one that will have lasting effect and you will do wisely in commencing any undertaking, fresh venture or important step which may now present itself. You will find all your affairs and projects tending to turn out well, and the social side of your life will also improve, advancement and progress being the keynote of this benefic and fortunate conjunction. Make the most of all your opportunities, and make hay while the Sun shines.

**xiv.** The Sun is now in BENEFIC aspect with the fortunate Jupiter, a good influence lasting for a period long enough in duration for you to feel its beneficial effects. You have now arrived at a stage in your evolution wherein opportunities will come to you, not only to develop the best side of your nature, but also to greatly improve your moral and social standing with the world. You will assuredly gain either worldly success or spiritual progress in proportion to the strength of your desires and wishes, much of this influence depending upon your power to respond to the opportunities that come in your way. However, all new and fresh undertakings commenced at this period will succeed, and you may expect eventual prosperity. This may be made the best period of your life, if your opportunities are used rightly and the fullest advantage taken.

**xv.** With the Sun and Jupiter now in ADVERSE aspect by progression you must be careful with regard to your health, especially so far as the condition of the blood is concerned. This aspect tends to waste and extravagance, and will bring obstacles into your life in connection with religious affairs or matters of the heart. It will be well to see that your expenditure does not exceed your income or you may be involved in legal troubles or difficulties in which finance will play a prominent part. As regards health, your liver is likely to suffer. "Moderation in all things" should be your watchword while under this influence, which may be made beneficial if you use discretion and self-control.

**xvi.** The CONJUNCTION of the Sun and Saturn is now in operation, one of the most important and powerful positions that can take place at any period of the life. It marks a critical stage in your life, bringing you a grave and serious responsibility and marked changes that will in many ways affect your future life and destiny. If you find your mind depressed or tending to take a gloomy view of things take it as a sign of danger that is threatening you and avoid all new undertakings, or those in which there is risk involved, in fact be more than usually on the alert for trouble and disaster generally. You will, under this conjunction, be liable to some severe illness arising from imperfect and interrupted circulation of the blood, springing from colds, chills, or congestion, the life forces being checked by the Saturnine influence.

**xvii.** The Sun has now progressed to a BENEFIC aspect with the planet Saturn, bringing you many benefits and opportunities. You will now have the possibility of gaining more recognition for your efforts, and will find yourself coming in touch with wiser and older men and women than yourself and with persons of influence; also forming friendships that will be lasting and beneficial. You should now prepare to come under one of the best directions of your life, for this influence generally lasts several years, unless other aspects mitigate it. You will find yourself more contemplative and thoughtful, and also more patient, prudent and virtuous, and possessed of much more self-control.

**xviii.** The Sun and Saturn in ADVERSE aspect will tend during this period to bring you trouble and disappointment, hindering your progress, affecting also your general health as well, while the good lunar influences will all tend to be nullified and hindered by this evil aspect. You must take great care of your health, avoiding chills or cold, and should embark on no new undertakings or fresh effort in business matters or enterprise.   During all this period it will be as well to act cautiously, doing nothing likely to cause scandal, or disgrace of any sort.   A death may occur within your circle about this time.   Avoid giving any offence to elderly persons, especially superiors, for the whole period tends to be very unfortunate.

**xix.**   The CONJUNCTION of the Sun with the mystic planet Uranus will now bring great changes and remarkable experiences into your life.   They may be sudden and extraordinary, according to your response to this unique influence, but it will not pass without bringing you either an inner, or outer change, or some sudden and unforeseen event.   To those who are seeking to raise their consciousness to a higher level it is one of the opportunities of a lifetime, but to the person who has not yet realised the true purpose, and vital import of life it will simply bring some external changes which tend to break up and alter existing conditions ; so that it will be as well for you now to examine yourself, and be prepared for either internal or external change according to your stage of development, which can be seen by a study of your nativity, or yourself.

**xx.**   The Sun has now progressed to a BENEFIC aspect with Uranus which promises you much expansion of consciousness, either produced through successful journeys, voyages, or by travelling or through changes ; through publicity or making acquaintance with those who will benefit you, and coming in contact with those who have a wider know- ledge than yourself, and also a greater influence over others.   This aspect sometimes brings unprecedented benefits, or affairs of a sudden and unexpected nature that eventually lead to good.   To those who can fully respond it signifies a mystical period, when new thoughts and ideas come to the mind bringing originality, foresight, etc.   You will awaken some of your inner faculties.

**xxi.**   The Sun has progressed to an ADVERSE aspect with Uranus, an influence depending upon those lunar influences in operation while it lasts.   Generally it brings very sudden and unexpected difficulties, obstacles to progress and sorrow following upon any impulsive, or rash, action.   If you act in any way without thought, this aspect will bring you many serious troubles, which may then cause some unlooked-for change, and the sudden break-up of existing conditions.   But this influence does not operate upon all alike, and it is difficult to deal with it alone, it being necessary to study the lunar aspects, and positions.   The unlooked for nearly always happens under this aspect; therefore it is difficult to say exactly how it will operate.

**xxii.** The Sun has now reached the CONJUNCTION of the planet Neptune, an influence that will largely depend upon the strength of Neptune in your nativity, and your ability to respond to its vibrations as to how it will affect you. But it is in any case a very strange and uncommon influence, and is sure to affect your emotional nature in some deep and lasting manner. It is possible you may be called upon to take a journey to some distant part, or you may in some other way be cut off temporarily from your friends and fellowmen, so that you will feel isolated and solitary. In what particular way it is likely to affect you, it is difficult to say, but, directly or indirectly, the sea will be associated with the experience that is before you.

**xxiii.** The Sun and the planet Neptune are now in BENEFIC aspect, and this is in itself a very good and favourable influence, depending however upon the prominence of Neptune in your nativity. To those who are sensitive to the planet's influence this aspect promises a very prosperous time in either a worldly, emotional or spiritual sense, and in any case this aspect is sure to have a beneficial effect, even if it is not a very obvious one. Neptune is especially related to the sympathetic nature, and your sympathies are sure to be broadened and stirred into fuller activity by this influence. It is very probable that you may take a sea voyage or make a prolonged stay at the seaside at this time, for there is a mysterious connection between this planet and the sea, in spite of its name having been given to it as we say "by chance."

**xxiv.** The Sun and Neptune are now in ADVERSE aspect, and this is an unfavourable influence that is likely to cause you some very peculiar experiences, perhaps connected in some way with the psychic plane or the after-death state, or perhaps on the other hand in ordinary everyday life, through some fraudulent person or persons. For the influence of the planet Neptune is very far-reaching and subtle, and covers a very wide field; but it may be said in general to be concerned with the psychic plane, with emotional states, with gigantic and unwieldy enterprises, and with frauds, shams, and deceitful doings. But in its true or inner nature it is specially related to the realities of life, and it is by means of the experiences that you are now about to go through that a deeper consciousness will in some measure be awakened within you.

## INTERPLANETARY OR "MUTUAL" ASPECTS.

### MERCURY.

**xxv.** The planet Mercury has reached the CONJUNCTION of the benefic Venus. It is on the whole a very good position, but acts rather upon the mind and the higher feelings and emotions than upon the senses or physical environment. Hence if the full advantage of this very exalted position is to be reaped, your mind must be very refined and inclined towards the higher things of life. For it is an influence through which the mind and feelings are blended, and only those who are pure in their intentions can absorb the good influence that will come from Venus at this conjunction. If however the general directions operating at this time permit you will now have some favourable opportunities to benefit your circumstances either by coming into a better environment, or by meeting persons who are favourably disposed towards you.

**xxvi.** The planets Mercury and Venus are now in BENEFIC aspect, which will improve your mind, cause you to seek for knowledge, and greatly improve your mental condition. It cannot be said to be a powerful influence, as indeed, it is not; still, it is more or less favourable, and helps considerably to break up any adverse aspect that may be operating. It should cause you to see clearly your way out of difficulties, and bring help in some way from those who will be inclined to benefit you. It also favours correspondence, legal affairs and financial matters generally, but especially mental conditions and all those matters where the mind is engaged in refined artistic work.

**xxvii.** The general tendency of the ADVERSE aspect between the planets Mercury and Venus seen in operation is to cause the mind and feelings to be temporarily separated, the mental conditions tending to go against the feeling or emotional side of the nature. This will often bring errors of judgment and a general condition in which affairs for the time may go adversely so far as minor details are concerned. It will cause you to mildly criticise, and feel somewhat out of gear in parts of your composition. It will be to your advantage to carefully watch your financial affairs, more especially where correspondence is concerned, avoiding litigation and general dealings with solicitors.

**xxviii.** The planets Mercury and Mars are now in CONJUNCTION, a position that will stir your mental conditions into great activity.

You will be more than usually alert, and keenly alive to your own interests, being generally enterprising and resourceful. You will meet persons who will be far too assertive : they will become quarrelsome, or too personal with you if you are not on your guard to avoid disputes, and if you do not keep clear of all impulsive action and hasty speech. Do not go to law during this period, or write letters that will bring you sorrow. Seek as far as possible to act with more than your usual tact, discretion and thoughtfulness. Avoid all rash conduct and try to curb the tendency to unpremeditated action.

**xxix.** There is now in operation a BENEFIC aspect between the planets Mercury and Mars, an influence which in a general sense tends to make your mind more active and more ambitious. It is an influence which is good for all business purposes, promising success to undertakings arising out of the activities of the brain, or the formation of new schemes and plans, and it will keep you busy during the whole of this period, though you should avoid extremes, or too much excitement. You will now feel full of confidence in yourself and your own abilities, and some new business enterprise is sure to occupy your attention. You will be involved in much correspondence, or have much to do with printing, literary affairs, and all matters to do with papers, legal affairs, and, Mercurial activities generally.

**xxx.** The planets Mercury and Mars will be in ADVERSE aspect during this period. The nature of this influence is such as to cause some mental anxiety, usually arising from a nervous state or condition such as is due either to your having overtaxed yourself or taken upon yourself too great a mental strain. This then eventually precipitates itself upon the body, thus affecting the general health. Therefore great care in regard to all dealings with others is advisable while under this aspect, especially to avoid hasty speech. Do not commit yourself in writing, and be careful to avoid legal difficulties. See that you get plenty of sleep.

**xxxi.** The CONJUNCTION of Mercury with the planet Jupiter is a most beneficial position, giving you an opportunity to join your higher and lower mind, in which wisdom represented by Jupiter, and intellect by Mercury, will so improve your judgment as to enable you to successfully arrange your affairs and thus to gain either mentally or physically by the union. To those who are in a condition to embrace the higher religious and philosophical side of life it will awaken the intuition and bring that illumination which is so much desired by all who are more spiritually than worldly minded. But to those who have not these aspirations it marks a period of profit and gain according to the mental abilities shown in the nativity at birth. You should endeavour to make the most of this benefic conjunction.

**xxxii.** The planets Mercury and Jupiter have now progressed to a BENEFIC aspect. The planet Mercury governing knowledge, and Jupiter wisdom, you may now turn much of the knowledge you possess into fruit and wisdom by calm reflection, and by meditation upon all that comes under your notice, throughout this period. You will find your judgment improve ; it will be well to listen to your intuition, as your mind will be in a better condition than it has ever been before. You will gain much by study, and also by your philosophical attitude to all that interests your higher thought, for wisdom is the goal to be sought. Financial affairs should improve, especially pursuits in which the mind is employed.

**xxxiii.** The planets Mercury and Jupiter have now progressed to an ADVERSE aspect, and this will probably incline you to err in judgment or cause you to have losses, arising from your condition of mind, or through correspondence or legal affairs. You should act with much caution during this period, and avoid law, and also be as careful in all writings as is possible. Think and judge very carefully before acting, as you may make some serious error in judgment which would bring you pecuniary losses. Your mind will be rather cloudy while under this influence ; great care will be needed in signing anything of importance. You should not borrow or lend under this aspect, but watch all financial affairs carefully.

**xxxiv.** The CONJUNCTION of Mercury with the planet Saturn will tend to solidify your mind, and thus cause you to be more practical and critical, with a thoughtful and grave attitude towards things. You will experience some sorrows, if you allow a materialistic or desponding mood to control you, for there is an evil side to this conjunction when the mind is tempted by Saturn to become in any way concrete, or disposed to melancholy. To those who have not risen above the personal and sensitive side of their nature this period will bring many annoyances, much worry, anxiety, and depression, but to the thoughtful student it is beneficial owing to its concentrative power, and the opportunity it gives to take on greater responsibilities, and become more earnest and thorough.

To all it will give opportunities to exercise patience and endurance, also to think.

**xxxv.** There is now in operation a BENEFIC aspect between the mental ruler Mercury and the slow and steady planet Saturn, which will bring you under a period of deep and earnest thought, so that a change will come over your demeanour and you will ponder more deeply the inner things of life, using your reflective powers more fully. You will come into contact with those older than yourself, grave and serious persons or those who have a purpose in life, so that you yourself will be inclined to become more earnest. By the study of things relating to the occult side of life your mind will become steadier and more concentrative, and you will tend to become more meditative, thoughtful and studious.

**xxxvi.** The ADVERSE aspect in operation during this period between Saturn and Mercury is an influence likely to cause worry, anxiety, much difficulty in matters connected with correspondence, writings, etc. Therefore you must use care in dealing with solicitors, trustees, or persons concerned at all with literary affairs and matters of correspondence. This is a rather adverse aspect, apt to cause disappointments, and tending to bring some treachery or unforeseen difficulty into your life which will make you anxious and easily upset. Thus it will be well to offend none. Be careful in speech; also very particular in matters of correspondence and in dealings with inferiors, the aged, partners, etc.

**xxxvii.** The CONJUNCTION of Mercury with the planet Uranus is a very important conjunction as it will awaken the metaphysical, and occult tendencies in you and incline your mind towards astrological and kindred subjects. It marks, however, a period in which care must be exercised, for besides giving originality of thought and inventive inclinations, it also tends to bring some eccentricity, and the excitation of the mind, which at times is unsafe when mental balance has not been cultivated, as it tends to quicken the vibrations too rapidly, and thus brings about nervous disorders, and severe headaches; but to those who are seeking higher mental development, this is the period to gather those higher thoughts which will come in their way, whether sought after or not, for this position of Mercury creates better facilities for receiving occult knowledge than any other in which Mercury is concerned.

**xxxviii.** The mental planets Mercury and Uranus having progressed to a BENEFIC aspect, a very good period is denoted while the influence lasts,—generally several years. This influence will awaken interest in occult study, and cause you to exhibit some originality in your mental pursuits ; it will also quicken your mind, making it witty, active, philosophical or original. You will be drawn to occultism, and could now take up a study of Astrology to advantage. You will be able to manage all your affairs with prudence, and so arrange matters as to bring yourself into favourable conditions enabling you to make the most of all your opportunities. You will gain in many ways under this exceptional influence.

**xxxix.** During this period an ADVERSE aspect is formed between your mental ruler, Mercury, and Uranus. Whenever Mercury and Uranus come into mutual affliction, the mind generally becomes very sarcastic and altogether unsettled in its condition. In all probability you will be attached to some unpopular pursuit or else take up some work or study that will bring to you discredit from friends and acquaintances, and you will tend to hold peculiar views generally. Therefore, keep your mental balance, avoiding extremes in thought, and all irritable and excitable tendencies.

**xl.** The CONJUNCTION of the planets Neptune and Mercury is now in operation, and this is sure to have some special influence upon your mind, the nature of which may be gathered from what has been said concerning the mental characteristics generally, although it will depend largely upon the susceptibility to the Neptunian influence which is indicated by the horoscope as a whole. The good influence of this vibration is to exalt the mind by the play upon it of the broader sympathies and the higher emotions—the lower is to incline the mind to nebulous and visionary fancies or, worse still, to nefarious schemes and vicious imaginings. But the true influence is to exalt the mind to the highest possible conceptions of poetry and philosophy.

**xli.** The planets Mercury and Neptune are now in BENEFIC aspect, a favourable influence for those who can respond to it, inclining the mind towards the refined sensuous side of art, and, in the case of those who are by nature spiritually inclined, also to the mystical view of life. In any case you are likely to take an added interest in symbolic studies, such as mystery plays, mythological dramas, folklore and kindred subjects ; and if you wish to derive the highest benefit from this aspect, you will take care that the sensuous beauty of art or poetry does not blind you to its spiritual meaning. The nervous system is benefited by this aspect, and some short trip or excursion made at this time is likely to live long in your memory.

**xlii.** The ADVERSE aspect between Mercury and Neptune which is now in operation is likely to have an unsatisfactory and perhaps distressing effect upon the mind, inclining it to morbid imaginings, baseless fears and questionable tastes.  Much depends, however, upon the aspects received by these two planets at birth, and if you wish for further information on this point I should advise you to study what is said about Neptune in *How to Judge a Nativity, Part II.*, as it is not possible to go fully into the matter here.  You should be careful to see that your mind is fully self-possessed, and not unduly influenced by others.  Remember that it is essential to allow principles, and not impulses, to regulate one's thinking.

## VENUS.

**xliii.** The CONJUNCTION of Venus with the planet Mars is a very interesting conjunction, indicating the quickening of the senses, and the association with the opposite sex produced by a magnetic and passional attraction which causes you to fascinate and physically affect those who are psychically or emotionally attracted to you.  The conjunction will bring you attachments, or unions with others which you will be unable to avoid unless you have gained control over your own feelings and emotions, and in any case you will be more easily persuaded to live more in your feelings than in your mind.  You will be drawn toward pleasures of various kinds, and if you avoid impulsive conduct, you will experience a feeling of exhilaration which will be pleasurable and beneficial to all with whom you come in contact.  More physical ties and unions are formed under this conjunction than any other aspect; therefore, the present period is an important one for you, and if you study the above thoroughly the position will aid you.

**xliv.** The planets Venus and Mars have arrived at a BENEFIC aspect with each other, and this tends to very much excite your feelings and emotions, or to stimulate them into activity.  You will now be more inclined for pleasures, and social intercourse, or to the exchange of pleasantries with the opposite sex, and the tendencies of the period will be such as to bring you into touch with those who will excite your nature with pleasure, awakening all your feelings and also causing you to express yourself through the avenues of the senses, in accord with the surroundings and those circumstances in which you may be placed. It is good for all love affairs and, in a general sense, is beneficial for matters financial, pleasurable and social.

**xlv.** The planets Venus and Mars being now in ADVERSE aspect, denotes a conflict between the higher and lower emotions, and under this influence the feelings are, as a rule, quickly excited and troubles arise from any impulsive action in connection with the emotions, and their connection with matters of a physical nature. Thus, temperance of all kinds is advisable, and particular care should be paid to expenditure, as there may be monetary loss through some extravagance, or foolish generosity. It is by no means a favourable aspect, especially where feelings are concerned, as desire may carry you into acts of indiscretion, which you will regret in your calmer moments.

**xlvi.** The CONJUNCTION of Venus with the benefic and fortunate planet Jupiter is not a very important conjunction, but it adds to the fortunes at the time of its operation, and brings more peace in the life than would be the case if the position were not so beneficial in nature. It will bring you some opportunity to gain financially or socially, probably more social advantages or pleasurable association with others will now be the order than was formerly the case. It is in many respects a case of likes and attraction and there is not enough of the differing elements to make the conjunction pronounced, but it is of course more favourable than adverse, so that my judgment enables me to conclude that a quiet and peaceful period is now before you while the good conjunction is in operation.

**xlvii.** The planets Venus and Jupiter have now progressed to a mutually BENEFIC aspect, and during this period they will favour you with many blessings and will bring you success in many ways, more particularly through your social intercourse with others. To obtain the full benefit of this aspect it will be well for you to make as many friends and acquaintances as you can, especially among the opposite sex. Your own conduct during this period will be sober and circumspect, tending to prudence and forethought, and thus aiding your physical, mental and moral progress. But much depends upon the lunar aspects in operation at the present time.

**xlviii.** During this period, Venus and Jupiter are in ADVERSE aspect, and although this aspect is not altogether important, both planets being benefics, it still indicates some extravagance or increased expenditure, and matters in connection with social life will not go so easily as formerly, and you may find expenditure a little heavier than usual. Generally, it is an aspect under which carefulness and prudence should be ,exercised. Avoid conflict with religious bodies or persons connected therewith. It is not altogether good for travel, but all these things may be overcome easily, owing to the planets being benefic. There is no absolute fate indicated by these aspects.

xlix. The planet Venus since your birth has progressed to the CONJUNCTION of Saturn's place in your nativity. This is not wholly an adverse influence, although it will cause a great deal of trouble and affliction to those whose horoscopes are strongly marked by Saturn's position. It will bring you into contact with persons older than yourself, and will also considerably steady your feelings and emotions. For the events now coming into your life will be of such a nature as to make you reflect and lead you to preserve a calm attitude in your affairs, thus tending to make you more serious. You will find yourself placed in a far more responsible position than any you have hitherto held. You will also be more acquisitive, persevering, patient and enduring, while the events now occurring will teach you, and add to the soul, qualities which Venus can only acquire by a conjunction with the 'solidifying' Saturn.

l. The planets Venus. and Saturn are now in BENEFIC aspect with each other, bringing an influence into your life, which will favour and benefit you as you are able to respond to the several opportunities it will afford. You will be unusually careful, prudent, and economical, and you will also gain through elderly persons, partners and domestic affairs, your feelings and affections being more steady and reliable than formerly. In some way you may gain honour and credit and financial affairs will improve with you, bringing gain through others, for the general tendency is toward financial gain. This influence will also benefit your mental conditions, making you very intuitive.

li. Venus and Saturn have now progressed to a mutually ADVERSE aspect, which will cause you to suffer losses, and to meet with sorrow and disappointment. Be ready for adverse circumstances, and conditions likely to be in any way unfavourable to you so far as material things are concerned. It is an aspect that usually causes grief through the loss by death of someone in the family circle, or it produces a great disappointment, with difficulties of progress. It is a period when temperance and care in living should be exercised, as the kidneys and circulatory system are liable to disorder. It will be well for you to be guarded in all your acquaintanceships with others.

**lii.** The CONJUNCTION of Venus with the planet of mystery, Uranus, will bring some romantic or very unusual attachment into your life. This is the position that awakens the dormant or latent and slumbering feelings that have hitherto lain in your composition unknown or unheeded. This is one of those powerful conjunctions which at the first opportunity may awaken a streak of genius, and to those who are musically inclined it stirs the soul to expression hitherto undreamed of ; and whatever latent power may be hidden in you, it is now that you should search your inner nature for its revelation. To those who are still deep in the throes of the materialistic world, it is an unfortunate aspect, yet it awakens to a real sensing of the world that is beyond the outer and physical. To all it marks a crisis of some kind, but more often it is a crisis in feeling than in any other direction.

**liii.** The influence of Venus and Uranus, now in BENEFIC aspect, is especially good for those who are naturally intuitive and inclined towards metaphysical and occult subjects, as it raises the feelings and higher emotions to a much higher condition of expression, almost eliminating the selfish element and giving a feeling of love and goodwill to all. It also widens the mental sympathies and I judge that you will feel more for strangers, will come into direct soul communion with persons of broader views than yourself, while materially, it will bring you into the society of those who will draw out the affectional side of your nature, as your magnetism will now draw others round you.

**liv.** There is during this period an ADVERSE aspect between the planets Uranus and Venus. This is an influence chiefly acting on love affairs, or matters connected with the opposite sex ; though it is liable to concern finance as well, to some extent. It will be well for you to be careful just now in all dealings with the other sex or you may become involved in difficulties or sorrows which you yourself would seek to avoid, since a peculiar fascination will tend to draw you into various complications eventually leading to scandal. It is well to be forewarned, for this aspect usually tends towards some secret alliance or peculiar experience affecting feeling and emotion, therefore act with prudence in all things.

**lv.** Venus has by progression arrived at the CONJUNCTION of the distant and mysterious planet Neptune, and this is an influence the exact nature of which it is difficult to foretell, depending much on your sensitiveness to Neptune's influence, and also on how far you are able to transcend the merely personal influence of this position, which inclines to an indulgence of the sensuous side of the nature. But its true meaning is to exalt and extend the love nature beyond all the limitations of selfishness into that pure devotion which seeks no return for the love which it freely bestows, and it is quite possible that a new conception of love may dawn upon you at this time. Beware of yielding to worldly considerations, however, if you would secure the greatest advantages of this influence.

lvi. The planets Neptune and Venus have now progressed to a BENEFIC aspect, and this although not of very great effect in ordinary matters, is likely to bring you some happiness and pleasure at this time. Things will go smoothly with you, your affairs will prosper and the more you can raise yourself above personal aims and wishes the more will your happiness increase. Your sympathies will be broadened and your mental outlook enlarged, while art and poetry will seem to open a new world to you. Much, however, depends upon the strength of Neptune in the nativity, and on your ability to respond to the higher side of its influence. You will gain in dealings with those of a lower social rank than yourself.

lvii. The progression of your horoscope has brought Venus into an ADVERSE aspect with the planet Neptune, and as this is an influence to which the majority of mankind cannot fully respond at present, it is likely to be somewhat unfavourable for you. It is difficult to give precise advice, but speaking generally you should beware of being placed in a false position through any unwise act of your own, or through undue influence of others—in short, beware of all things that are not perfectly open and straightforward, whether in monetary matters or in affairs of the heart. Beware of " grasping at shadows "; for Neptune is the planet of illusion, whereby we are taught to distinguish between the real and the unreal, the permanent and the changing, and this aspect is likely to bring you some experience of the hollowness of earthly pleasures.

## MARS.

lviii. The planets Mars and Jupiter are now in CONJUNCTION, a position that promises you an unusual access of enthusiasm energy and keen ardour. Do not allow it to carry you to extremes, either in the direction of speculative enterprise, impulsive adventure or unrestrained pleasure-seeking. Avoid over-enthusiasm in any religious cause. For this influence will manifest in one of these or in some kindred direction, according to the predominant bias of your character; there is sure to be a vivid awakening of the emotional nature. This is an influence that frequently brings about the phenomenon known as religious "conversion," should it do so in your case, do not expect the first glow of devotion to maintain its white heat indefinitely, but seek to turn your fervour into the calm flame of true devotion which no breeze can fan into a furnace nor any tempest extinguish.

lix.      The BENEFIC aspect of Mars and Jupiter now in operation, will increase your mental energy, and stimulate you to fresh enterprise and new undertakings. You will be more than usually generous, and free, and will tend to be very liberal minded, but you must be careful to guard against expenditure exceeding your receipts; because you may now be inclined to over-estimate things, and to spend more money than is wise. This aspect will benefit your health, and incline you to be more hopeful, free, and buoyant; and you will also benefit by superiors and persons having authority, and those who are religiously minded. This is a good aspect for both travel and changes, but thrift and prudence are necessary.

lx.      The ADVERSE aspect between the planets Mars and Jupiter at this period warns you to use very great care in all matters connected with or concerning finance. There is also some possibility of waste or extravagance; and expenditure is likely to exceed receipts. You will do well to avoid becoming surety for anyone or lending money, and should avoid litigation and anything that is likely to involve you in any monetary loss. About this period your health will suffer, may be through the inflammatory condition of the blood, there being a tendency for the blood to become overheated; therefore temperance in all things will be necessary, to avoid sickness. Especially avoid impulse.

lxi.      The planet Mars having arrived at a CONJUNCTION with Saturn at this period of your life, some important changes are probable and, when the "Directions" denote it, you will find yourself more assertive and confident than usual, possessing a much greater determination to carry out your desires and wishes. You will feel the effects of this conjunction whenever the Moon arrives at an aspect to these planets, and then much change and activity will be experienced.  During this period your ambitions will increase and the passional side of your nature will be stirred up.  This aspect usually ushers in an entirely new state of affairs, the nature of which will be indicated by the " directions " operating at this period of your existence.

lxii.    The two planets Mars and Saturn having now progressed to a BENEFIC aspect, you will come under very powerful influences, which will greatly increase your energy, and may make you more venturesome, persevering, earnest, and self-reliant.   Your mind will become much more courageous and there will also be a tendency for you to embark on undertakings which, at other times, you may have dreaded. A certain steadiness will come into your character and your influence to others will be more beneficial than it may have been before.   This position indicates that you are now entering upon a period of success, and you may safely take the necessary steps to secure better conditions and greater progress.

lxiii.    The planets Mars and Saturn have now progressed to an ADVERSE aspect, the former representing the emotional nature, the latter the selfish mental, or concrete conditions.   Therefore the two will struggle one against the other, and you may be called on to decide between feeling and the impulse of your emotions, and reason.   It is thus a somewhat critical period in which you yourself must decide as to the best line of action to pursue in whatever crisis, no matter how small, that may come under your notice.   You should avoid impulse, and paradoxical as it may seem, also avoid premeditation where feeling is concerned, or you may become very selfish.

lxiv.    The progression of your horoscope has now brought about the CONJUNCTION of the planets Mars and Uranus, a very important and eventful position, and one that calls for considerable self-control. The nervous energies will be brought up to a high pitch, and the whole of the psychic nature will receive an unwonted stimulus, which may result in those intermittent flashes of clairvoyant or other astral perceptions that are sometimes classed as hallucinations.   How this influence may result will largely depend upon the innate purity of the nature, but in any case it is sure to mark a memorable period in your life.   Beware of giving way to enthusiastic impulses, subject all your projects to the calm scrutiny of reason, and try to maintain a firm and dispassionate attitude whatever troubles may beset you.

**lxv.** The planet Mars is now in BENEFIC aspect with Uranus, which indicates a very active period with regard to good thought, denoting that the mind may be turned to metaphysical subjects, thus giving you a tendency to be more original than usual. This is the period for using the inventive faculties, also for quickening your perception and in generally toning up the whole condition of your mind. But as a rule this influence has more to do with other planes than this, and it is very probable that you may come into touch with some higher knowledge, either during sleep, or through the influence of others. It is a good time for investigating all kinds of metaphysical subjects, especially astrology.

**lxvi.** The planets Mars and Uranus are now in ADVERSE aspect, which will bring misfortunes upon you, and good fortune according to your power to respond to the peculiar vibrations produced by these two forceful planets. In a general sense, there will be a great deal more activity in your nature, and you will find your mind more inclined to irritability and nervous tension. It will also make you wish to investigate mystical and occult matters, or enter upon uncommon, and original pursuits. It will be a period in which difficulty may come, and it will be favourable or not according to your actions and mental attitude to events that may be occurring. Avoid all excitement, and minimise the risk of sudden accidents.

**lxvii.** Mars has now arrived at the CONJUNCTION of the planet Neptune, and this is likely to bring you some peculiar experiences as it is not altogether a favourable influence, owing to the contrary nature of these two planets. Beware of trusting too confidently to your impulses at this time, and shun "wild cat" schemes, being careful not to undertake any work that you are not justified in entering upon with a reasonable expectation of success. For a new-born spirit of confidence is likely to come upon you at this time and unless you exercise discretion you may court disaster. Let moderation be your watchword in all things, in play as well as in work.

**lxviii.** Mars and the planet Neptune are now in BENEFIC aspect, and this is a very favourable influence, when things tend to go smoothly with you and your general concerns prosper well. Your physical energy will increase and your personal magnetism become more attractive, so that people will deal readily with you and you will find yourself agreeably served by all inferiors, servants and the common people generally. Beware of losing your sense of caution, however, and becoming involved in more than you can reasonably expect to carry through efficiently, for there is a slight tendency to extravagance about this aspect. A sea voyage at this time would be very beneficial to your health.

lxix. The planets Mars and Neptune have now arrived at an ADVERSE aspect and although the direct influence of the latter planet upon humanity is at present but slight, you are likely to be somewhat adversely aspected by it at this time. Beware of emotional extravagances of any kind. Do not run undue risks in any attempts to add to your income, and seek to curtail unnecessary expenses, for there is a decidedly prodigal tendency about this influence. Be careful in your dealings with what are known as the "lower classes," with servants and with all social inferiors, for you are likely to come into antagonism with them at this time to your hurt.

## JUPITER.*

lxx. The ponderous planets Jupiter and Saturn are now in BENEFIC aspect to each other. This is a very fortunate position, bringing you success and good fortune. You will now be able to undertake any responsibility and commence any new venture which it will be to your advantage to engage in. All things tend to go well when Jupiter and Saturn are in harmonious vibration. It promises you some financial gain and many privileges and opportunities according to your power to in any way respond to the vibration. It is an indication of honour and favours in dealing with persons older than yourself, or those possessing power and authority. You may get help from such persons and win their favour.

lxxi. The planets Jupiter and Saturn have now progressed to an ADVERSE aspect. This promises no success in any matter connected with the law or where finance is concerned, for it threatens you with troubles and with difficulties, and altogether hinders your progress, involving loss of friends, with many unpleasant experiences. It will be well to avoid any new undertaking under the aspect: avoid also, giving way to feelings of depression, by checking every tendency

---

* *Note.*—The CONJUNCTION of Jupiter and Saturn is rarely formed. It may be treated the same as a benefic aspect. The aspects of Jupiter and Neptune are not important and may be neglected, except perhaps the square which may be treated much the same as the affliction to Uranus. *See also footnote to* SATURN, p. 266.

towards melancholia or hypochondria. Avoid everything that is likely to result in complications, which this adverse aspect usually brings about. You may suffer also through your liver and by blood disorders. Take abundant exercise, with light diet.

**lxxii.** The CONJUNCTION of the planets Jupiter and Uranus is at times favourable, and at others very much the opposite ; for it may bring you very sudden gain and success, but it will also bring equally sudden losses and misfortune. This is an influence most difficult to gauge at our present state of evolution. Uranus is an uncertain planet, bringing benefit only to those who are students of occult and mystical subjects. To speculators or investors it may mean either fortune or ruin; which can to a certain extent be known by studying all the " Directions " in operation. But even then the calculations require very great care, to see how the conjunction will act ; for it brings good luck which is often followed by bad, etc.

**lxxiii.** The planet Jupiter having progressed to a BENEFIC aspect with the mystic Uranus, creates an aspect that very few persons can hope to fully respond to. It simply means that the ' Manas ' or Higher Mind is able to inform the personality of higher things and a more advanced state of existence. It awakens all the intuitive faculties, and gives a peculiar, higher kind of mentality which sometimes is summed up in the words " whatever is, is best," this being the expression that one coming fully under the influence would be most likely to use in all the affairs of daily life. Materially it gives benefits through touches of genius or inventiveness, and originality.

**lxxiv.** The planets Jupiter and Uranus are in ADVERSE aspect at the present time, and as these planets move slowly, their adverse and unfortunate influence is likely to remain in force for some time, therefore commence no new undertakings, avoid speculation, and do not act impulsively where money or financial matters are concerned. Avoid conflict with religious persons ; also keep clear of those who are possessed of strange notions and are eccentric and erratic. This will not be a good period to deal with strangers, and you would act wisely to live quietly, and avoid all excitement; for things will now tend to go wrong under the slightest provocation and discretion will be the better part of valour.

## SATURN.*

lxxv.    The CONJUNCTION of Saturn with the planet Uranus is not a very important conjunction, but it will act very powerfully if you have any very important " Directions " operating about this time.   It will be necessary to make many calculations, coming under the heading of " Directions " before anything definite can be said about its influence. However, it will in a general sense cause you to investigate the occult and mystical side of things, and incline your mind toward Astrology, and science generally.   The attitude of your mind will undergo a change with regard to former conventional ideas that you may have held, and if these changes in your mind are not too sudden you will have opportunity to look deeper, and more toward the subjective side of life than formerly. There are but a few who can understand the importance of this great conjunction, and they are the fully awakened.

lxxvi.    The progress of the planet Saturn to a BENEFIC aspect with Uranus is remarkably good, showing some advancement along occult lines, and an awakening of the lower nature towards higher things. During the period that this influence operates you will have opportunity to come in touch with advanced people, and will be brought in contact with metaphysical subjects, and will, in all probability, take an interest in all things that are deep and profound.   This influence is peculiarly beneficial to those who can respond to all matters connected with higher thought, and I judge that you will gain from its influence.

lxxvii.    The ADVERSE aspect of Saturn with Uranus, which becomes completed during this period, is unlikely to affect you in any immediate manner at this time, for its influence will probably have begun to make itself felt earlier and the completion of the aspect will therefore probably only mark one of the minor crises in the chain of events to which this aspect will give rise.   On those who are not yet capable of responding to the true nature of this influence at any time, it will probably have little effect, but it tends always to bring a complete separa-

---

* Both Jupiter and Saturn in the progressed horoscope move so slowly that they are unable (except very rarely) to form any aspect by progression which is not within " orbs " at birth.   This should be borne in mind when studying the paragraphs here given.

   The progression of Saturn to an aspect with NEPTUNE is so rare, and its influence so obscure, as to make it unnecessary to include it in such a book as this.   It may be interpreted in much the same general sense as the aspect to Uranus.

tion between custom and tradition on the one hand, and originality and independence on the other, so that you will be forced to decide whether you will go with the majority, or be "in the right with two or three" rather than prove false to a principle.

## LUNAR POSITIONS AND ASPECTS.

### The Moon progressing through the Signs.

**lxxviii.** The Moon is passing through the sign ARIES, so all matters to do with the mental sphere will be prominent during this time. In character you will be somewhat assertive, enterprising and impulsive, desiring to be at the very head of things, wanting very much to rule and lead. Mentally you will be more irritable than you usually are and certainly more active and ambitious. You will find yourself prone to make changes and desirous of altering existing conditions. Your personality will be stronger, and the life force more abundant than usual. You should therefore avoid rashness or too much enthusiasm.

**lxxix.** During this period the Moon will be in TAURUS, and financial matters may now engage your attention. You will try to be more practical and fixed, not desiring to change so much as to settle peacefully. It will, however, cause your feelings to be more than usually excited, and a kind of sensuous tendency will pass over you. You should carefully guard against inclinations to obstinacy or dogmatism, and should try to learn the true nature of what is called obedience. This influence tends to make you more determined, although feeling may be too strong to allow you to exercise all your will, the negative influence being more powerful than the positive.

**lxxx.** The Moon passing by progression through GEMINI will cause many dual experiences to come under your notice. You may now enter on two different undertakings or have two quite contrary experiences. This influence will cause you to reason upon your sensations and feelings: occasions also will arise that will require you to take a decided attitude, yet you will tend to waver and be undecided. Experiences in connection with relatives and travel will engage your attention, and you may incline to learning and be more eager for knowledge than usual; but all your experiences will be more or less of a dual nature. This being a Mutable sign you can expect nothing very definite or fixed, the mind being now difficult to concentrate.

**lxxxi.** The Moon has now progressed to the sign CANCER, a sign governing home-life and all domestic affairs, also the negative side of life generally. During this period domestic matters will come much under your notice and you will gain experience through them. You will make new ties and attach yourself to people or objects. You will become very sensitive, inclined to moods, able to feel the vibrations passing round you; but much will depend upon the circumstances in which you are placed, as to how the Moon's passage through this sign affects you. In character you will have the opportunity to become more tenacious, but also to become much more impressionable and receptive.

**lxxxii.** Whilst the Moon passes through the sign LEO your condition will be light-hearted and harmonious. You will take greater delight in pleasure, and possibly seek it more than usual. This sign governing all matters to do with the heart it will cause you to have various experiences in connection with the feelings, such as social affairs and matters connected with the joyous side of life. You will be inclined to speculate or invest money and your mind will tend to improve also. This is a good sign for the lunar orb to be passing through, being better able to meet adverse aspects, and accentuating the good. You are now under an influence that allows the aspects to express themselves positively.

**lxxxiii.** The sign through which the Moon is now progressing, VIRGO, will tend to make you express whatever discriminative powers you possess, and also accentuate your critical ability. Your mind will be engaged upon various undertakings and all business matters should increase, and much activity is denoted in connection therewith. This sign is not so good for your health, and you must not despond, or become melancholy, as your mind is apt to become rather too sensitive and critical and to see things less hopefully than is good for you. You may now interest yourself in a study of hygiene to advantage. You will be drawn more toward persons below you in the social sphere, and may do much to benefit them at this period.

**lxxxiv.** The Moon is now passing through LIBRA. While in this sign matters dealing with partnerships and marriage may occupy your attention; you will have more intercourse with strangers and friends than formerly, and will in some way be benefited by linking yourself with another. Your mind will be more equable and artistic, more affable and courteous, and much more inclined to look at things from a balanced point of view. It would be well to use caution in regard to legal affairs.

Your faculty of comparison should be much improved, and you should be able to judge how matters would be likely to end. You have now a good opportunity to become more tolerant and look at things impersonally.

lxxxv. During this period the Moon will be passing through the sign SCORPIO. Your mind will be very curious and will tend to enquire into the mystical and long to know the hidden things of nature, but you will also have a tendency to be more than usually dogmatic and proud. You should guard against jealousy or any condition that would cause you to live in the lower mind. It will, however, give you powers of self-control, and you may be raised to a higher condition of thought in which you will eventually seek to live. You may be attracted to some strange characters whilst the Moon is passing through the sign Scorpio. A loss in your circle is probable, this being the sign connected with what is called death.

lxxxvi. Whilst the Moon is passing through the sign SAGITTARIUS, the house of Jupiter, you will find your energies increasing, and you will tend to much activity. You will incline to higher thought, and a more philosophical spirit will now take possession of you than is usual to you. Long journeys may also be undertaken during this period, and your mind may be anxious in regard to travel. Still it is a good position, being the house of Jupiter; thus the evil aspects will not affect you so much as they would in any other sign. You must avoid being rebellious, and try to understand the meaning of law, and harmony; this being the sign that makes for prophecy, philosophy, science, and religion.

lxxxvii. While the Moon is passing through the sign CAPRICORN you will tend to become more ambitious as well as anxious for recognition, will make some efforts to advance yourself both socially and financially and therefore your mind will be prone to change, because you will desire to improve your general surroundings, yourself included. You will be much more contemplative and thoughtful, though more practical at the same time; you will also incline to look upon the graver side of life, and will come in touch with elderly persons and take much thought regarding your actions. But much depends on the aspects of the Moon, this being the sign of her fall, in which she has little power unless affected by the aspects from other planets, which can only be seen by a study of the " Directions " now in operation.

lxxxviii. The Moon has now progressed to the sign AQUARIUS. You will come more in touch with groups of persons, associations and societies and come into contact with many friends, or acquaintances. Your hopes and wishes will increase, and you will find yourself more refined and artistically inclined, also in possession of humanitarian ideas, tending to greatly improve your general surroundings and conditions; you will also be able to concentrate and think more deeply. This is a good position for the Moon; it gives you the ability to study human nature, the personality becoming now more anxious to gain a knowledge of humanity than at any other time of life. You will have opportunities to refine your lower nature and obtain more control over your mind.

**lxxxix.** The Moon has progressed to the sign PISCES, indicating a very receptive period, dual experiences, not altogether fortunate. Sorrows and disappointments may arise, and you will not always regard things from the bright side. You will be inclined to look into spiritualism or to study the occult, but you must avoid giving way to a more dreamy state than usual, as this is not a practical sign. You will now find yourself very much interested in psychism, or will have certain experiences in connection with public institutions, asylums and large buildings. You should be very careful to do nothing to give offence to others. This sign awakens the inner and softer side of the character, and usually makes the mind very receptive and inclined to be mediumistic, or affected by other minds.

## THE MOON PASSING THROUGH THE HOUSES*

**xc.** The Moon in her passage through the FIRST HOUSE of your nativity will now awaken the personality into fuller activity, and you will find yourself gaining more special and personal experiences which will affect, not only your environment, but also your mind and to some extent your disposition. You will feel most keenly the vibrations around you, and will desire changes, or may feel somewhat restless and unsettled. You will also come more prominently to the front, advancing your interests and seeking to stimulate the energetic side of your nature more than was formerly the case. You may now either travel or make removals, or make desirable changes in your surroundings and environment.

---

* The house-positions here referred to are of course those of the birth-horoscope. The position of the Moon in the houses of the progressed horoscope is comparatively unimportant.

**xci.** The Moon has now progressed to the SECOND HOUSE of your horoscope, and whilst it is passing through this house your financial affairs will be the cause of more concern than before, and you will either have more to do with finance, or your income will fluctuate and cause your mind to be more than usually taken up with monetary or business affairs. This has also to do with the thoughts in some way, as it is a succedent house, in which the thoughts are matured, but not immediately brought into action. You will in all probability pass through some experiences that will arrest your attention and cause you to think; it is very probable that these will be occasioned by your financial affairs, more than by any other means; therefore you should be prepared for some changes in this respect.

**xcii.** The Moon by progression since your birth has passed into the THIRD HOUSE of your nativity, the house of mind. You will now find your mental powers increase, and become more active than usual. You will either take some special journey, or travel during this period, or the third house having connection with relatives and brethren, you may expect to be concerned with their affairs more or less, during the time that the Moon takes to pass through the third house. Removals, but more probably travelling, will now .occupy much of your time and attention. This will be a good period wherein to study and energise your mind, either by reading or by engaging in those mental pursuits which tend to improve the mind generally.

**xciii.** The Lunar orb is now occupying the FOURTH HOUSE of your nativity by progression since your birth, this house being connected with home and domestic affairs, also the end of things. You may now expect some changes, either removals or alterations, variable conditions, etc., which will tend, in a certain measure, to upset your plans. Domestic and home affairs will now be very active, and you will in all probability have fresh occupants in your residence or abode, or have persons in the same house as yourself who will in some manner affect you. In many respects this is rather an unimportant house for the Moon to be passing through by progression except for the fact that it generally has more to do with the parents or elderly persons and home affairs particularly.

**xciv.** During this period the Moon's position by progression will be in the FIFTH HOUSE of your radical figure. This influence will incline you to matters of enterprise and will cause an activity in your sensational conditions, and thus awaken your desire-nature in many ways. You will be more than usually anxious to have pleasures and will either invest and speculate or desire to increase your income. You will be drawn toward social gatherings and favour entertainments and pleasurable undertakings, etc., the fifth house signifying pleasures, profit and success, also all matters connected with children and their affairs. You will now in all probability be concerned with some or all of these various indications, according to your ability to respond or restrain.

xcv. The Moon's position is now that of the SIXTH HOUSE of the natal chart, therefore all matters connected with the sixth house of your nativity will come to the front. It will be as well for you to safeguard your health, for sickness being often threatened whenever the Moon passes through this house necessitates the use of caution. This house has also some connection with phenomenal magic, and matters relating to the psychic world. It is also the house that is concerned with your inferiors, servants, and those who rank in a lower social scale than yourself; but the chief influence is generally that of health. You should take care to live carefully, and never allow yourself to become despondent. This period inclines to obscurity, and not much good fortune.

xcvi. The Moon in her revolution by what is termed secondary direction, or progression, has passed into the SEVENTH HOUSE of your horoscope. This will bring you in contact with partners, or those with whom your life will be linked in some way, as the seventh house of the nativity is the house of unions, and it is often found that when the Moon passes through this part of the horoscope marriages take place in the family, or some binding partnership is entered upon. It will bring you more before the public than usual, or you will take some very prominent position which will make you noted in the sphere in which you move. Avoid all legal disputes; for this is the house that is often productive of lawsuits and litigation.

xcvii. The Lunar orb is now in the EIGHTH HOUSE of your radical figure. This is the house of deaths, wills, legacies, and all matters that are connected with the dead and their affairs. Someone in your circle may pass over during the passage of the Moon through this house. You will gain money through co-workers, or the goods of the dead. This is rather a critical position for your affairs, although it will bring you nearer to the occult life, and it is quite probable that you will put your mind into occult and mystical matters much more deeply than you have hitherto done. You will either become a member of some occult school, or else find yourself more than usually psychic and mystical. This is a position which often brings the news of death.

**xcviii.** The Moon has now progressed to the NINTH HOUSE and in passing through this portion of your horoscope it will incline your mind and thought toward philosophical and scientific pursuits. You will either take a long journey or travel during the operation of this influence. It indicates that your mental vision will be widened, and your outlook will be more philosophical than usual. You will come in contact with either religious persons or some very deep thinkers. You will be active and alert, and will study deeper subjects than formerly. The ninth house is connected with what is termed the "higher mind," wherein the soul is more earnestly concerned with the subjective experiences than the objective and concrete. Your aspirations will now tend to quicken.

**xcix.** The Moon is now in the TENTH HOUSE of your nativity, the Midheaven, which has chief concern with honour, profession, and external matters generally. You will now come more to the front than formerly, obtaining either publicity, advancement or recognition from your efforts. You should seek to make all the progress that you can; for you will be able to command authority, and have far greater opportunities to advance in life, and make your activities more useful than hitherto. This position sometimes brings success, also the acquisition of power and responsibility. The whole of your horoscope is strengthened by this progressed position of the Moon, and much depends upon your abilities as to how it will benefit you ; but it brings opportunity.

**c.** The Moon has progressed into the ELEVENTH HOUSE of your Nativity, the house concerning desires, hopes, wishes, and friendships, etc. You will now meet with new friends, and find yourself coming in contact with associations and groups of people. You will make many new acquaintances and have many opportunities to form some permanent friendships. This is in many respects a favourable position for the Moon and some success will come to you while the Moon is in this house. You will now use your mind to advantage in artistic matters, and your desires will be more likely to be fulfilled, as this house favours all wishes. You will find yourself more than usually drawn toward the study of human nature and character.

**ci.** The Moon has now by progression passed into the mysterious TWELFTH HOUSE. You will now have some troubles and sorrows, and may perhaps suffer through enemies and accusations, etc., while the Moon is so posited. For this house is the position that stirs up the worst and most disagreeable influences in the Nativity. But it is a good position for the working out of destiny, and if you so regard it you will have various and many opportunities and realisations. You will probably have something to do with hospitals or places of confinement, or, it may be, duty in connection with such institutions during this period. You will be more drawn toward the psychic world and generally interested in the deeper side of life; occultism, etc. Your sympathies will be awakened for the suffering and needy.

## Lunar Aspects.

**cii.** The progression of the Moon has brought her to the CONJUNCTION of the Sun, an important position, usually indicating some important change that is about to take place in the circumstances, consequent upon the influx of the Solar life into the Lunar personality whereby the latter receives a new charge of life. This change is usually preceded by a period of more or less uncertainty and indecision, the coming events casting their shadows before, as it were. It indicates changes in the system and is sometimes accompanied by an indisposition of some kind whereby the system is accommodated to the new life flowing into it. This change is more beneficial as a rule to males than to females. Be careful of the health at this period, and avoid all indiscretions in diet, etc.

**ciii.** The Moon and Sun are now in BENEFIC aspect, tending to bring you some honour, success and credit. You may gain favour of those in a superior position ; and those in authority will also be able to render you aid if necessary. Your mind will tend to be somewhat ambitious and anxious for prosperity and advancement. You will have more than usual self-confidence and will gain by your association with others. You will also be inclined to form some binding and beneficial attachments. It is a favourable time for important changes, and under this aspect your moral growth will be stimulated, and your mental abilities increased. This is an opportunity which you would do well to make the most of materially.

**civ.** The Moon and the Sun are now in ADVERSE aspect, which is unfavourable for health, and brings troubles connected with parents, or those who are in any sense your superiors. Your mind will be rather assertive and contrary, and you will be liable to acts that may bring you into some disfavour. You may find yourself losing helpers or friends owing to the condition of your magnetism, or through your attitude to others, and you may lose some honour or feel yourself working against adverse influences. But much will depend upon the attitude of your mind as to how this aspect will operate, therefore control your mind and do not allow it to control you. Guard your health also, as the system will be somewhat run down.

cv.  The CONJUNCTION of the Moon with the planet Mercury will awaken your mental activities to the full, bringing activity in all business and enterprising affairs. You will either travel or undertake some new pursuits, or engage in those mental flights of imagination which will cause you to carry out new plans and schemes. It will be an excellent time for you to study, write or speak; in fact, wherever activity of the mental faculties is required you will be able to use and employ your mind to advantage. You will not lack power of expression while this conjunction is in operation, because it will allow you to use and energise your mind according to your mental and intellectual ability as shown by your nativity. To every person there are "times and, seasons," and this is the time to expand your mind to the full, its elasticity now being greater than at any other period of your life.

cvi.  During this period the Moon and Mercury are in BENEFIC aspect, bringing activity in writings, correspondence, literature, travel, commissions and business affairs generally. You may now expect some changes, your mind being restless and very desirous for changes of a beneficial nature. Your ideas will also be brighter and clearer, and general progress and prosperity will wait on nearly all your efforts where the mind is employed. Thus, mental pursuits may engage your attention to advantage during this period. A great deal of course depends on the nature of Mercury, in his aspect with the other planets at your birth, which may be learned from a study of the horoscope, but in a general sense the mind will be more than usually active and eager for improvement during this period.

cvii.  The Moon and Mercury are now in ADVERSE aspect, causing your mind to be in a restless and anxious condition; many petty worries will now tend to upset your affairs, and you will be over-anxious about any contemplated plans. You will do well to avoid correspondence as much as possible, and you should also sign no papers, or contracts and agreements, it being advisable to have as little to do with solicitors, clerks or literary persons as possible.  This influence is such as to produce mental anxiety, and troubles affecting the mind will react upon the health, affecting the whole system.  Keep your mind free from anxiety, or you will become involved in various troubles.  Avoid becoming too sarcastic or indiscreet in speech, and endeavour to keep your own counsel until this aspect passes away.

cviii.  The CONJUNCTION of the Moon with Venus denotes a very happy and pleasurable time, and in accordance with your power to enjoy, so will this conjunction benefit you.  Everything in any way connected with the emotional side of your nature will now be awakened, and a favourable time is reached for engagements and social intercourse and unions with others, also for everything wherein your love nature will be able to find its expression.  You will meet with persons who will minister to your happiness and you will have opportunities to enjoy life to the full.  To some people this conjunction marks the epoch of their life, bringing another life into it and from that union establishing the fate or fortune of the whole future.  To others who have not the responsive horoscope it merely brings a more or less favourable and pleasant period.

cix.  The Moon and Venus being now in BENEFIC aspect may bring success in your financial affairs, but more especially in matters to do with pleasure and domestic concerns.  You may now engage your mind with advantage in matters relating to the opposite sex, for a happy and prosperous time is now foreshadowed.  You will find your disposition very peaceful and happy, and all things will tend to go forward, especially matters dealing with society and friendship.  It is good for all matters connected with partnerships, and love affairs generally, or where finance is concerned in any very particular sense.  This period should prove a prosperous one for your worldly welfare.

cx.  The Moon and Venus are now in ADVERSE aspect, bringing some sorrow and disappointment, especially in your domestic affairs.  Your feelings will be affected, and you will be in danger of acting carelessly, and may expect disappointments, and also disagreement with the opposite sex.  Any matters having to do with pleasure are better avoided, for little success in happiness or pleasure is indicated.  You will do well to practise restraint, avoiding excess of feeling, grief, or sorrow. This aspect usually causes some extravagance or excess in some way, and also sometimes affects the health; it is, however, an influence that can be overcome by care, and by avoiding conflict with the feminine sex generally.

**cxi.** The Moon in CONJUNCTION with the planet Mars is not a favourable position, and much will depend upon whether you stop to think before you act, or whether impulse prompts all your actions during the period that it is in operation. It is one of the most unfortunate periods of a life, bringing a liability to accidents, disputes, and danger of many misfortunes through associates or dealings with the opposite sex. To some persons this conjunction marks the most unfortunate and disastrous epoch in the life, but only those who will not stop to think carefully ere action is taken. To all, however, it is a period to guard against, nothing of importance being undertaken while this conjunction lasts. The health is liable to suffer from feverish conditions, and functional disorders are threatened while it is operating, therefore more than usual caution and discretion are necessary to avoid mishaps. The overplus of physical energy that accompanies this position may be advantageously used if applied to existing conditions. Seek to control restlessness.

**cxii.** The Moon has now advanced to a BENEFIC aspect with the planet Mars, which will tone up your affairs in general, and give you an inclination to travel or take journeys, your mind being more than usually active and prone to changes, exercise, and activity generally. You will be more courageous, loving freedom and seeking independence. But you must avoid everything impulsive, and not act rashly in any way, for your inclinations will tend very strongly in the direction of doing things suddenly and from impulse. The positive element predominating, all matters connected with the male sex will prove beneficial to you. Business affairs will also go well, your activity allowing you to embark upon new schemes and undertakings. The emotional side of your nature will now be active.

**cxiii.** The Moon has now reached an ADVERSE aspect with Mars This influence generally causes a feverish state of the blood, and gives a liability to fevers, and accidents of some kind, and if you are at all impulsive you will be liable to several dangers. It makes you mentally inclined to dispute; you will, under provocation, be likely to rush into litigation ; therefore avoid being over hasty and rash in your judgments. Be careful if you travel to avoid risk of accidents, and avoid all impulses and excesses. Do nothing hurriedly, and take time to think before you act, as you may now get into trouble through hastiness. All that happens to you during this period will be partially the result of impulsive thought or action, and any tendency to be rash in speech will bring trouble upon you. Avoid over-stimulating foods.

**cxiv.** The CONJUNCTION of the Moon with the planet Jupiter is a very benefic and fortunate influence, which will make this period one of the important portions of your life. Your general health and prosperity will improve, and social intercourse with others will be advantageous and profitable. To those who are seeking spiritual advancement, this is the best period for aspiration and higher thought. It forms the apex point of the benefic influence, and brings many blessings which only those who are sensitive to the perfume of the inner and more subtle vibrations can appreciate. But for those also who are seeking worldly welfare this is the time not only to commence new undertakings, but also to make the best of existing conditions, success following all efforts that may be made to bring prosperity and financial gain. Honours, preferment and fame come to those who have the natal marks of elevation and promotion indicated for this time.

**cxv.** The Moon and Jupiter in BENEFIC aspect will make this period a very successful one, nearly all your efforts being attended with prosperity and success. Your mind will be free and generous, frank and jovial, and your body healthy. You are now entering on a hopeful and promising period, during which you will form some honourable and beneficial attachments and friendships. You may now embark on any serious undertakings for future gain and happiness, and generally all will go well. Your mind will be more inclined to higher thought, and your mental and moral character improve. You may now push all important matters well forward, for eventual success. "Make hay while the sun shines."

**cxvi.** The Moon is now in ADVERSE aspect with Jupiter, indicating some monetary losses or financial changes. It is a bad influence for new undertakings, or having anything to do with business, unless extreme care is used. All speculation should now be avoided, also dealings with solicitors or with persons in authority, holding property, or governing bodies. Matters to do with law are likely to cause you loss, and you are apt to be extravagant and over free during the period of this direction. It is not by any means a good aspect for finance, so do not borrow or lend; beware also of letting expenditure exceed receipts. Keep your blood pure, or your health may suffer.

cxvii. The Moon has now advanced to the CONJUNCTION of the planet Saturn, an aspect that is not often favourable or productive of worldly fortune. It is considered a restricting and binding influence and as such it limits and restrains, thus appearing to hinder progress. It is however an indirect blessing, for it produces stability, thoughtfulness, and a certain degree of firmness. It is in reality an influence that brings a period of responsibility upon those who are progressive, and during the period that it operates you should not shirk any old or new responsibilities. To some it lowers the vitality and gives a liability to take chill or become subject to colds, and thus causes the health to get below par and makes it difficult to recuperate if the vital forces are allowed to run down; therefore use care while it is in operation.

cxviii. The Moon and Saturn in BENEFIC aspect to each other during this period, indicates general success in business matters, and promises a steady and prosperous time. Your mind will be more concentrative and thoughtful and quietly industrious and you will do well in all Saturnine pursuits or investments, such as mining, building, etc., or through business connected therewith. Mentally it will make you sober, grave, calm and persistent, always taking due forethought before action. It brings success to efforts where severe labour is employed or careful planning needed, and you may now sow thoughts that will produce lasting effects. This is an excellent opportunity for you to study science or any subject requiring very clear or profound thought.

cxix. The Moon and Saturn are now in ADVERSE aspect. This will bring you disappointment and sorrow, causing the period to be an unfortunate one. Your mind will tend to despond and you may suffer from morbid and melancholy tendencies which will cause you to take cold easily, and thereby make you suffer in health. You will find yourself more than usually cold in manner and suspicious in thought, and your disposition will now be more reserved, and reticent, making you feel more cramped than usual. You will do well not to begin any new undertaking of importance under this influence, and should use caution in all your actions when dealing with others, especially your elders. At the same time do not exaggerate prudence. Your mind will be fearful and anxious, but you must avoid suspicion and mistrust.

cxx. The Moon has progressed to the CONJUNCTION of the planet Uranus, a position that denotes that some sudden or unexpected event is likely to take place, the nature of which it is difficult to foresee.

This influence may act mentally, emotionally, or physically, but its ultimate will be some change, in all probability of a temporary nature, either in consciousness or in your environment.  It will be a favourable time to entertain new thought or to come into touch with advanced views in order that your mental outlook may be widened, and your sphere of influence expanded.  With some it signifies a romance, or new enterprises, and with all it tends to increase the personal magnetism and attract those who are responsive to its higher rate of vibration.  For Uranus is the planet of mysteries, wonders and development, therefore pay great attention to your conditions while under this influence.

**cxxi.**  The Moon is now in BENEFIC aspect to Uranus, a position which promises some sudden or unexpected benefits, and perhaps some strange or uncommon travelling.  Removals or changes are promised which will prove beneficial, and any adventures you may engage in should turn out well.  You will find your mind more than usually eager, more inclined for out-of-the-way studies, and disposed to look into the deeper side of life, while your disposition will be somewhat unconventional, seeing things from a new standpoint; hence this influence is favourable for the study of Astrology.  Your magnetic power will increase, and you will have influence over others, bringing you success with societies and public bodies.

**cxxii.**  The Moon and Uranus being now in ADVERSE aspect your affairs are likely to go unexpectedly wrong, entailing disappointment and disagreeable consequences.  You should be cautious, and guard against accidents while travelling; in fact, it is advisable to avoid travel if possible while under this influence, there being some liability to untoward events.  Be guarded in speech, as you will tend to be more brusque than usual, and your mind either more aggressive, or troubled and anxious. It is an unfortunate aspect, denoting a very critical time, when matters go wrong unexpectedly and things over which you have no control turn out adversely.  Avoid dealing with public bodies, societies and associations. Take extra pains to understand another's point of view, for you may tend to be hasty and make mistakes at this time.

**cxxiii.**  The Moon has now arrived at the CONJUNCTION of the planet Neptune, and you are sure to feel this influence in some peculiar psychic way, though possibly it will not bring any marked change of circumstances in its train.  Its real effect will depend very largely on your sensitiveness to the Neptunian influence, and whether this affects you physically, emotionally or mentally.  To the majority of people very little if anything happens under this conjunction, save perhaps that they meet with some uncommon person or undergo some insignificant but peculiar and uncommon experiences.  The emotional nature is sure to be strangely stirred at this time, and you should be very careful that you are not led into indiscreet acts that your calmer judgment would not approve.

**cxxiv.** The Moon is now in BENEFIC aspect with the planet Neptune, and this is favourable in the main, though greatly subject to the general influences in operation as to the way in which it acts.  Your personal conditions are now likely to be harmonious and you will get on well with those with whom you are brought into contact.  Probably some excursion or seaside trip will bring a week or two of pleasant experiences; for the sea generally has some bearing, direct or indirect, upon all matters under the influence of Neptune, the planet being related to the deeper emotions of human nature, symbolised by the sea.  Do not, however, expect too much lasting good from this aspect, which is only transient.

**cxxv.** The Moon has now arrived at an ADVERSE aspect with Neptune, and this will or will not affect you, in accordance with your sensitiveness to the Neptunian vibrations.  It is an influence that passes many people entirely by, but it chiefly affects the psychic or emotional nature.  It is rather unfortunate in the main, rendering one liable to fraud and deception, or to be victimised in some way; and you should be on your guard while it operates, being careful not to place yourself unduly under the influence of any person, or group of persons, of whose *bona fides* you are not quite sure.  Beware of bogus schemes offering great returns for a small outlay, and do not allow yourself to be greatly influenced by " personal magnetism."

# CHAPTER XXXVI.

## CONCLUSION.

IN order that this book may be used to the best advantage, a special Chart should be prepared,* similar to that printed on the following page, the numbers of the paragraphs, as given in the REFERENCE CHART at the beginning of the book, should then be carefully filled in opposite to the descriptions as in the Example Chart facing title-page.

When the special Chart sheet has been prepared, reference should be made to the various paragraphs containing the required delineations. They may be read from the book, or written out in their order so as to form a complete delineation. The whole reading may however be considerably amplified and extended by reference to the other volumes of this series, in the following order :

*Astrology for All, Part I.*, for :—

Delineations based on the Rising Sign, pp. 164-184
Individual and Personal Characteristics „ 13-47
The Moon in the signs „ 63-70
The Polarities „ 71-156
Also the planets and their sign-positions „ 189-238

*Astrology for All, Part II.* The Horoscope may be correctly cast from the Condensed Ephemeris from 1850 to 1911.

*How to Judge a Nativity, Part I.*, may be referred to for further details concerning each of the twelve houses and the planetary positions with their aspects.

*How to Judge a Nativity, Part II.*, in like manner may be turned to for a full description of the planets, and for useful hints upon the *synthesising* of a horoscope. Finally

*The Progressed Horoscope* may be studied if it is desired to examine the Future in detail.

---

* These special Charts may be obtained from the office of *Modern Astrology* at the following rates : 100 at 2s. 6d., 50 at 1s. 6d., 25 at 1s., post free.

# The Key to Your Own Nativity
# Special Chart

| Description of Paragraph | Number of Paragraph |
|---|---|
| INTRODUCTION | |
| §1 RISING SIGN | |
| RULING PLANET | |
| Ruler's House | |
| Ruler's Sign | |
| Ruler's Aspects | |
| *Extra Par.* | |
| §2 INDIVIDUALITY | |
| Sun in Sign | |
| Sun's Aspects | |
| „ „ | |
| §3 PERSONALITY | |
| Moon in Sign | |
| Moon in House | |
| Moon's Aspects | |
| „ „ | |
| POLARITY | |
| §4 MENTAL QUALIFICATIONS | |
| Mercury in Sign | |
| Mercury in House | |
| Mercury's Aspects | |
| „ „ | |

| Description of Paragraph | Number of Paragraph |
|---|---|
| §5 FINANCE | |
| TRAVEL | |
| ENVIRONMENT | |
| ENTERPRISE | |
| SICKNESS | |
| MARRIAGE | |
| LEGACIES | |
| PHILOSOPHY | |
| PROFESSION | |
| FRIENDS | |
| OCCULTISM | |
| *Supplementary Paragraphs* | |
| Rising Planet | |
| Personal Colouring | |
| Planet in Sign | |
| *Extra Par.* | |
| §6 SUMMARY | |
| Planetary Positions | |
| Quality | |
| ☉ & ☽ | |
| *Extra Par.* | |

## §7 FUTURE PROSPECTS

| *Year* | *Aspect* | *Paragraph* |
|---|---|---|
| | | |
| | | |
| | | |

# APPENDIX.

## An Example Delineation.

THE reader may possibly feel that however simple the plan of this book, and however clear the instructions, an Example in Full would help him to feel certain that he had grasped the whole idea in a satisfactory manner. And therefore it has been thought well to reprint in their proper order the paragraphs relating to the Chart which forms the Frontispiece to this work.

The choice of this nativity for such a purpose will hardly need explanation, since in the year of his accession the figure of HIS MOST GRACIOUS MAJESTY KING GEORGE THE FIFTH is emphatically the cynosure of the whole world.

It may be wondered, perhaps, why the paragraphs are reprinted just as they stand in the body of the book, why at least they are not diverted from the second person to the third. Is there not a certain impertinence, it may be argued, in thus addressing what will seem to be a personal admonition, couched in the familiar " you " and " your " of ordinary speech, to one of such exalted station ?

This possibility was clearly foreseen, and the two alternatives considered before the present course was taken. To take another Example seemed a pity when His Majesty's character and temperament were being made the theme of newspaper and magazine articles by the score— for where could a better test of the truth of Astrology *as a science* be found than this?

On the other hand, to modify the wording of each paragraph would have been to invite a charge of " doctoring " the delineation. The alteration of the second to the third person would, it is true, entail no such consequences; but it would involve a certain disadvantage by robbing the delineation of that vigour and directness which arise out of the use of the second person, and so weaken it of some of its force.

In the end it was thought that readers generally, and even the august native himself (should he ever honour this book with a perusal),

284

would find the apparent familiarity void of offence, considering the purpose which the delineation is intended to serve. And therefore the paragraphs are reproduced word for word, the same as in the earlier chapters, the Delineation thus being strictly representative of the value and use of the book.

The following Delineation may therefore be regarded as a model or pattern for beginners to imitate, when drawing up delineations for their friends.

In cases where a written delineation is given, it is well worth while to arrange that every paragraph has a page to itself. As each contains just about enough to go comfortably on a page of an ordinary exercise book, there need be no difficulty about this, and the advantage of having the reader's attention concentrated on one paragraph at a time is obvious. To use only the right-hand page, leaving the left blank, also makes for clearness, and besides leaves room for additions or comments to be made without spoiling what has been written. Indeed, most who have tried this plan are agreed that it is false economy to write on both sides of the paper. But each reader will find out for himself the plan that suits him best. No method suits all equally well, and these hints are only offered as suggestions which may appeal to some.

## THE NATIVITY OF HIS MAJESTY KING GEORGE V. *

### INTRODUCTION.

630. The True Purpose of Astrology is to serve as a guide through
A b   physical life, but the soul must have awakened before the real value of a horoscope can be fully appreciated. The writer believes that CHARACTER IS DESTINY and that we, in our past lives, have woven the web of destiny by our own thinking, and thus to-day are weaving the web of our future horoscope. All sin is a result of ignorance or non-knowledge, therefore to KNOW ourselves is to become wise and thus to master fate. All fate, good or evil, is made originally by our own thoughts and actions and has its roots in our *character*. The horoscope

---

* The reader is requested to bear in mind through this delineation what is sai on p. 284.

is the indicator of the Divine Law in action and thus helps us to discover much of our destiny.

## "What Sign am I Born Under?"

630.   The following quotation from *Everybody's Astrology* will serve
   C   to clear up an element of doubt that often arises in connection with this question.

"Astrologers use the expression 'under' any sign, or 'under the influence of' any sign in three quite different ways, as follows :

> (1)   When under the Sun's influence through that sign, *i.e.*, the Sun is in that sign at birth.
> (2)   When the Moon is in that sign at birth.
> (3)   When born under a certain sign of the Zodiac, *i.e.*, that sign is on the horizon at birth.   (" Rising Sign.")

.   .   .   .   .   Thus, in the case of any given man or woman for (1) it would merely be necessary to know the month of birth, for (2) it would also be needful to know the very day, and for (3) the actual time and place of birth.   This fact gives us a hint as to the relative importance of the three senses in which the phrase is used."

In the popular articles on Astrology which appear from time to time in the weekly papers the term " born under " such and such a sign usually refers to the sign occupied by the Sun, and *not* to the Rising Sign, a practice which is to be regretted as it often causes confusion.

## What is Meant by the Term "Rising Sign."

630.   Each point of the zodiac rises, culminates, and sets once in every
   D   24 hours; this is caused by the turning of the earth on its axis. The zodiac, consisting of 360 degrees, is divided into 12 "signs," or portions of 30 degrees each, and the sign which is on the Eastern horizon at birth is known as the Rising Sign or Ascendant.   (See *Everybody's Astrology*, pp. 93, 94.)

The "Rising Sign" describes your form and temperament, your disposition and general tastes and likings.   It denotes the form fitted for the environment, and it is the most important point in your nativity to consider.   Next comes the planet which governs your sign, your " Ruling Planet," together with any planets that may be rising upon the Eastern Horizon at birth; and after that the Sun and Moon.

## The Ascendant or Rising Sign.

**1.** ARIES was rising at your birth. This is a cardinal, movable and fiery sign. This gives much energy and activity both of body and mind, much impulse and enthusiasm, with many changes in the course of life. You are courageous, enterprising, frank and outspoken. You can face difficulties promptly and bravely; you know your own mind, and are seldom at a loss what to do or say when called upon to decide. You are ambitious, self-reliant, and adventurous; and you will win your way in the world largely through these qualities and through your confidence in your own ability to succeed. You are a great lover of freedom and independence, and you get along badly when you are in any way hampered, restricted, or interfered with. You are generous and quickly responsive to appeals to the emotions. You are a zealous and energetic supporter of any person or cause that enlists your sympathies. Most of your misfortunes will arise through too much hastiness and impulse, whether in action, in judgment, or in the feelings. You are somewhat lacking in coolness, in calm deliberation, and self-restraint; and you do not find it easy to give way to others even when justice or prudence demands it. Mars is the ruling planet of the sign Aries.

## The Ruling Planet.

**17.** The planet MARS is the ruler of the signs Aries and Scorpio. It is the planet of fire, energy, and expansion. It gives you a disposition that is ardent, active, positive, impulsive, and impetuous. You are a lover of freedom and independence, and cannot endure restraint, confinement or delay. You are generous and frank, an admirer of openness, bravery and courage, both physical and moral. You have much self-confidence, and are usually able to hold your own easily, being prompt in word and action. You need to beware of being too rash and headstrong, for you are rather inclined to be aggressive and self-willed; and you are likely to bring many troubles upon yourself through this. You have a good deal of pride, which is easily wounded, and you do not find it easy to remain cool and self-restrained under provocation. You are an active and energetic worker and can accomplish much in a short time, and you have it in you to become very practical and capable in the world if you exercise a little self-discipline.

## THE RULER'S POSITION.

26. The ruling planet is in the FIFTH HOUSE. This brings out the social and pleasure-loving side of the nature, giving warmth to the affections and ardour to the feelings. Amusements and occupations are taken up because they give you pleasure rather than for any use you intend to put them to, and you extract a good deal of enjoyment from life. In some cases the person who has this position at birth follows some pursuit or takes up some hobby that gives pleasure to others, such as music, art, the theatre, etc., and there is often decided taste in one of these directions. You must beware of going too far in matters of pleasure and the senses. You may be able to gain through judicious speculation when under favourable directions. You will be interested in children and fond of them. Your love nature will be strong and easily moved. You are generous, sincere, and honourable. Vitality and bodily health are strengthened by this position.

## THE INFLUENCE OF MARS.

86. MARS IN LEO. This is a strong position for Mars, giving some success through matters governed by the planet. It makes you energetic, active, and independent, and contributes strength of will and character. It indicates that you are sincere, honourable, open, candid, and generous ; it fits you for a position of responsibility where you would have to control others, to manage, order, and command. It brings you recognition and respect from superiors and those in authority, and possibly may lift you up in life and give honour or preferment. It is apt to make you a little too positive or militant in manner, so that when you are under bad directions you may make enemies and meet with opposition and contention. This increases the fire and vitality of the body but gives a little liability to fevers, accidents, and high temperature. You may suffer from social opposition or from family disputes ; there is danger of too much impulsiveness or rashness in love matters ; and there may be death of a child. The heart or back may be affected, but no serious evil need be feared as Mars is strong here.

## MARS' ASPECT.

267. Venus and the planet Mars were in an ADVERSE aspect in your nativity. Although this is an unfortunate aspect it will in many

ways stimulate your feelings, making your emotional nature very keen and active. It is rather an improvident aspect, tending to make you over generous and impulsive, and through this you may lose financially, and through excess of feeling may in some way be imposed upon. You should be guarded in all your dealings with the opposite sex and never let yourself be drawn into any scheme or plan that might be misconstrued. *This aspect is not favourable for love, or marriage, denoting dangers from quarrels and jealousy. It spoils financial prospects.* (See special note.)

## THE RISING PLANET.

**473.** NEPTUNE rising at the time of your birth, will affect your life in an uncommon manner. You will be romantic and mediumistic, or psychically inclined. Some very strange experiences and also some remarkable episodes will occur in your life. It is only the very few who can in any way respond to the subtle, spiritual vibrations of the planet Neptune, and they are the souls that live the purest lives. You must be on your guard against hypnotic suggestion, and should be very choice in your associates and acquaintances. You will in all probability have some very remarkable dreams, which you should endeavour to remember. You will not escape being very mediumistic and hypersensitive at times.

## INDIVIDUAL CHARACTERISTICS.

**144.** SUN IN GEMINI. The vitalising principle of the solar rays in this sign will make you quick-witted, mentally impulsive, and inclined to be imperative. You will be intellectual, interested in literature, science or art, and also somewhat ambitious and aspiring. You should cultivate concentration if you would become clever, for you have latent ability in connection with literature or public speaking. There will be restlessness in your internal character which will lead to nervousness and irritability, and when not guarded against, there will be a tendency for you to become volatile, indecisive and unreliable. It will be well for your comfort and happiness in life, if you learn to avoid worry and restlessness. A study of thought control would enable you to turn much of your intellectual ability to good account.

**212.** The Sun and the planet Mars in BENEFIC aspect, is remarkably good for your health and vitality generally. It will give you courage, and a strong constitution. Your will power and desire nature are blended, which will enable you to force your way in life with an intensity of purpose, energy, and perseverance that will seldom, if ever, be thwarted. You can control and command others, you will generally carry your point through energy and strength of will more than through tact and diplomacy. You may accomplish great things if you let your individual nature act more often than the personal desires and wishes. This very powerful influence often gives too much life, and it is necessary to either have plenty of exercise, or live an active life to distribute it through the system evenly.

224. The Sun was in a BENEFIC aspect with Neptune indicating that the influence of this mystical planet is beneficial to your spiritual growth, and probably you will find your greatest expansion of consciousness will arise out of experiences which you would have a great difficulty in adequately describing to others. The real paradoxes of life will be always more or less present to your consciousness, and certain truths that can only be expressed in the form of a paradox will always have a special meaning and reality for you, if you can rise to the highest side of this influence. You will be, in the general sense of the word, lucky (though you may not consider yourself so), and you will be much liked by other people as a rule. You should, however, beware lest the sensuous side of life dominate you.

## PERSONAL CHARACTERISTICS.

160. MOON IN LIBRA. This position confers upon you personally a refined character. It will make you love ease and pleasure, the arts, and social gatherings. You will always be kindly, genial, affable, and courteous, and will try to preserve a happy disposition. You will like approval, and life will be sweet to you when you are appreciated, but not so when you remain unnoticed. You will be just as well as generous, and love order and refinement. You have good powers of imitation and perception, and love of comparison. Always endeavour to be even-tempered, and try to keep the " Balance." It will not be well to carry comparison too far, and activity may at times be beneficial. You have some artistic tastes.

172. THE MOON IN THE SEVENTH HOUSE will bring you into intimate relation with the public, and you will be popular in your own sphere, though at times you may have to contend with some public

opposition. You will come into contact with those who travel much, and make acquaintance with some who lead Bohemian or roving lives. Your chances of success in law will fluctuate, at times going well, at other times adversely, according to the aspects. Another life will surely be mixed up with your own, causing you anxiety as well as pleasure and happiness, for your fortunes will always be strangely bound up with those of another, either in marriage, partnerships, or where there is more than a single and separate interest.

233.
The Moon and the planet Mars were in BENEFIC aspect at your birth. This aspect will make you fearless, enterprising, and courageous. You can exhibit much pluck and endurance, being resolute and full of that confidence in yourself which will enable you to deal successfully with others. You are fully competent to undertake anything upon which you set your mind. It is a very hopeful aspect, provided you are not too free and generous, as you may then tend to become rather prodigal or too extravagant. This influence will strengthen and tone up your constitution, enabling you to resist disease. It will also make you bright and cheerful, improving your disposition.

## The Polarity.

5i0.
Blending the influence of the Sun in GEMINI and Moon in Libra, representing your individual and personal character, this is a combination which shows that you have a peculiar spiritual tendency with a love of the occult and the unseen, also a very intuitive and far-seeing mind. You have great accuracy and quickness of decision and will appreciate the study of nature and philosophy. You have good imitative powers and these will enable you to hold your own in all departments of life, but you are more especially fitted for literary pursuits. You often come to your decisions quickly through intuition rather than reason, and have a wonderful appreciation of beauty, art, and everything of an ennobling character. You are liable to be affected by others, and it is essential that you associate with pure persons, if not, you will absorb much of their influence and perhaps be led to think that it is your own. Learn to distinguish between your own views and opinions and those of others.

## Mental Qualifications.

179.
MERCURY IN TAURUS indicates that you are slow to make up your mind, but that it is immovable when once it is made up.

You can, however, exercise much patience and perseverance in all mental pursuits, and it makes you disposed to be sociable, friendly and affectionate. It also inclines you towards religion, and gives you a taste for art, music or poetry. You can exercise much endurance in all you undertake mentally, and I judge that you possess good memory. This position of Mercury in a fixed sign, makes you just, constant, firm, industrious, strict, sincere, and uncompromising, but you must guard against a danger of becoming mentally obstinate.

191. MERCURY IN THE SECOND HOUSE. This is favourable for gaining by correspondence, letters, and writing, also for financial success in literary pursuits, and in professional and artistic affairs generally. Although a good position for Mercury on the whole, and when under favourable directions you would be successful as regards travel and short journeys, it is on the other hand not very favourable when afflicted. You have mental abilities for finance and would gain either by trading, or through scientific pursuits, lectures, etc. *But you should guard against theft and fraud, as at some time of your life you may be the victim of sharp practice.* (See special note on p. 300.)

247. Mercury in CONJUNCTION with Venus is a very good position, refining the mental qualities and causing your mind to be sympathetic, artistic and poetical: you are thus able to appreciate all matters connected with art. Possessing a good eye for colour, and loving all things beautiful, you naturally incline to painting, music, poetry or singing, everything in fact that is likely to give pleasure to yourself and others. Science is not likely to attract you, but you delight in reading, especially the lighter form of literature, though your mind will not be very concentrative or studious. You will be well-disposed and affable in disposition, ever choosing the social and pleasurable side of life, not the laborious.

## FINANCE.

311. MERCURY governs the house of finance in your nativity, and thus promises gain through literary matters, agencies, papers, etc.; in short, all stationery occupation in which the mind is more employed than the body. You have good business abilities, and you are inventive as well as rather acquisitive where money is concerned, but you should guard against fraud and theft, and also be cautious in signing all financial

documents. You would do well in all professions where a quick and rapid movement is required, and journalism or businesses and professions connected with printing, commission, agencies, etc., would furnish the most remunerative mode of income for you.

## TRAVEL.

323. THE SUN governing the third house of your nativity is rather favourable for any travelling that you may take during life, but in a general sense it does not indicate much moving about. You may come into contact with or meet persons of high and noble birth while taking journeys, as the Sun signifies all things connected with rank and high estate. All your travels should have some high mission connected with them, or you may have some commission to perform that necessitates your moving from place to place occasionally. You have a very high spirit and agree well with your brethren, and benefit by or through them in some manner. The mind is broad and generally impartial and there is agreement with relatives.

## ENVIRONMENT.

342. URANUS having rule over the fourth house of your nativity indicates that the latter portion of your life is to be somewhat peculiar and eccentric. You will take up studies towards the close of life of which in the earlier part you had little if any idea. This position of the planet Uranus is not altogether favourable, as it indicates some sudden surprises and unexpected events in the closing years of life, and you may come into some environment that you will not be able to respond to unless you have made great progress in occult matters. You have some ability to study astrology and kindred subjects.

## ENTERPRISE.

348. MARS having rule over the fifth house of your nativity, denotes much energy and an enterprising spirit, and if you avoid impulse in matters of speculation, also with regard to certain investments, you may apply your energy to advantage in speculative matters, but you should carefully avoid gambling or any risky enterprises where you have to rely upon the honesty of others. You are somewhat free in matters connected with pleasure, and ardent in your affections, with a tendency to involve yourself with the opposite sex if you are not cautious in

dealing with them. This influence indicates some pain or some trouble through children, and warns you against all rash conduct in your enterprises.

## SICKNESS.

355. MERCURY having rule over the sixth house of your nativity most of your ills in life will arise through nervous and also mental troubles. You should be careful never on any account to worry, if you value your health at all, because a nervous breakdown is threatened you at any time when the mind lets you give way to worry and irritability. All your sicknesses will generally arise from the condition of your mind and the nervous system. You will have some psychic impressions that will in certain directions affect you, and there is more depending upon the peaceful condition of your mind than you will ever estimate. This influence is a dangerous one when mental troubles press heavily, affecting the mind.

## MARRIAGE.

368. SATURN governs the seventh house, the house of marriage, in your nativity. This planet tends to delay or hinder the marriage prospects. Should marriage take place however, it promises a faithful and steady partner, one who is just though rather grave and serious, very industrious, persevering, careful, thrifty and economical. There is some probability of your partner being older than yourself, with a tendency to court responsibility. It is not a very favourable testimony for prosperity, but it denotes a faithfulness in the marriage state, although care should be taken not to allow coldness to spring up between you at any time, for your partner will not be over demonstrative in affection, and will prefer action to speech and loving deeds in preference to the use of many words of endearment.

## LEGACIES.

387. MARS has chief influence over all matters connected with the eighth house of your nativity, the house concerned with deaths, wills or legacies. You may or may not, gain money by the death of others, but if you should it would be sudden, and in some way unexpected, for Mars is not a good planet to be concerned with money matters. You would find that you had been probably buoyed up by some false

hope, and would not gain so much as you had been led to expect.  Your own *terminus vitæ* will be somewhat sudden, although you may live to a good age, but it will be advisable to guard against accidents, and not to run any more risk than is absolutely necessary.  You would be drawn to public calamities, etc.

## PHILOSOPHY.

397.  JUPITER rules over the ninth house of your nativity, the house of science, philosophy, and religion.  This influence inclines you to philosophy and wisdom, in its widest sense.  You will not be so scientific, as philosophical and artistic, for you incline more to accept the broad outlines than the limited and precise details of the higher mind.  You would succeed in foreign lands, and probably gain in some way through foreign affairs.  This influence favours all legal affairs, and also religious matters in general.  It gives you some prophetic tendencies and the power to dream correctly and also to bring the dreams through into the physical brain.  Take note of them.

## PROFESSION.

407.  SATURN has rule over your profession or occupation and this denotes power and authority in some way, but brings most fortune and success through industry and perseverance.  You will either hold a leading position or have some kind of responsibility placed upon you.  This Saturnine influence is not good for business matters as there is always some danger threatened, either through the injury of others or the failure to carry to a successful issue whatever projects you have in hand.  Saturn favours gain by labour more than by good fortune.  Matters requiring patience, tact and caution succeed better than any other methods, therefore you should seek the pursuits requiring these qualifications.

## FRIENDS.

419.  SATURN governing the eleventh house of your nativity, will bring some very faithful and reliable friends into your life, but some trouble in connection with your friends and acquaintances is also denoted.  *You will have friends, in a general sense, amongst the aged or those who are much older than yourself.*  (See note, p. 300.)  You will have some bitter disappointments, in connection with either friends and

acquaintances, and you will not always realise your hopes and wishes with regard to them. Some of your so-called friends are liable to desert you, when you most require their aid, therefore do not rely too much upon all your friends, this influence giving but few real friends.

## OCCULTISM.

435. Your twelfth house, the house of occultism and secret affairs, was NOT OCCUPIED by any planet at your birth, therefore its influence over your life was not so strong as would have been the case had a planet stirred this house into activity. This may have the effect of delaying any special effort on your part to lead the occult life, and whatever tendencies you may have towards occultism will come from other influences in your nativity. There is one advantage that this gives you, it does not show any very marked sorrow through treachery or the deliberate evil intention of enemies, and all your troubles arising from enmity or jealousy will be more spontaneous, and the result of impulse rather than premeditation.

## PERSONAL COLOURING.

480. The Moon occupying the sign LIBRA at your birth will tinge your personal aura with light sky-blue, making you compassionate, affectionate, sympathetic and generally kind hearted. At the same time you must be careful not to let other people's minds and conditions affect you too much, for those who have this colour in their aura have a tendency to be swayed by environment and psychic emanations. It will make you very refined and religiously inclined, tending to bring out all the finer qualities which belong to the planet Venus which this colour is directly under, therefore all artistic pursuits will tend to accentuate this portion of your aura and you will view the world generally from a more balanced standpoint than the majority. This ray will strengthen your powers of comparison, and the more balanced you become, the more will you lean towards the side of justice and tend to harmonise yourself under the Venus principle. Therefore try to discover as much as possible the strength and influence of the planet Venus in your nativity.

## THE INFLUENCE OF VENUS.

71. VENUS IN TAURUS. This is considered a fortunate position for the planet Venus. It gives constancy to the affections, faithful-

ness in love, and, although the feelings are strong, the nature is fixed and not liable to change easily. Both likes and dislikes are maintained tenaciously, and while you can be an enduring friend you are also rather loth to give up feelings of prejudice or hostility. The social side of your nature is well developed and you can gain friends and be popular in your own circle. If you apply yourself to business or financial matters this position would be fortunate because it would help to win you the good opinion of people with whom you dealt and so would smooth your path. It is slightly favourable for money matters generally, especially through legacy, partnership, or marriage. You have some ability for dealing with money, but you can also be generous and kind.

## INDIVIDUALITY AND PERSONALITY.

630. Before summarising your horoscope it should first be explained
I that the nativity is divided into two parts: one half dealing with the internal or higher, subjective or " Individual " part of the nature; and the other concerned with the lower, external or objective manifestation, generally termed the " Personal." To go fully into the matter, however, demands a more detailed treatment than is possible in this class of horoscope, so that we will pass on to a study of the elements predominating at your birth and their general influence. Should you desire fuller information, in such books as *How to Judge a Nativity* and *The Art of Synthesis*, the subject is gone into more fully.

## GENERAL SUMMARY.

630. You have a favourable nativity, and will have opportunities to
K develop your character, and use your mental faculties wisely. You will gain by studying your horoscope, for you have the ability to profit by the good influences operating at your birth, the planetary positions giving you some power in the world, no less potent because it may not be open and public. The judgment has been given as succinctly and lucidly as possible, and you should ponder well what has been said, so as to catch any inner meaning that may attach to any paragraph, remembering that the whole delineation is given with the main view of helping you to progress. [The following is a brief judgment of the whole combinations denoted by the nativity.]

436. The majority of the planets were RISING AND NEAR THE EASTERN HORIZON at the time of your birth. This denotes

that you will rise in life by your own energy, enterprise, and perseverance, and attain to a good position in which you will have power and authority in the sphere in which you may be moving. You will have many opportunities, and the ability to seize them; thus you will prosper and advance. The majority of the planets rising at birth, denotes ability and self-control, and enables those who are born at this time to have the vibrations of the planets to their hand, so to speak, and thus you will make good use of the operating forces around your ascendant.

441. The majority of the planets were in AIRY SIGNS at the time of your birth. This will give you an inspirational and also an artistic temperament. You are essentially refined and can live much more in the mind than in the senses. You may love sensuous pleasures, but you will abhor all things sensual. Your soul is alive and you have that very rare quality of feeling things with your mind. You have good intellectual ability and could study with ease, but it is the artistic side of life that appeals to you more than the scientific, unless it be the philosophically intellectual aspect of science. You have splendid ideals, and may subjectively cultivate exquisite tastes.

## YOUR FUTURE PROSPECTS.

### Directions.

630. In certain horoscopes the word "Directions" may be mentioned, M  and as those unfamiliar with astrological terms may not understand what is meant, it may be well to give a brief explanation. The word "Directions" is used in reference to a judgment given upon the planetary positions since the time of birth, it being necessary to erect a fresh horoscope for every year after birth, so that by a study of the progressed positions we may discover the possibilities and influences operating for any given year of life. It is wise in certain cases to have the Directions calculated, for often detailed advice can be given for each month in any year.

The "Future Prospects" which follow give a rough outline of your Directions for the ensuing three years.

630. Although any attempts to give accurate predictions with regard N  to the future are based upon astrological laws, at the same time it must be remembered that astrologers are very far from being

infallible. These words of the wise Ptolemy to his pupils should be well pondered: "Judgment must be regulated by thyself, as well as by the Science. For it is not possible that particular forms of events should be declared by any person, however scientific, since the understanding conceives only a certain general idea of some sensible event, and not its particular form. It is, therefore, necessary for him who practises herein to adopt inference. They only who are inspired by the Deity can predict particulars."

### 1909-10-11.

lvi.
The planets Neptune and Venus have now progressed to a BENEFIC aspect, and this although not of very great effect in ordinary matters, is likely to bring you some happiness and pleasure at this time. Things will go smoothly with you, your affairs will prosper and the more you can raise yourself above personal aims and wishes the more will your happiness increase. Your sympathies will be broadened and your mental outlook enlarged, while art and poetry will seem to open a new world to you. Much, however, depends upon the strength of Neptune in the nativity, and on your ability to respond to the higher side of its influence. You will gain in dealings with those of a lower social rank than yourself.

### 1911.

xcii.
The Moon by progression since your birth has passed into the THIRD HOUSE of your nativity, the house of mind. You will now find your mental powers increase and become more active than usual. You will either take some special journey, or travel during this period, or the third house having connection with relatives and brethren, you may expect to be concerned with their affairs more or less, during the time that the Moon takes to pass through the third house. Removals, but more probably travelling, will now occupy much of your time and attention. This will be a good period wherein to study and energise your mind, either by reading or by engaging in those mental pursuits which tend to improve the mind generally.

### 1911-12-13.

cii.
The progression of the Moon has brought her to the CONJUNCTION of the Sun, an important position, usually indicating some important change that is about to take place in the circumstances, consequent

upon the influx of the Solar life into the Lunar personality whereby the latter receives a new charge of life.   This change is usually preceded by a period of more or less uncertainty and indecision, the coming events casting their shadows before, as it were.   It indicates changes in the system and is sometimes accompanied by an indisposition of some kind whereby the system is accommodated to the new life flowing into it. This change is more beneficial as a rule to males than to females.   Be careful of the health at this period, and avoid all indiscretions in diet, etc.

## CONCLUSION.

630.   As time goes on you will have opportunities to awaken that
   R    which is latent in your nativity, and in accordance with your earnestness and adaptability you will be enabled to live up to all that your planets indicate.   You may not recognise the whole of the foregoing characteristics perhaps, yet if your birth-time has been correctly taken every word should appeal to you.   Astrologers believe that " Character is Destiny," and that during this life we must work to develop our characters.   In the far future we are destined to take an active part in the management of the world's evolution, and to this end we should fit ourselves; for eventually we must become perfect.

----

SPECIAL NOTE TO THIS NATIVITY.—Those sentences that are in italics in this delineation would be omitted when writing out the judgment, owing to their contradicting that which has gone before, or is due to other aspects, as for instance 267 ♀ ♂ ☿ refines the mind and modifies the □ of ♀ and ♂ , improving the *love* nature and freeing it from the martial sense strain as noted in 247.   Paragraph 473 is the top note, so to speak, of the horoscope, its receptive tendencies modify the other martial or positive notes, and it will act like sweet music in tuning up the whole nature.

Then again 191 is much improved by the one that follows, 247. Paragraphs 436 and 441 shew how the summaries fall appropriate to the horoscope and great care should always be taken in choosing them.

## How May a King's Horoscope be Known?

ONE question sure to rise to the lips on coming to the end of this delineation of King George's horoscope, is: How are we to tell that a given horoscope is that of a monarch? The answer may be given plainly, *we cannot tell*—that is, we cannot tell if the horoscope is that of a person actually of Royal blood, though it can certainly be seen at once if it is the nativity of a born ruler.

But before going further it may be interesting to give an account of the astrological "doubles" of Kings George III. and George IV.

I. In Raphael's *Manual of Astrology* (R. C. Smith), published in 1837, and printed by Thomas Tegg & Son, 73, Cheapside, we find the following on p. xvi.:

" In the newspapers of February, 1820, the death of a Mr. Samuel Hemmings was noticed. It was stated that he had been an ironmonger and prosperous in trade—that he was born on the 4th of June 1738, at nearly the same moment as his late majesty, GEORGE THE THIRD, and in the same parish of St. Martin's-in-the-Fields : that he went into business for himself in October, 1760, when his late majesty came to the throne ; that he married on the 8th of September 1761, the same day as the king ; and finally, after other events of his life had resembled those which happened to the late king, that *he died on Saturday, January 29th*, 1820, *on the same day and nearly the same hour as his late majesty.*"

II. In a book entitled *Shadow Land, or the Seer,* by Mrs. E. Oakes-Smith, and published in 1852 by Fowler & Wells, of 131, Nassau Street, New York, on p. 89 we find the following statement:

" I lately found, in an old astrological work, the horoscope of the Prince of Wales (GEORGE THE FOURTH), together with that of a little chimney-sweep, ushered into the world the same day and hour that witnessed the birth of the slip of royalty, and who was therefore christened by the name of ' Prince George.' One child wrapped in purple, the other rolled in its sooty blanket : yet the same *stars*, indicating a similarity of destiny, and in result whimsically verified. Of the career of the Prince of Wales it is unnecessary to speak—his vices, his follies, his perjuries were all royal, and his fellow, the sweep, was not a jot behind him. The broom and scraper were found as ill-adapted to the hands of one as the

sceptre to the hands of the other.   The parents of ' Prince George,' tired
of his profligacy, which shamed their profession, finally established him
as a tallow chandler.   He was now a *ruler*, with apprentices and coteries
about him, and could follow the bent of his genius.   He was handsome,
courteous, gallant, a spendthrift, and a gamester, as testified before the
age of twenty, the fortune and reputation of the family having suffered
much through his tendencies of this kind.   He soon became famous in
his own sphere, dressed in the best style of his class, was the idol of the
women, the essence of politeness, the greatest *bettor* and gamester at all
the races and fairs within ten miles of London, and finally kept the best
asses, and ran the best donkey races of the day.   All this time his royal
compeer was working out a destiny perfectly analogous, except that one
is ' high life above, the other below, stairs '—the one races with a blood
horse, the other with a donkey.   But all glory must have an end; the
Prince of Wales became bankrupt, and the Prince George ' smashed '—
*the very day that the stud of His Royal Highness, Prince of Wales,*
*was sold by Tattersall, the racing donkeys and ponies of the other*
*' Prince George' were put to the hammer.*   SIC TRANSIT GLORIA
MUNDI ! "

To these instances might be added a third, the late King Edward
VII., for in the Manchester edition of the *Daily Sketch* for the
Saturday following his death there appeared an account of a similar
astrological " double," an inhabitant of Walthamstow, born 9/11/'41, died
May 6th, 1910, the same day as King Edward, and various incidents of
parallel fortune were noticed.   There is also the well-known case of
the Kaiser's " double," an artisan whose children have been born on the
same dates as those of William II., and who has in sundry other ways
reflected in his own career the fortunes of his Royal patron—for on the
story coming to His Majesty's ears he bestowed the Royal bounty upon
him.

These facts serve to illustrate a very important point in Natal
Astrology, namely that in certain rare instances two people are born at
the same time in the same locality, and therefore have the same horoscope.
Yet while we see that their lives run strangely parallel, they are not
identical. Thus, at a certain time Prince George inherited the throne of
England; but his contemporary, the ironmonger, merely went into
business on his own account.   In each case there was an accession of

honour and responsibility, to the prince a crown, to the tradesman independence.

The horoscope shows the inborn tendencies, and by its progression it shows the times at which opportunities will present themselves for the fruition of those tendencies—opportunities of expansion, honour—occasions of self-examination, suffering or disgrace.

In other words, the horoscope shows the influences at work, be the subject peer or peasant; but to the peer honour means the purple, to the peasant at best but the parish council. The horoscope is written in a symbology that speaks of *principles*, not particulars; and the same planetary map may disclose to the astrologer the character of an infant, the fate of a nation, or the whereabouts of a missing child, according to the method of interpretation.

Hence it is essential to remember when considering the delineation of a horoscope, that all references to environment and fortune are RELATIVE to the social and civil sphere into which the native is born. Just as the manifestation of character—though not the character itself— will be modified by education or lack of it, so the benefic influence of Jupiter will work upon a larger or smaller social and financial scale according to the sphere into which the native is born. It must be borne in mind that physical heredity counts for something, that there is a something real in "blue blood," and that though it is said that a strong soul may under some circumstances deliberately *choose* a cramped and plebeian environment, yet in spite of the spiritual strength that can be gained thereby there will never be the same degree of success, *as the world counts success*, where a lowly birth is chosen. Even the divine must work with physical implements, and even in the hands of a great artist a dull chisel is but a dull chisel.

At the same time there is truth in the saying that "a live dog is better than a dead lion." The born ruler is a ruler, even if his subjects be but a group of fishermen, and Astrology can say if the nativity shows power to rule, and favourable opportunity to exercise that power. In this sense, we can say that it is possible to tell a Royal Horoscope at sight. Not otherwise.

# THE ALAN LEO ASTROLOGER'S LIBRARY

The most renowned, complete course in Astrology ever to appear! The Alan Leo Astrologer's Library has become the undisputed source for self-instruction in Astrology.

### ASTROLOGY FOR ALL $12.95

A concise, easy to understand introduction to astrology, which presents the major astrological principles in a simple and fascinating manner, developed especially for the reader without prior knowledge. This, Leo's most general text, is specifically designed for the beginning student and therefore includes background material, an analysis of the characteristics of each of the signs, a description of the sun and moon through the signs, and of the significance of the planets in each of the signs. The body of the work concerns the influence of the two major luminaries, the sun and moon, on character and offers a complete delineation of the twelve zodiacal types and the 144 sub-types born each year.

### CASTING THE HOROSCOPE $12.95

Fundamental to astrology is the horoscope, a map of the heavens for the time and place of an individual's birth, from which astrological interpretation begins. In this book, Leo teaches everything one needs to know to cast a natal horoscope, including calculation of the ascendant, the use of the table of houses, how to read an ephemeris, the conversion of birth time to sidereal time and adjustments of planetary motions. For the more advanced student, there is information on rectification, directions, methods of house division, lessons in astronomy and sample tables. The coverage is comprehensive and includes areas not detailed in other works.

### HOW TO JUDGE A NATIVITY $12.95

HOW TO JUDGE A NATIVITY is a storehouse of general information concerning planetary and zodiacal influences. It deals with the nativity almost entirely on a purely practical level, explaining how to assess the occupations and activities of life in great detail, from health, wealth and the home to philosophy and travel. All the necessary rules and references are presented with a view to helping the student learn to give a reliable reading of any nativity. Comprehensive analysis of the individual houses as they relate to chart interpretation is included, as well as planetary positions and aspects.

### THE ART OF SYNTHESIS $12.95

In this work, Alan Leo stresses the esoteric and intuitional aspects of astrology, along with the philosophical and psychological. He provides a richly detailed study of the relation between planets and consciousness, based upon first-hand experience. Particularly interesting are the planetary correlations to the types of temperament, e.g. martial, saturnine, jovial, etc., accompanied by illustrations of the types. The triplicities are analysed comprehensively. Twelve sample horoscopes of famous individuals, including Rudolph Steiner, Robespierre and John Ruskin are discussed as examples of how to synthesize the many elements which come into play in a single, natal chart. A handy astro-theosophical dictionary is provided for the reader's convenience. Where HOW TO JUDGE A NATIVITY emphasizes the scientific-technical aspect of astrological interpretation, THE ART OF SYNTHESIS demonstrates the intuitional dimension. Intuition is soul penetration; it sees through the veil that divides the subjective from the objective universe and brings knowledge that the mind alone cannot obtain from the objective world. THE ART OF SYNTHESIS brings this intuitive penetration to astrology.

## THE PROGRESSED HOROSCOPE $12.95

THE PROGRESSED HOROSCOPE is the most comprehensive guide to the system of predicting the future. The methods for drawing up annual forecasts and divining upcoming influences are completely outlined. Included are a detailed and full delineation of every possible progressed aspect; solar, mutual and lunar. Their influences on character and destiny are fully described, enabling the student to form a firm foundation on which to base his judgment of any progressed horoscope he may wish to interpret. There is a lengthy chapter dealing with Transits in their exoteric and esoteric aspects. The last section, "The Art and Practice of Directing" is a complete handbook on "Primary Directions". The YES! Guide calls this "... the most detailed examination of progression available. Includes a great deal of background information on the why of progressions, in addition to detailed instructions on calculating the progressed ascendant, solar and lunar positions and aspects, solar revolutions and transits and primary directions."

## THE KEY TO YOUR OWN NATIVITY $12.95

A complete and comprehensive analysis of all the elements of the horoscope, giving full descriptions of every position in the nativity. With the assistance of this book, any person can learn to interpret a natal chart. Shows where to find indications in the horoscope related to topics such as, finance, travel, environment, enterprise, sickness, marriage, legacies, philosophy, profession, friends, occultism. Here is the master astrologer's easy to follow method for delineation and interpretation. A must for the beginner and an essential reference for the advanced astrologer.

## ESOTERIC ASTROLOGY $12.95

This work deals with Natal Astrology in a manner never before attempted by any writer on Astrology. Divided into three parts, the first part explains the theoretical aspect of Esoteric Astrology; the second demonstrates the practical side of Esoteric Astrology with many examples and complete explanations and the third part deals with the subdivisions of the Zodiac.

For the first time in the history of Astrology, an entirely new method of reading horoscopes is given. The *individual* and *personal* Stars of all persons are explained by a series of *Star Maps,* showing how the age of the soul may be astrologically discovered. It shows how the Horoscope may be changed into a Star Map.

Along with chart interpretation in terms of reincarnation, the methods for the working out of Karma are covered in detail.

## THE COMPLETE DICTIONARY OF ASTROLOGY $12.95

A handy reference text of all the terms and concepts you will need to understand astrology in its technical and philosophical dimensions. Useful for quick reference to the signs, planets, houses, ascendants, aspects, decanates, planetary herbs, etc. An extensive section on Hindu astrology. An analysis of horary astrology. Simple explanations of technical terms. Esoteric interpretation of the different elements of astrology. Indispensable to the study of the other Leo textbooks and a useful companion to any study of astrology.

These and other titles in the Alan Leo Astrologer's Library are available at many fine bookstores or, to order direct, send a check or money order for the total amount, plus $2.00 shipping and handling for the first book and 75¢ for each additional book to:

Inner Traditions International
P.O. Box 1534
Hagerstown, MD 21741

To order with a credit card, call toll-free:

1-800-638-3030

For a complete catalog of books from Inner Traditions International, write to:

Inner Traditions International
One Park Street
Rochester, VT 05767